NEW MERM

General editors:
William C. Carroll, Boston University
Brian Gibbons, University of Münster
Tiffany Stern, University College, University of Oxford

General editor for the Bernard Shaw titles:
L. W. Conolly, Trent University

NEW MERMAIDS

BERNARD SHAW

PYGMALION

A Romance in Five Acts

Definitive Text

Edited by L. W. Conolly

Professor of English, Trent University

Methuen Drama • London

New Mermaids

1 3 5 7 9 10 8 6 4 2

First published 2008

Methuen Drama
A & C Black Publishers Limited
38 Soho Square
London W1D 3HB
www.acblack.com

ISBN 978–0–7136–7997–7

Application for performing rights in Bernard Shaw's plays should be made to the Society of Authors, 84 Drayton Gardens, London SW10 9SB, phone: (020) 7373 6642.

A CIP catalogue record for this book is available from the British Library

This book is produced using paper made from wood grown in managed, sustainable forests. It is natural, renewable and recyclable. The logging and manufacturing processes conform to the environmental regulations of the country of origin.

Typeset by RefineCatch Limited, Bungay, Suffolk
Printed in the UK by CPI Cox & Wyman, Reading, RG1 8EX

CONTENTS

ACKNOWLEDGEMENTS

I am grateful to many friends and colleagues for their guidance, advice, and encouragement while I have been working on this edition of *Pygmalion*. I express thanks in particular to Eugene Benson, Jeremy Crow, James Ellison, and Michel Pharand. My fellow New Mermaids Shaw editors Jean Chotia, Nicholas Grene, Norma Jenckes, and Peter Wearing have generously shared their own frustrations, challenges, and solutions with me, and Jenny Ridout and Katie Taylor at New Mermaids have been a constant source of support. The editorial guidance of Sue Gibbons has been invaluable and is much appreciated.

Library staff at the University of Guelph, the British Library, the British Theatre Museum, and the University of Texas at Austin have been unfailingly helpful, and I am grateful to the Trustees of the British Library and to the Harry Ransom Humanities Research Center at the University of Texas for permission to publish materials from their collections in Appendices I, II, and III.

Family members have once more been patient with my Shavian preoccupations. I thank my daughter Rebecca for editorial advice, my son James for technical advice, and my wife Barbara for her proofreading skills and for her astute insights into what Shaw was up to in *Pygmalion*.

L. W. C.
March 2008

BERNARD SHAW: A CHRONOLOGY

For a comprehensive and detailed chronology of Shaw's life, see A.M. Gibbs, *A Bernard Shaw Chronology* (Basingstoke, 2001). Dates of British and foreign productions of Shaw's plays are given in Raymond Mander and Joe Mitchenson, *Theatrical Companion to Shaw* (New York, 1955), and definitive bibliographical information on Shaw can be found in Dan H. Laurence, *Bernard Shaw: A Bibliography*, 2 vols. (Oxford, 1983).

1856	Born in Dublin, 26 July, to George Carr Shaw and Lucinda Elizabeth Shaw.
1871	Leaves school and takes an office job with a Dublin property agency.
1876	Moves from Dublin to London.
1879	Completes his first novel, *Immaturity* (first published 1930).
1880	Completes his second novel, *The Irrational Knot* (first published in serial form in *Our Corner*, 1885–7, and in book form 1905).
1881	Completes his third novel, *Love Among the Artists* (first published in serial form in *Our Corner*, 1887–8, and in book form 1900).
1883	Completes his fourth and fifth (his last completed) novels, *Cashel Byron's Profession* (first published in serial form in *To-Day*, 1885–6, and in book form 1886) and *An Unsocial Socialist* (first published in serial form in *To-Day*, 1884, and in book form 1887).
1884	Joins the Fabian Society.
1885	Publishes first music and drama criticism in the *Dramatic Review*. Shaw's criticism (including art and literary criticism) also appeared in periodicals such as the *Pall Mall Gazette*, *The World*, and *The Star* before he began a three-year stint as drama critic for the *Saturday Review* (1895–8).
1891	Publishes *The Quintessence of Ibsenism*.
1892	His first play, *Widowers' Houses* (begun 1884) performed by the Independent Theatre Society, London.
1893	Completes *The Philanderer* and *Mrs Warren's Profession*.
1894	*Arms and the Man* performed at the Avenue Theatre, London, and the Herald Square Theatre, New York; completes *Candida*.
1896	Meets Charlotte Payne-Townshend, his future wife. Completes *You Never Can Tell* and *The Devil's Disciple*.

1897   *Candida* performed by the Independent Theatre Company, Aberdeen. *The Man of Destiny* performed at the Grand Theatre, Croydon. American actor Richard Mansfield produces *The Devil's Disciple* in Albany and New York.

1898   Marries Charlotte Payne-Townshend. Publishes (in two volumes) *Plays Pleasant and Unpleasant*, containing four 'pleasant' plays (*Arms and the Man, Candida, The Man of Destiny, You Never Can Tell*) and three 'unpleasant' plays (*Widowers' Houses, The Philanderer, Mrs Warren's Profession*). Completes *Caesar and Cleopatra*. *Mrs Warren's Profession* is banned by the Lord Chamberlain from public performance in England. Publishes *The Perfect Wagnerite* (on the *Ring* cycle).

1899   *You Never Can Tell* performed by the Stage Society. Writes *Captain Brassbound's Conversion*.

1901   Publishes *Three Plays for Puritans* (*The Devil's Disciple, Caesar and Cleopatra, Captain Brassbound's Conversion*). Writes *The Admirable Bashville*.

1902   *Mrs Warren's Profession* performed (a private production) by the Stage Society.

1903   Publishes *Man and Superman* (begun in 1901).

1904   Begins his partnership with Harley Granville Barker and J.E. Vedrenne at the Royal Court Theatre (until 1907). Eleven Shaw plays are produced there, including *Major Barbara* (1905).

1905   *Mrs Warren's Profession* performed (then banned) in New Haven and New York. *The Philanderer* performed by the New Stage Club, London.

1906   *Caesar and Cleopatra* performed (in German) in Berlin. Publishes *Dramatic Opinions and Essays*, and writes *The Doctor's Dilemma*.

1908   Writes *Getting Married*.

1909   *The Shewing-up of Blanco Posnet* banned in England, but performed in Dublin. *Press Cuttings* banned in England. Completes *Misalliance*.

1911   *Fanny's First Play* performed at the Little Theatre, London. Runs for 622 performances (a record for a Shaw première).

1912   Completes *Pygmalion*.

1913   *Pygmalion* performed (in German) in Vienna.

1914   *Mrs Warren's Profession* performed by the Dublin Repertory Theatre. *Pygmalion* performed at His Majesty's Theatre, London. Outbreak of World War One. Publishes *Common Sense about the War*.

1917	Visits front line sites in France. Completes *Heartbreak House*.
1918	End of World War One.
1920	*Heartbreak House* performed by the Theatre Guild, New York. Completes *Back to Methuselah*.
1922	*Back to Methuselah* performed by the Theatre Guild, New York.
1923	Completes *Saint Joan*. It is performed in New York by the Theatre Guild.
1924	First British production of *Saint Joan*, New Theatre, London. The Lord Chamberlain's ban on *Mrs Warren's Profession* is removed.
1925	First public performances in England of *Mrs Warren's Profession* (in Birmingham and London).
1926	Awarded the 1925 Nobel Prize for Literature.
1928	Publishes *The Intelligent Woman's Guide to Socialism and Capitalism*.
1929	*The Apple Cart* performed (in Polish) in Warsaw, followed by the British première at the Malvern Festival, where other British premières (*Too True to be Good*, *The Simpleton of the Unexpected Isles*, *Buoyant Billions*) and world premières (*Geneva* and *In Good King Charles's Golden Days*) of Shaw's plays were produced between 1932 and 1949.
1930	Begins publication of *The Works of Bernard Shaw*, completed (in 33 volumes) in 1938.
1931	Visits Russia; meets Gorky and Stalin.
1933	Writes *On the Rocks*.
1936	*The Millionairess* performed (in German) in Vienna.
1938	*Pygmalion* is filmed, starring Leslie Howard and Wendy Hiller.
1939	Outbreak of World War Two. Wins an Oscar for the screenplay of *Pygmalion*.
1940	*Major Barbara* is filmed, starring Rex Harrison and Wendy Hiller.
1943	Charlotte Shaw dies.
1944	Publishes *Everybody's Political What's What?*
1945	*Caesar and Cleopatra* is filmed, starring Claude Rains and Vivien Leigh. End of World War Two.
1950	Dies, 2 November, aged 94, from complications after a fall while pruning a shrub in his garden. Cremated at Golders Green Crematorium on 6 November, his ashes (mixed with his wife's) scattered at his country home in Ayot St Lawrence, Hertfordshire (now a National Trust property), on 23 November.

ABBREVIATIONS

BH   *The Bodley Head Bernard Shaw. Collected Plays with their
           Prefaces.* Volume IV. *Misalliance, The Dark Lady of the
           Sonnets, Fanny's First Play, Androcles and the Lion,
           Pygmalion, Overruled, The Music-Cure, Great Catherine,
           The Inca of Perusalem, O'Flaherty, V.C.* London: Max
           Reinhardt, The Bodley Head, 1972.

CL   *Bernard Shaw: Collected Letters.* 4 vols. Dan H. Laurence,
           ed. New York: Viking Penguin, 1985–8.

C1916   Bernard Shaw, *Androcles and the Lion, Overruled,
           Pygmalion.* London: Constable, 1916.

C1931   Bernard Shaw, *Androcles and the Lion, Overruled,
           Pygmalion.* London: Constable, 1931.

C1939   Bernard Shaw, *Androcles and the Lion, Overruled,
           Pygmalion.* London: Constable, 1939.

C1941   Bernard Shaw, *Androcles and the Lion, Overruled,
           Pygmalion.* London: Constable, 1941.

Dukore   Bernard Dukore, *Shaw's Theater.* Gainesville, FL:
           University Press of Florida, 2000.

EM/NASH   *Everybody's Magazine* (New York) 31 (November 1914),
           577–612. The first English-language publication of
           Pygmalion. Simultaneously published in London (with
           minor variations) in *Nash's and Pall Mall Magazine* 53
           (November 1914), 147–69, and 53 (December 1914),
           305–25.

HRC   Harry Ransom Humanities Research Center, University
           of Texas at Austin, Texas.

LB   Dan H. Laurence, *Bernard Shaw: A Bibliography.* 2 vols.
           Oxford: Clarendon Press, 1983.

LC   Licensing Copy. A printed proof copy (Constable, 1913), 'by a Fellow of the Royal Society of Literature', submitted to the Lord Chamberlain for a licence for public performance. British Library Add MS 66056F. The licence is dated 26 February 1914.

MS   Manuscript of Shaw's original text of the play (written in shorthand), 7 March–[10 June] 1912. Harry Ransom Humanities Research Center, University of Texas at Austin, Texas. SHAW 24.7.

RC1   Shaw's rehearsal copy of *Pygmalion*, His Majesty's Theatre, 11 April 1914; a printed proof copy (Constable 1913), 'by a Fellow of the Royal Society of Literature'. British Library Add MS 50629.

RC2   Mrs Patrick Campbell's rehearsal copy; typescript, with Mrs Campbell's notes. British Theatre Museum.

RN1   Shaw's rehearsal notes for productions of *Pygmalion* at the Strand Theatre (1920), Academy of Dramatic Art (1920), and Malvern Festival (1936); British Library Add MS 50644, ff. 36–55, 59–60, 303–8.

RN2   Shaw's rehearsal notes for the production of *Pygmalion* at His Majesty's Theatre, 11 April 1914. Harry Ransom Humanities Research Center, University of Texas at Austin, Texas. SHAW 60.4.

Shaw/   *Bernard Shaw and Mrs Patrick Campbell: Their*
Campbell   *Correspondence.* Alan Dent, ed. New York: Alfred A. Knopf, 1952.

Theatrics   *Bernard Shaw Theatrics.* Dan H. Laurence, ed. *Selected Correspondence of Bernard Shaw.* Toronto: University of Toronto Press, 1995.

TS   Typescript of Shaw's original shorthand manuscript of *Pygmalion*, with Shaw's corrections and revisions. Harry Ransom Humanities Research Center, University of Texas at Austin, Texas. SHAW 24.5.

INTRODUCTION

The Author

Eliza's seriously unladylike response – 'Not bloody likely' – to Freddy's enquiry about walking across the park after Mrs Higgins's at-home in Act III of *Pygmalion* shocked audiences at the play's British première at His Majesty's Theatre in London in 1914. But whereas Eliza's scandalous behaviour is innocent, instinctive, and momentary, Bernard Shaw's behaviour – in words and in deeds – for almost all his life was predicated on a conviction that controversy was both a necessary and desirable pre-condition for social, political, and cultural progress.

When *Pygmalion* opened in London, Shaw was in his fifty-sixth year, already a veteran of several controversies, with more to come. Since arriving in London on April Fool's Day in 1876 from Dublin (where he was born on 26 July 1856), he had worked hard to establish himself as a leading figure in literary, theatrical, and political circles. The success that he had achieved in this regard by 1914 had not come easily. Largely self-educated (he had left school when he was fifteen) by regular visits to Dublin's National Gallery and the city's concert halls and theatres, supplemented by voracious reading (especially of Shakespeare), he eked out a living for his first few months in London by ghost-writing music criticism (on behalf of his mother's singing teacher) for a satirical magazine called *The Hornet*, and worked briefly in 1880 for the Edison Telephone Company. He depended largely, however, on his mother (who had left her husband, Shaw's father, in 1873 and moved to London) for financial support in his early London years – 'I did not throw myself into the struggle for life: I threw my mother into it', he quipped in the preface to his (second) novel *The Irrational Knot*. Writing novels was among Shaw's first literary endeavours, and he was spectacularly unsuccessful, all five (written between 1879 and 1883) being rejected (some several times) by London publishers.[1] In his spare time – and he had plenty of it – Shaw continued his self-education in the Reading Room of the British Museum, where he

---

1 See Richard F. Dietrich, *Portrait of the Artist as a Young Superman: A Study of Shaw's Novels* (Gainesville, FL, 1969).

(Unless otherwise noted, the place of publication for books cited in the footnotes is London. The full title and publication details of books and articles are given in the first citation only. All subsequent citations are abbreviated to author and title. Other abbreviations are listed above, p. xi.)

first encountered (in a French translation) Marx's *Das Kapital*, a work that was central to his subsequent political thinking and values.

Not quite as radical as Marx, however, Shaw found a more congenial political home with the Fabian Society, which he joined in 1884, shortly after it was formed. There he encountered writers and political activists such as H.G. Wells and Sydney and Beatrice Webb, committed – as all Fabians were – to fundamental social and political reform, but through debate and legislation rather than revolution. The Fabian Society gave Shaw a valuable platform as a writer for the Society's famous 'tracts' – on subjects such as socialism and anarchism – and as a public speaker and debater. The year 1884 was also important for Shaw in that it marked a turning point in his professional career from disillusioned novelist to aspiring playwright. The Reading Room of the British Museum had brought Shaw and Marx together, and another meeting there – this one in person – also had momentous significance for Shaw's career. In the autumn of 1883 Shaw had encountered William Archer in the Reading Room. One of London's leading theatre critics, Archer discussed with Shaw an idea for a play that sparked Shaw's imagination and that he began working on in earnest in November 1884. After numerous interruptions, Shaw completed the play – *Widowers' Houses*, his first – in October 1892 and it was produced the following month in London by the Independent Theatre Society, a private club founded in 1891 by Dutch-born critic and playwright Jacob Thomas Grein for the purpose of producing work whose experimental or controversial nature made it unpalatable to commercial theatre. As a private club, the Society's productions were also exempt from the censorship to which all commercial productions had been subject in Britain since 1737.

Widowers' Houses, which exposes the scourge of slum landlords in London, defined the kind of playwright Shaw wanted to be, at least in the early years of his playwriting career – trenchant social critic reaching as wide a public as possible through accessible (and often very amusing) plays, plays written with a view, Shaw later declared in the preface of his 1909 play *The Shewing-up of Blanco Posnet*, 'with the deliberate object of converting the nation to my opinions'. *Widowers' Houses*, in which, Shaw claimed, he had shown 'middle-class respectability . . . fattening on the poverty of the slum as flies fatten on filth', was published in 1898 in a volume called *Plays Unpleasant*, which also contains *The Philanderer* (about the 'blundering abominations' of Victorian marriage laws) and *Mrs Warren's Profession*, a play that – audaciously for its time – treats prostitution as an economic rather than moral problem, a position that caused the play to be banned from public stages in Britain for over twenty-five years.[2] Shaw published a companion volume with *Plays Unpleasant* that, while treating – as its title, *Plays Pleasant*, suggests – subjects in a lighter manner nonetheless reflected Shaw's ongoing concern with serious matters – particularly warfare (*Arms and the Man* and *The Man of Destiny*) and sexual politics (*Candida* and *You Never Can Tell*).

That British Museum meeting with Archer had the further benefit for Shaw of leading to some regular employment, Archer helping Shaw secure posts as music and art critic with the *Dramatic Review* and *The World*. That experience opened up later appointments as art, music, and drama critic with other newspapers and periodicals, including a long and productive stint as drama critic for the *Saturday Review* from January 1895 to May 1898. In his weekly articles for the *Saturday Review* Shaw frequently excoriated London theatre for its shallowness, predictability, and triteness, making exceptions for writers such as Henrik Ibsen (another important early influence on Shaw) whose plays (translated and championed by William Archer) shocked and outraged some of Shaw's fellow critics for their daring treatment of issues such as sexual disease (*Ghosts*) and women's rights (*A Doll's House*). (Shaw had already expounded at some length on his admiration for Ibsen in his 1891 book *The Quintessence of Ibsenism*.) Shaw's frustration with the London theatre was exacerbated by the power of actor-managers such as Henry Irving (at the Lyceum Theatre), Beerbohm Tree (at the Haymarket – where, ironically, *Pygmalion* would subsequently be so successful), and Charles Wyndham (at the Criterion). The priorities of such actor-managers, Shaw argued, were leading parts for themselves and handsome financial returns rather than worthwhile plays.[3]

By the 1890s, despite his unpromising start, Shaw was a striking and well-known figure in London. Tall, red-bearded, dressed in distinctive Jaeger woollen suits, this Dublin-accented vegetarian teetotaller was a

2 Shaw's comments on *Widowers' Houses* and *The Philanderer* are in the Preface to *Plays Unpleasant* (1898). Written in 1893, *Mrs Warren's Profession* was banned from public performance in England until 1925. See L.W. Conolly, '*Mrs Warren's Profession* and the Lord Chamberlain', *SHAW: The Annual of Bernard Shaw Studies*, 24 (2004), 46–95. For Shaw's views on censorship, see *Mrs Warren's Profession*, ed. L.W. Conolly (Peterborough, ON, 2005), pp. 64–9 and 206–14, and Celia Marshik, *British Modernism and Censorship* (Cambridge, 2006), pp. 46–87.

3 See Shaw's preface to William Archer's *The Theatrical 'World' of 1894* (1895). See George Rowell, *Theatre in the Age of Irving* (1981) for a good introduction to the theatre of this period. Shaw's dramatic criticism was collected in his *Our Theatres in the Nineties* (3 vols., 1932) and, more fully, in Bernard F. Dukore, ed., *The Drama Observed* (4 vols., University Park, PA, 1993).

much sought after dinner guest, lecturer, and journalist. Far from shy about seeking publicity, and increasingly adept at self-promotion, Shaw had become, as Dan H. Laurence has put it, 'something of a celebrity'. 'Everybody in London knows Shaw', said the *Sunday World*: 'Fabian, Socialist, art and musical critic, vegetarian, ascetic, humourist, artist to the tips of his boots. The most original and inspiring of men – fiercely uncompromising, full of ideas, irrepressibly brilliant – an Irishman'.[4] He was an Irishman, however, like many before him, with his sights set on London, not Dublin, particularly London theatre, where it wasn't until a run of seventy-six performances of *Arms and the Man* at the Avenue Theatre in the spring and early summer of 1894 that he began to achieve commercial success, albeit as yet of modest proportions. W.B. Yeats, who was at the first night of *Arms and the Man*, later declared that 'from that moment Bernard Shaw became the most formidable man in modern letters, and even the most drunken of medical students knew it'.[5]

The income from *Arms and the Man* was welcome, but from a financial point of view Shaw's marriage to Irish heiress Charlotte Payne-Townshend in June 1898 was a much more significant turn of events. While sexual attraction was not a prominent feature of the relationship – the marriage was probably never consummated – their devoted companionship, which lasted until Charlotte's death in 1943, gave Shaw not only financial security but also the personal stability on which he could base his increasingly hectic and productive career. Playwriting had now become Shaw's major preoccupation, but it could hardly be said that he had withdrawn from other interests and activities: writing provocative articles for and letters to the press (his first of many letters to *The Times* – on the British jury system – was published on 27 September 1898[6]); supporting unpopular causes (such as Oscar Wilde during his trial and imprisonment for gross indecency in 1895); travelling (including a cruise on the SS *Lusitania* in 1899 – 'a godless cruise with godless people ... a guzzling, lounging, gambling, dog's life'[7]); being elected to the St Pancras Borough Council in 1897 and defeated when running for election to the London County Council in 1904; advocating women's rights; fighting against theatre censorship; sitting for a bust by August Rodin in 1906; and almost drowning while swimming off the coast of Wales in 1907.

---

4 Qtd in CL I, 106–7.

5 W.B. Yeats, *Autobiographies* (1961), p. 282.

6 See Ronald Ford, ed., *The Letters of Bernard Shaw to 'The Times', 1898–1950* (Dublin, 2007).

7 Qtd in A.M. Gibbs, *A Bernard Shaw Chronology* (Basingstoke, 2001), p. 144. (The SS *Lusitania* was not the same *Lusitania* that was sunk by a German torpedo in 1915.)

After the publication of *Plays Pleasant and Unpleasant* and the success of *Arms and the Man*, the plays came thick and fast. They continued to be characterized, for the most part, by social and political imperatives, and, increasingly, were first produced abroad (as was *Pygmalion*), a reflection both of Shaw's international stature and of his sense that his plays would be received more sympathetically by theatre managers and critics in, say, New York or Vienna than by the undiscerning and conservative London impresarios and critics.[8] Thus *The Devil's Disciple* (appropriately enough, given its subject of America's revolutionary war against Great Britain) opened in Albany, New York, on 1 October 1897, while the first professional production of *Caesar and Cleopatra* was in Berlin on 31 March 1906. Thanks, however, to the theatrical drive of actor and playwright (and Fabian) Harley Granville Barker and the business acumen of J.E. Vedrenne, Shaw was prompted to stage several of his plays in the welcoming environs of the small Royal Court Theatre in Sloane Square, London, where, for three heady seasons under the Barker–Vedrenne partnership (1904–07), eleven of Shaw's plays were presented, for a total of 701 performances – among them some of his greatest: *Man and Superman, You Never Can Tell, Major Barbara, The Doctor's Dilemma*, and *Candida*,[9] all of which, in their different ways, heightened Shaw's reputation for writing argumentative (and, his critics, complained, wordy) plays.

The five years between the end of the Barker–Vedrenne partnership at the Royal Court and Shaw's start on *Pygmalion* saw more controversy and more acclaim. In 1909 a short play about a horse thief set in the American west, *The Shewing-up of Blanco Posnet*, was banned in England on grounds of blasphemy,[10] and there were censorship problems as well with another 1909 short piece called *Press Cuttings*, a farce (written in aid of the London Society for Women's Suffrage) that was banned until Shaw removed allegedly satiric allusions to Prime Minister Herbert Asquith and Boer War hero General Kitchener.[11] It was also in 1909 (on 30 July) that Shaw appeared as a witness before a Joint Parliamentary Committee

---

8   Shaw told *The Observer* (2 November 1913) that 'It is the custom of the English Press, when a play of mine is produced, to inform the world that it is not a play – that it is dull, blasphemous, unpopular and financially unsuccessful', thus discouraging managers abroad, Shaw argued, from producing his work.

9   Raymond Mander and Joe Mitchenson, *Theatrical Companion to Shaw* (New York, 1955), p. 287. The other plays were *John Bull's Other Island, The Admirable Bashville, How He Lied to Her Husband, The Philanderer*, and *The Man of Destiny*.

10 Written early in 1909, *Blanco Posnet* was performed at Dublin's Abbey Theatre (Ireland was outside the Lord Chamberlain's jurisdiction) on 25 August 1909.

11 BH III, 884–95.

set up to investigate the censorship of plays, specifically the system that since 1737 had given the Lord Chamberlain (a senior official of the royal household) absolute power to determine what could or could not be seen on the British stage. Shaw's view was clear: the system 'ought to be abolished', and the drama, he argued, like other forms of creative work, should be subject to normal legal restraints (e.g., the laws of libel or blasphemy) through the courts. Many other leading writers supported Shaw, but to no avail. The Lord Chamberlain retained control over the drama until the 1968 Theatres Act did exactly what Shaw had urged in 1909.[12]

There were no censorship problems – despite its suffragette theme – with *Fanny's First Play*, which ran for 622 performances (a record for a Shaw première) at the Avenue Theatre, where it opened on 19 April 1911. *Misalliance* (Duke of York's Theatre, 23 February 1910, eleven performances) was initially less successful, but *Androcles and the Lion* (St James's Theatre, 1 September 1913, sixty-three performances) and *Pygmalion* at His Majesty's in 1914 (118 performances) enhanced Shaw's status as the leading playwright of his generation.

But Shaw and controversy were never far apart. Eliza's (and Clara's) expletive in *Pygmalion* scandalized many, but the scandal was but a leaf in the wind compared to the furore created by Shaw's iconoclastic and courageous criticism of Britain's involvement in the First World War, particularly as expressed in his book *Common Sense about the War*, published in 1914. Shaw's curse on *all* the combatants for the obscene folly of the war they had created pleased hardly anyone and antagonized almost everyone, friends shunning him and librarians and booksellers removing his books from their shelves – the ultimate form of censorship. Theatres continued to produce his plays, but Shaw himself withheld *Heartbreak House*, written in 1916–17, from publication and production until 1919 and 1920 (in the United States) respectively, even Shaw considering the ending of the play – a bomb dropping on an English country house – too provocative during wartime.

Heartbreak House was followed by the mammoth five-part *Back to Methuselah* (1923), which takes some fifteen hours to produce in full, and then *Saint Joan* (1923), which became a huge international success, but which upset the Catholic Church for treating Joan as an ordinary human being. In *The Apple Cart* (1929) Shaw pitted democratic against monarchical government (with the monarchy coming out of it

---

12 For Shaw's comments to the 1909 Joint Committee, see Conolly, ed., *Mrs Warren's Profession*, pp. 209–12. For a history of British theatre censorship, see Dominic Shellard and Steve Nicholson, *The Lord Chamberlain Regrets. A History of British Theatre Censorship* (2004).

surprisingly well) and in *The Millionairess* (1936) he presented a farcical disquisition on capitalist economics, with a lead character, Epifania Fitzfassenden, who has attracted actors such as Katharine Hepburn and Sophia Loren (who played opposite Peter Sellers in an appallingly bad 1960 film adaptation).[13] In 1929 the Malvern Festival in Worcestershire was founded by Sir Barry Jackson to honour and celebrate Shaw,[14] but other honours were declined, including a knighthood offered in 1926. Shaw did accept the Nobel Prize for 1925, but only on condition that the prize money be used to establish a foundation to encourage and support the translation of Swedish literature into English. Shaw's political agitations continued with the publication of *The Intelligent Woman's Guide to Socialism and Capitalism* in 1928, a book that was praised by Labour Prime Minister Ramsay MacDonald as 'after the Bible ... the most important book that humanity possesses', a remark that revealed MacDonald to be 'more of a wit than I suspected', Shaw said.[15] But even Winston Churchill, no political ally of Shaw's, considered him (writing in 1937) 'the greatest living master of letters in the English-speaking world'.[16]

During the 1930s and 1940s Shaw – who turned eighty in 1936 – showed no sign of slowing down as playwright or political activist, and he continued to court controversy. His respect for Hitler and Stalin (whom he met on a visit to Russia in 1931) provoked considerable fury, but was justified in Shaw's mind by the pressing need for strong leadership to combat the widespread unemployment, poverty, and inequality that constituted palpable evidence of the failings of capitalism in Britain and the United States. As the humanitarian crimes of Stalin and Hitler became more apparent, Shaw repudiated them both, and also mocked them (and Mussolini) in his play *Geneva* (1938). But as late as 1940, in a radio talk commissioned by the BBC but banned by the government, Shaw praised Hitler's 'physical and moral

---

13 For film adaptations of Shaw's plays, see Donald P. Costello, *The Serpent's Eye: Shaw and the Cinema* (Notre Dame, IN, 1965) and Bernard F. Dukore, ed., *The Collected Screenplays of Bernard Shaw* (Athens, GA, 1980).

14 See L.W. Conolly, ed., *Bernard Shaw and Barry Jackson* (Toronto, 2002). The Malvern Festival continued until 1949 and has been held intermittently since then (with or without a Shaw play). The Shaw Festival in Niagara-on-the-Lake, Ontario, has been held annually since 1962, always with two or three Shaw plays in the repertoire.

15 Michael Holroyd, *Bernard Shaw* III (*The Lure of Fantasy 1918–1950*), p. 133.

16 Holroyd III, 226. Shaw invited Churchill to the opening night of *Pygmalion*. 'I am sending you a couple of tickets for the first performance of *Pygmalion*', Shaw wrote. 'Bring a friend – if you have one'. Churchill replied: 'I deeply regret that I am unable to attend the first performance of *Pygmalion*, but I will gladly attend the second – if you have one'. (Richard Huggett, *The Truth about 'Pygmalion'* [New York, 1969], p. 114.)

courage, his diplomatic sagacity, and his triumphant rescue of his country from the yoke the Allies imposed on it in 1918'.[17]

After the death of his wife in 1943, Shaw lived – for him – a relatively reclusive life in his country home in the village of Ayot St Lawrence, Hertfordshire. But through the letters and articles he still wrote to and for the press, productions of his plays in many languages in theatres around the world, radio and television broadcasts of his plays and talks,[18] and films of his plays, Shaw remained very much in the international public eye. His death on 2 November 1950 was front-page headline news in newspapers and news bulletins everywhere, and the lights of Times Square and Broadway theatre marquees were blacked out in respect. Shaw was cremated at Golders Green Crematorium on 6 November 1950 and his ashes, mixed with his wife's, were scattered in the garden of their Ayot home (now a National Trust property) on 23 November 1950.

The Genesis and Composition of *Pygmalion*

Shaw began writing *Pygmalion* on 7 March 1912, and took just over three months to complete it. The play had been in his mind, however, since at least September 1897, when he wrote to actor Richard Mansfield (who had introduced Shaw's plays to American audiences with his September 1894 production of *Arms and the Man* in New York) that he would like to write a play for Johnston Forbes-Robertson and Mrs Patrick Campbell 'in which he shall be a west end gentleman and she an east end dona in an apron and three orange and red ostrich feathers'.[19] In the same letter Shaw also refers to Mrs Campbell as that 'rapscallionly flower girl'. Shaw had read his new play *Caesar and Cleopatra* to Forbes-Robertson and Mrs Campbell in February 1897, and they subsequently played opposite each other in a copyright performance of the play (i.e., a performance – barely more than a staged reading – mounted specifically to establish legal copyright for the author) in Newcastle on 15 March 1899. Mrs Campbell had come to prominence in the West End as Paula Tanqueray in Arthur Wing Pinero's *The Second Mrs Tanqueray* in 1893, and Shaw was later to cast her as his first English-speaking Eliza – and to fall in love with her.[20] In a letter to another actress with whom Shaw was smitten – Ellen Terry – Shaw

---

17 'The Unavoidable Subject', in Bernard Shaw, *Platform and Pulpit*, ed. Dan H. Laurence (New York, 1961), p. 289.

18 Shaw's BBC radio broadcasts are available on a British Library 2-CD set, *The Spoken Word: Bernard Shaw* (2006), with introduction and notes by L.W. Conolly.

19 CL I, 803.

20 Their stormy relationship is best experienced through their correspondence, published in *Bernard Shaw and Mrs Patrick Campbell: Their Correspondence*, ed. Alan Dent (New York, 1952).

described reading *Pygmalion* to actor-manager George Alexander (on 20 June 1912) with a view to his producing it (and playing Higgins) at his St James's Theatre. Alexander told Shaw that he would play Higgins 'with anyone in the world but Mrs P.C.', to which Shaw replied that 'it couldnt be played with anyone else'. A few days later Shaw read the play to his friend Dame Edith Lyttleton, and 'contrived' (Shaw's word) for Mrs Campbell to be present. He worried – with good cause – that his play about 'a flower girl, using awful language and wearing an apron and three ostrich feathers, and having her hat put in the oven to slay the creepy-crawlies, and being taken off the stage and washed'[21] would be beneath the dignity of the notoriously haughty and egotistical actress (hence Alexander's antipathy to working with her) who, he told the Austrian translator of his plays into German, 'has never appeared in a low life part'.[22] Shaw complicated matters by falling 'head over heels in love with her in thirty seconds'[23] when he went to her house to discuss business aspects of her involvement. Mrs Campbell did not go gently into the role of Eliza; Shaw had to plead relentlessly with her – 'I must have my Liza and no other Liza. There is no other Liza and can be no other Liza. I wrote the play to have my Liza'[24] – and they argued relentlessly about who should play Higgins until finally settling on Herbert Beerbohm Tree, generally viewed by Shaw (in the words of Tree's biographer) with 'cheerful contempt, lightened with occasional dabs of appreciation'.[25] Tree was also manager of His Majesty's Theatre, which, since its opening in 1897 (then as *Her* Majesty's) had been London's most fashionable theatre.

By the time that rehearsals began at His Majesty's on 19 February 1914 *Pygmalion* had had its world première in a German translation by Siegfried Trebitsch at the Hofburg Theatre in Vienna on 16 October 1913,[26] followed on 1 November by a production in Berlin. Both productions were well received, but the ensuing London rehearsals, directed by Shaw, were a nightmare. Tree thought the character of Higgins insufficiently flamboyant and histrionic for his abilities, and sought to enhance his interpretation by inducing Shaw – mostly to no avail – to let him 'take large quantities of snuff, to use a Scots accent, to vault on the piano from

21 CL III, 110–11 (20 August 1912).

22 CL III, 147 (Shaw to Siegfried Trebitsch, 29 January 1913).

23 CL III, 111 (20 August 1912).

24 CL III, 97 (5 July 1912).

25 Madeleine Bingham, *'The Great Lover'. The Life and Art of Herbert Beerbohm Tree* (New York, 1952), p. 218.

26 The Vienna opening was attended by Archduke Francis Ferdinand, whose assassination some six months later (on 1 June 1914) sparked the outbreak of the First World War.

time to time, [and] to indicate an addiction to port by walking with a limp and a stick'.[27] Mrs Campbell – at age forty-nine a good thirty years too old for the part of Eliza (Shaw describes Eliza in Act I as 'perhaps eighteen, perhaps twenty, hardly older') – was prone to frequent temper tantrums, and at one point – just a week before the opening – disappeared entirely from rehearsals to get married (her second) to George Cornwallis-West (recently divorced from Winston Churchill's mother), and then spent a three-day golfing honeymoon near Tunbridge Wells. And Shaw could throw his own temper tantrums, on one occasion leaving the rehearsals in a huff and staying away until Tree begged him to return.[28] As Henry Dana, Tree's manager, put it, 'if you put a cat, a dog and a monkey into a sack together, what can you expect but ructions?'[29]

Opening Night, 11 April 1914

Somehow, it all came together in time for opening night at His Majesty's Theatre on 11 April 1914, though far from perfectly. The *Westminster Gazette* pointed out in its review on 14 April 1914, that 'the characters work ill together, suggesting insufficiency of rehearsal', particularly, perhaps, from Tree, whose part, said the *Gazette*, 'sometimes appears to be improvised', with Tree seeming to rely more on his 'invention than his memory'.[30] Stories had been circulating in the press for some time (aided and abetted by numerous interviews given by Tree and Shaw) about the turbulent and erratic nature of the rehearsals for *Pygmalion*, and there were also rumours that there was something scandalous about Shaw's new play, rumours that culminated in a *Daily Sketch* headline on the day of the opening that '*Pygmalion* May Cause Sensation To-Night', with several sub-headlines, including 'Mr Shaw Introduces A Forbidden Word'. The *Sketch*, like other newspapers, wouldn't bring itself to print the word (a handful subsequently did), but predicted that unless the Lord Chamberlain intervened (he didn't) a 'dreadful word' would 'fall with bombshell suddenness from the lips of Mrs Patrick Campbell'.

Shaw's only regret over giving Eliza her famous 'Not bloody likely' response to Freddy's innocent enquiry (Act III, line 421) about whether

27 Holroyd II, 335.

28 CL III, 221.

29 Stanley Weintraub, *Journey to Heartbreak: The Crucible Years of Bernard Shaw 1914–1918* (New York, 1971), p. 4.

30 The *Westminster Gazette* review of *Pygmalion*, together with reviews from the *Clarion* (17 April 1914) and the *Nation* (18 April 1914) are included in *Shaw: The Critical Heritage*, ed. T.F. Evans (1976), pp. 223–9.

she intended to walk across the park after Mrs Higgins's at-home was that the uproarious reaction it provoked distracted attention from the rest of the play. He resolutely defended the epithet as a 'familiar and quite harmless word', 'in common use as an expletive by four-fifths of the English nation' (*Daily News*, 17 April 1914). And the word had certainly been heard on the English stage previously,[31] Shaw himself telling the *Daily Chronicle* (17 April 1914), perhaps with a touch of hyperbole, that 'it has been used of late years over and over again on the stage'. Nonetheless, this was a time when the word 'damn' was routinely banned from the English stage as blasphemous, so when Mrs Campbell actually dropped the bombshell predicted by the *Daily Sketch* something close to pandemonium broke out in His Majesty's Theatre, but it was the pandemonium of laughter, not protest. The *Daily Sketch* (13 April 1914) was but one of several newspapers that reported that the audience 'rocked to and fro in their seats and shook with laughter. They roared with laughter. They cried with laughter'. In his account to Charlotte of the opening night – Charlotte had sailed for America on 8 April to avoid the opening night distress of watching her husband's current paramour – Shaw said that the performance was 'nearly wrecked' by 'Not bloody likely'. The audience, he said, 'laughed themselves into such utter abandonment and disorder that it was really doubtful for some time whether they could recover themselves and let the play go on'.[32] True, there were some complaints; the *Sketch* thought the phrase 'absolutely appropriate in the moment', and that Mrs Campbell's 'consummate comedy acting' robbed the phrase 'of all offensiveness, making it only extraordinarily funny', but found Clara's 'Such bloody nonsense!' a few moments later 'inartistic and unpleasant'. 'It must be altered', the *Sketch* demanded. (It wasn't.) A few boos at the end of the opening night performance perhaps reflected disapproval of Eliza's and Clara's language (though Mrs Campbell thought they were directed at Tree's acting[33]), and there were mild protests from some church representatives (reported in the *Sketch*, 13 April 1914). Tree had initially had qualms about the word (even asking Shaw just a few

---

31 In, for example, *Admiral Guinea*, by W.E. Henley and R.L. Stevenson (Avenue Theatre, 29 November 1897). It is worth noting as well that every 'damn' (and its variants) was cut from the film version of *Pygmalion* for American distribution in 1938, as was any reference to Doolittle's not being married to the woman he is living with. But Eliza's 'Not bloody likely' somehow survived the censorship. (See Dukore, *The Collected Screenplays of Bernard Shaw*, p. 76.)

32 CL III, 227. According to stage manager Stanley Bell's stopwatch, the laughter lasted a minute and a quarter (Huggett, *The Truth about Pygmalion*, p. 137).

33 CL III, 228.

hours before the curtain went up on opening night if 'bloody' could be changed to 'ruddy'[34]), but when the Theatrical Managers' Association, worried about 'retaining the respect of the public for the theatre', asked Tree to remove it from the play he flatly refused.[35]

It was all great fun, and it sold tickets. But for Shaw it was also a problem in that the palaver over 'bloody' had become a major distraction from the more serious elements of the play. He told the *Daily News* (17 April 1914) that when 'the nine days' wonder about the word "bloody", and the laughter at the superficial fun of the play is over – as I hope it soon will be – the scene in the third act will be more interesting than it is now, not less'. Two days later (19 April 1914) Shaw sent Charlotte some 'dreary bundles of press cuttings' that showed, he told her, that 'all political and social questions have been swept from the public mind by Eliza's expletive'.[36]

But the laughter wasn't the only problem on the opening night of *Pygmalion*. While describing to Charlotte the impact of 'Not bloody likely' on the play as a whole, Shaw also fretted about the tensions between his two star actors. Tree had complained to him that the play was too long, blaming Mrs Campbell for spending too much time over her costume changes. Mrs Campbell, on the other hand, complained that Tree 'takes thirty seconds between each word and five minutes between each bite of the apple he munches in Act IV'. Shaw's sympathies were with Mrs Campbell, though factors other than her acting ability perhaps coloured his judgment. In any event, Shaw reported to Charlotte that he had told Tree that though he was 'a man in a thousand' (an enigmatic compliment at best) he was 'for my purposes, an infamous actor, and had better drop Higgins as soon as he has got through the present run'.[37]

Largely because of Tree's acting, 'the raving absurdity' of which 'was quite beyond description',[38] Shaw told Charlotte he had 'writhed in hell' for the last two acts, and he bolted from the theatre as quickly as he could at the end – but not quickly enough to miss Tree's final outrage.

34 CL III, 226–7.

35 Bingham, '*The Great Lover*', pp. 229–30.

36 CL III, 229.

37 CL III, 229. Shaw also wrote to American producer Lee Shubert the day after the opening of *Pygmalion* to tell him 'to leave Sir Herbert Tree out of your plans as far as they concern *Pygmalion* in America', for 'it would clearly be a mistake for Sir Herbert to stake his next visit to the States on a part so ill adapted to his personality and his methods' (*Theatrics*, 119).

38 CL III, 227.

The Ending(s) of *Pygmalion*

Shaw had worked particularly hard during rehearsals on impressing both Tree and Mrs Campbell that the ending of *his* version of the Pygmalion myth did not correspond with the version from classical mythology, at the end of which Pygmalion marries Galatea (see below, p. xxxiii). As Shaw makes very clear in his Sequel to the play (below, pp. 129–40), *Pygmalion* is a 'romance' only because 'the transfiguration it records seems exceedingly improbable' (though, Shaw adds, it is 'common enough'). 'Nevertheless', Shaw continues, 'people in all directions have assumed, for no other reason than that she [Eliza] became the heroine of a romance, that she must have married the hero [i.e., Higgins] of it'. What Shaw declared to be an 'unbearable' outcome began with Herbert Tree's performance at His Majesty's Theatre.

Shaw had carefully directed Tree in the final moments of the play to 'occupy himself affectionately with his mother, & throw Eliza the commission to buy the ham &c. over his shoulder'.[39] That is, there was to be no suggestion of a romantic future for Higgins and Eliza. Shaw did, however, provide engagingly ambiguous dialogue and stage directions in the original text of the play (the text used at His Majesty's). After Higgins has given his shopping orders to Eliza, she '*disdainfully*' retorts 'Buy them yourself' and '*sweeps out*'. Mrs Higgins then offers to do some clothes shopping for Henry, but Henry tells her not to bother because Eliza will 'buy em all right enough'. Mrs Higgins exits (for Doolittle's wedding), leaving Higgins alone on stage. Higgins says nothing else, but '*rattles his cash in his pocket; chuckles; and disports himself in a highly self-satisfied manner*'. And the curtain falls.[40]

This 'richly suggestive' ending, as A.M. Gibbs has aptly described it,[41] provides interesting talking points for the audience as they leave the theatre. Is Higgins's self-satisfied confidence that Eliza will return justified? And if she does return, what will her relationship with Higgins be? Does Eliza's imperious exit indicate emancipation from her teacher and a new life independent of him? The questions may have remained but for Tree's sabotaging of Shaw's intentions. As Shaw described it to Charlotte, the 'last thing' he saw as he hastily left the theatre on opening night was Higgins 'shoving his mother rudely out of his way and wooing Eliza with appeals to buy a ham for his lonely home like a bereaved Romeo'.[42]

---

39 CL III, 227.
40 See Appendix III.1 for the full text of the original ending of the play.
41 A.M. Gibbs, *Bernard Shaw: A Life* (Gainesville, FL, 2005), p. 331.
42 CL III, 227–8.

Things got worse as the run continued. When Shaw saw *Pygmalion* again – at the 100th performance on 15 July 1914 – Tree's Romeo imitation had been embellished by his throwing flowers after Eliza as she leaves the stage at the end of the play. Mrs Campbell had also succumbed to romanticizing the relationship, countermanding Shaw's direction at the end of (the original) Act IV that Eliza merely looks for the ring that Higgins has just flung away by not only finding it but then, on her knees, gazing 'feelingly' at it. It was all, Shaw later complained to Tree's daughter Viola, a 'breach of faith', and he resolved never to see the production again – though he knew by then that it was shortly to close.[43]

Shaw's first decisive – and startlingly innovative – step to counteract the damage that he believed had been done by Tree's shenanigans at the end of the play was to write the Sequel that first appeared with the 1916 publication of the play by Constable. The Sequel is a prose narrative that mingles the after-play lives of his *Pygmalion* characters with contemporary figures such as novelist H.G. Wells, General William Booth (founder of the Salvation Army), novelist and playwright John Galsworthy, and others. Shaw makes it clear that while Higgins would remain 'one of the strongest personal interests' in Eliza's life, her instinct tells her 'not to marry' him, and that Higgins's 'indifference to young women on the ground that they had an irresistible rival in his mother' is 'the clue to his inveterate old-bachelordom'. On the other hand, Freddy Eynsford Hill, whom Eliza first meets at Mrs Higgins's at-home in Act III, is soon 'pouring out his love for her daily through the post', so will Eliza 'look forward to a lifetime of fetching Higgins's slippers or to a lifetime of Freddy fetching hers?' Shaw asks. It's no contest. 'Unless Freddy is biologically repulsive to her, and Higgins biologically attractive to a degree that overwhelms all her other instincts, she will, if she marries either of them, marry Freddy'. 'And that', Shaw declares authoritatively and definitively, 'is just what Eliza did'. And, with the financial backing of Colonel Pickering, the Eynsford Hills set up a florist and greengrocer business 'in the arcade of a railway station not far from the Victoria and Albert Museum; and if you live in that neighborhood you may go there any day and buy a buttonhole from Eliza'.

43 Holroyd II, 340. *Pygmalion* ran at His Majesty's for 118 performances, closing on 24 July 1914. It could have run much longer, but Tree was getting bored and he announced the closing at the end of June, when, according to Mrs Campbell, box office revenue was some £2,000 a week (Dent, *Bernard Shaw and Mrs Patrick Campbell*, p. 184). St John Ervine believed the closing was prompted by the murder of Archduke Francis Fedinand in Sarajevo on 28 June 1914 and the imminent outbreak of World War I (*Bernard Shaw: His Life, Work and Friends* [New York, 1956], p. 459).

The Sequel was one way for Shaw to affirm how the play should end, but the text of the Sequel does not constitute a change to the text of the play itself, and Shaw continued to grapple with the issue of the ending as Mrs Campbell and various producers sought to exploit the commercial success of the production at His Majesty's. Tree was now out of the picture, but Mrs Campbell and several of the company from the production at His Majesty's opened the American English-language première of the play at New York's Park Theatre on 14 October 1914, Mrs Campbell playing opposite a new Higgins, Philip Merivale, who had played Pickering at His Majesty's.[44] Shaw told producer George Tyler that Merivale wouldn't sentimentalize the part, but Tyler confessed to Shaw that he had retained Tree's romantic London ending.[45] It was difficult for Shaw to exercise control over a New York production, but when the play came back to London – still with Mrs Campbell as Eliza, now opposite C. Aubrey Smith – in a production at the Aldwych Theatre that opened on 10 February 1920 directed by Tree's daughter Viola, Shaw experimented with a new ending. He gave instructions that after Eliza, maintaining her 'pride and triumph to the end', makes her final exit, Higgins must go to the balcony to watch her departure from his mother's home, and then 'come back triumphantly into the room' and exclaim 'Galatea!' as the curtain falls. Shaw believed that this would show that 'the statue has come to life at last', but such an explicit parallel between Eliza and Galatea also implies at least the possibility that the play follows the myth and that just as Pygmalion marries Galatea so Higgins marries Eliza. There is no record of this ending being used again.[46]

Eventually Shaw decided that the only way to make his intentions absolutely clear was to remove any inkling of ambiguity from the ending. An ideal opportunity arose when the idea was mooted to make a film version of *Pygmalion*. A film co-directed by Anthony Asquith and Leslie Howard (who also starred as Higgins, with Wendy Hiller as Eliza) was eventually released in London on 6 October 1938 (and in New York on 7 December 1938),[47] but Shaw had prepared a screenplay as early as 1934. The ending of the 1934 screenplay has Higgins on his mother's balcony

---

44 The American première of *Pygmalion* was a German production that opened at the Irving Place Theatre on 24 March 1914, with Hansi Arnstaedt as Eliza and Heinrich Marlowe as Higgins. The New York *Sun* (25 March 1914) said that the audience was 'mildy amused'.

45 CL III, 253.

46 The full description of the Aldwych ending is given in Appendix III.2.

47 German and Dutch film versions of *Pygmalion* were made in 1935 and 1937 respectively. See Costello, *The Serpent's Eye* and Dukore, *The Collected Screenplays of Bernard Shaw*. Neither version was faithful to Shaw's play, and both romanticized the ending (i.e., projecting a Higgins–Eliza marriage).

witnessing Eliza and Freddy kissing as they leave for Doolittle's wedding. Higgins shakes his fist at the couple, while Eliza '*cocks a snoot*' in response and Freddy '*takes off his hat to* HIGGINS *in the Chaplin manner*'.[48] Shaw wrote another screenplay in 1938, which has an even more explicit ending. It shows what Shaw calls a '*vision of the future*', with Eliza and Freddy in a florist's shop in South Kensington (as described in the Sequel). The shop is '*full of fashionable customers*'; Eliza is behind the counter '*in great splendor*' serving flowers; and Freddy, '*in apron and mild muttonchop whiskers*', looks after the vegetables.[49]

The clarity of these endings was first reflected in a relatively small but important change to the published text of the play when it was re-issued by Constable in 1939. Eliza still '*sweeps out*', but now, instead of offering to do some clothes shopping for Higgins ('I'll buy your tie and gloves'), Mrs Higgins reflects on the relationship between Eliza and her son: 'I should be uneasy about you and her', she says, 'if she were less fond of Colonel Pickering', a line that gives Higgins the lead-in to the unambiguous new conclusion: 'Pickering! Nonsense: she's going to marry Freddy. Ha ha! Freddy! Freddy!! Ha ha ha ha ha!!!!! [*He roars with laughter as the play ends.*]'[50]

What could be clearer? But still producers and directors have insisted on thwarting Shaw. The producer (Gabriel Pascal) and co-directors of the 1938 film of *Pygmalion* secretly shot a different ending to Shaw's screenplay, keeping it from him until he saw it at the press preview two days before the première, too late for him to do anything about it. Pascal's ending shows not the married independent business woman that Shaw wanted, but a subservient Eliza returning to Higgins's home helping a smug mentor and master find his slippers, 'leaving the public assured', as Pascal's wife astutely put it, 'that Eliza would be running for those slippers to the end of her days'.[51] How ironic, then, that Shaw should win an Oscar for the screenplay of *Pygmalion* (making him the first person to win both a Nobel Prize and an Oscar – matched subsequently only by former U.S. Vice-President Al Gore). The image of a subservient Eliza has been perpetuated most effectively, however, by the

---

48 See Appendix III.5.

49 See Appendix III.6.

50 See Appendix III.3.

51 Valerie Pascal, *The Disciple and His Devil* (1970), p. 85. The involvement of the Tree family in the history of *Pygmalion* continued with the casting in the film of Violet Tree in a bit part in the ballroom scene and of David Tree (Violet's daughter, Beerbohm Tree's grandson) as Freddy Eynsford Hill.

melodious but saccharine adaptation of *Pygmalion* as the 1956 Broadway musical *My Fair Lady* (starring Rex Harrison and Julie Andrews),[52] followed by the 1964 film version (in which the more chic but less melodic Audrey Hepburn replaced Julie Andrews as Eliza). The ending of *My Fair Lady* (on stage and on screen) is essentially the same as the ending of the 1938 Pascal film. And even critics and biographers otherwise sympathetic to Shaw have told him, in effect, that in rejecting the romantic ending he didn't know what he was talking about – witness St John Ervine's comment that all 'sensible people' conclude that Eliza 'married Henry Higgins and bore him many vigorous and intelligent children'.[53]

Which *Pygmalion*?

Any discussion, then, of 'Shaw's *Pygmalion*' must be prefaced by clarification of *which Pygmalion* is under consideration. The audience that saw *Pygmalion* at the Shaw Festival in Niagara-on-the-Lake, Ontario, in 2004, directed by Jackie Maxwell, for example, saw a very different play from that presented by the Peter Hall Company in England in 2007. Maxwell chose to use the version that incorporates scenes from the 1938 film, while Hall gave his audiences Shaw's original and significantly different 1916 version – roughly the one seen at His Majesty's Theatre in April 1914.

The textual history of *Pygmalion* is more complicated than most in the Shavian canon, but it is instructive to trace it. Shaw's original manuscript copy of the play, neatly written in shorthand, is held at the Harry Ransom Humanities Research Center (HRC) at the University of Texas at Austin (SHAW 24.7). The typed transcription of the shorthand manuscript, corrected and revised by Shaw (HRC SHAW 24.5), was the basis for the first publication of *Pygmalion*, a German translation by Siegfried Trebitsch, published in Berlin on 16 October 1913 (LB, A124a), simultaneously with the world première in Vienna. Hungarian and Swedish translations followed, in January and April 1914 respectively (LB, A124b, A124c). Unauthorized extracts translated from the German edition were published in the *New York Times* on 30 November 1913 (LB, C1918 and

---

52 Shaw had strenuously resisted attempts to turn *Pygmalion* into a musical – 'a Pygmalion operetta is quite out of the question', he told Siegfried Trebitsch, his German translator (CL III, 731, 28 August 1921) – and when the idea came up again in 1948 he said 'I absolutely forbid any such outrage' (CL IV, 813, 3 February 1948). The relationship between *Pygmalion* and *My Fair Lady* is well documented in Paul Bauschatz, 'The Uneasy Evolution of *My Fair Lady* from *Pygmalion*', *SHAW: The Annual of Bernard Shaw Studies*, 18 (1998), 181–98. See also Keith Garebian, *The Making of My Fair Lady* (Toronto, [1993]).

53 Ervine, *Bernard Shaw*, p. 460. For further misrepresentations of the ending of the play see below, 'Stage History', pp. xlv–xlix.

CL III, 213–14). The first full and authorized English-language publication of *Pygmalion* appeared roughly simultaneously in the United States in *Everybody's Magazine* in November 1914, and in England in *Nash's and Pall Mall Magazine* in November and December 1914 (both LB, C1959). There are minor spelling and punctuation variations between the two texts, mainly reflecting differences in British and American usage. Both are illustrated with line drawings of scenes from the play. An unauthorized bound edition of the *Pygmalion* text from *Everybody's Magazine* was issued in New York by Putnams in November 1914 (LB, A124d).

The first authorized English-language publication of *Pygmalion* in book form was in a three-play collection published in New York by Brentano's on 21 April 1916 (LB, A137a; the two other Shaw plays are *Androcles and the Lion* and *Overruled*) and by Constable in London on 25 May 1916 (LB, A137b). The 1916 *Pygmalion* is substantively the same as the 1914 magazine texts, though it now includes Shaw's Preface and Sequel. In response, however, to the determined efforts of Herbert Beerbohm Tree and others to put a sentimental gloss on the ending of the play, Shaw eventually decided that the published text had to be altered. He had an opportunity to do so when Constable began bringing out major collections of his work in the 1930s, beginning with a Collected Edition in 1930, but it was the misshapen ending of the 1938 film that probably prompted Shaw to act.

A strange edition of *Pygmalion* was published in the United States by Dodd, Mead in 1939 (LB, A198c) – strange in that although it contains several photographs from Gabriel Pascal's film of the play the text is the 1916 original. Readers who had seen the film and then decided to read the Dodd, Mead edition must have been puzzled by the huge discrepancies between the two forms (especially the ending).[54] Shaw's first major step towards removing the confusion came with a 1939 edition of *Pygmalion* in a volume (still also including *Androcles and the Lion* and *Overruled*) published in Constable's 'Standard Edition' of Shaw's works (LB, A207). For the first time, the ending was changed to Higgins's declaration that Eliza will marry Freddy (as in Appendix III.3).

And then, prompted by a proposal from Alan Lane at Penguin Books, Shaw finally decided to go the whole hog. On 9 November 1939 he wrote to William Maxwell at Constable to tell him that he had sent 'a fearful job' to Constable's printer in Edinburgh. The job was 'a new edition of

---

54 The 1939 Dodd, Mead edition prints the text (pp. ix–xi) of a trailer that Shaw made for American distribution of the film, in which he makes the curious statement that 'My friend, Mr Gabriel Pascal, who has made this production, has tried the extraordinary experiment of putting a play on the screen *just as the author wrote it and he wanted it produced*' [my italics].

Pygmalion with several screen scenes interpolated'. 'The occasion', Shaw said, was 'a proposal to Penguinize Pyg.', a proposal that Shaw had accepted on condition that the printing be done by Constable.[55] Constable were also free to publish the edition themselves, which they did on 14 February 1941. The Penguin edition, with illustrations by Feliks Topolski, was published (94,500 copies) on 19 September 1941 (LB, A241). The 'screen scenes' are of Shaw's, not Gabriel Pascal's, making, and represent Shaw's wishes about how the film *should* have ended, and how productions of the play should end. It was the 1941 Constable and Penguin text that was included in the definitive and authorized edition of Shaw's plays and prefaces published by Max Reinhardt at the Bodley Head in 1972,[56] and is the text used in this New Mermaids edition.

Sources and Influences

To some extent, Shaw himself was responsible for the abuse of the original ending of *Pygmalion*, much as he liked to blame actors and directors for their intransigence and shortsightedness. His decision to use the Pygmalion/Galatea myth as the basis of his plot was bound to raise expectations of a Higgins/Eliza marriage, though Ovid was far from the only influence at work on the play.

In fact, some influences on *Pygmalion* have been more evident to commentators on the play than they were to Shaw himself. Soon after the première of the play, similarities between Higgins's experiment with Eliza and an episode in Tobias Smollett's 1751 novel *Peregrine Pickle* were pointed out. Smollett's eponymous hero buys a bedraggled young beggar from her mother, has her scrubbed and dressed as a lady, teaches her to speak and behave fashionably, and successfully passes her off in society until in an argument in a card game, as Smollett describes it, 'the floodgates of her own natural repartee' burst open and she 'twanged off' at her opponent 'with the appelation of b—— and w——'. The appelations are repeated 'with great vehemence', and as the young lady angrily leaves the room she 'applied her hand to that part which was the last of her that disappeared, inviting the company to kiss it, by one of its coarsest denominations'.[57] When asked in 1925 about the similarities between this section of Smollett's novel and *Pygmalion*, Shaw replied (through his

---

55 HRC SHAW 25.5.

56 *The Bodley Bernard Shaw. Collected Plays with their Prefaces.* Volume IV. Editorial Supervisor, Dan H. Laurence. London: Max Reinhardt, The Bodley Head, 1972.

57 Tobias Smollett, *Peregrine Pickle* (1751), chapter 87, in which Peregrine 'meets with a Nymph of the Road, whom he takes into Keeping, and metamorphoses into a Fine Lady'.

secretary) that he had never read *Peregrine Pickle* and added that the 'experiment of two writers of fiction treating the same subject and producing the same series of incidents – the same results practically – shews that the human imagination always runs in the same grooves, and that this is the explanation of almost all the alleged plagiarisms'.[58]

Many parallels between *Pygmalion* and the novels of Charles Dickens (with which Shaw was intimately familiar) have also been pointed out – the early scene in *Pickwick Papers* where Pickwick's note-taking, like Higgins's, creates suspicion in the gathering crowd; Boffin, the dustman in *Our Mutual Friend*, who, like Doolittle, inherits a fortune – and problems to go with it; Lizzie Hexman (also in *Our Mutual Friend*), who, like Shaw's Eliza, escapes from poverty; Pip, in *Great Expectations*, and Eliza, both of whom, it has been noted, 'are virtually recreated by their social sculptors and both [of whom] end up resenting their respective benefactors'; and several others.[59] *Pygmalion* has been linked as well to the Victorian writer William Ernest Henley (particularly his sonnet 'Eliza'); to a short story, 'The Lady Automaton', by Ernest Edward Kellett; to a 1909 novel, *Our Adversary*, by Mary Elizabeth Braddon; to a short story by Henry James called 'The Real Thing' (1892); to Florence Marryat's 1879 novel, *Out of His Reckoning*; to Gilbert and Sullivan's *Pygmalion and Galatea* (1871); to Somerset Maugham's *Liza of Lambeth* (1897); and to many other works. Even Eliza's hat gets into the game, one writer arguing that its '*three ostrich feathers, orange, sky-blue, and red*' (Act II, lines 95–6) derive from an eighteenth-century production of Rousseau's opera *Pygmalion*.[60] Whatever the validity

58 CL III, 912. See E.S. Noyes, 'A Note on *Peregrine Pickle* and *Pygmalion*', *Modern Language Notes* 41 (1926), 327–30, and Valerie Grosvenor Myer, '*Peregrine Pickle* and *Pygmalion*', *Notes and Queries* 226 (1981), 430–31.

59 See Michael Goldberg, 'The Informing Presence of Charles Dickens in Bernard Shaw's *Pygmalion*', *The Dickensian* 80.3 (1984), 144–50, and Michael Goldberg, 'Shaw's *Pygmalion*: The Reworking of *Great Expectations*', *The Shaw Review* 22.3 (1979), 114–22. The quoted comment on Pip and Eliza is from Goldberg 115.

60 On these and other influences and parallels see Julie A. Sparks, 'An Overlooked Source for Eliza? W.E. Henley's *London Types*', *SHAW: The Annual of Bernard Shaw Studies* 18 (1998), 161–71; Philip Klass, ' "The Lady Automaton" by E.E. Kellett: A *Pygmalion* Source?', *SHAW: The Annual of Bernard Shaw Studies*, 2 (1982), 75–82; Sara Moore Putzell, 'Another Source for *Pygmalion*: G.B.S. and M.E. Braddon', *The Shaw Review*, 22.1 (1979), 29–32; E.F. Briden, 'James's Miss Churm: Another of Eliza's Prototypes?', *The Shaw Review*, 19.1 (1976), 17–21; Jule Eisenbud, 'Possible Sources of Shaw's *Pygmalion*', *Notes and Queries*, 222 (1977), 442–4; Virginia E. de Moss, 'The Probable Source of Eliza Doolittle's Plumed Hat in Shaw's *Pygmalion*', *Notes and Queries* 220 (1975), 203. There is extended discussion of the presentation of the Pygmalion myth (and the related Cinderella story) on the nineteenth-century stage in Essaka Joshua, *Pygmalion and Galatea. The History of a Narrative in English Literature* (Aldershot, 2001), pp. 97–133. Charles Berst's book, *Pygmalion: Shaw's Spin on Myth and Cinderella* (New York, 1995) is premised largely on the Cinderella parallel, as is Maurice Valency's discussion of the play in *The Cart and The Trumpet* (New York, 1973), pp. 312–28.

of these claims and conjectures, from Shaw's point of view it was all grist to his mill: 'If I find in a book anything I can make use of, I take it gratefully. My plays are full of pillage of this kind'. Shaw's own image for the process was not from milling, but from fishing – 'all is fish that comes to my net'.[61] Or, as stage designer and theatre historian Laurence Irving once neatly put it in a letter to the *Times Literary Supplement* (20 November 1959), 'GBS shared with Shakespeare an easy conscience in turning the ideas of others to his own account'.

One fish that Shaw acknowledged through his chosen title for the play was, of course, the myth of Pygmalion and Galatea, found most readily in Book X of Ovid's *Metamorphoses*. As Ovid put it, Pygmalion, 'horrified/ At all the countless vices nature gives/To womankind', decided to sculpt his own ideal female out of ivory, and promptly fell in love with it. He caressed the statue, kissed it, dressed it, spoke to it, and gave it gifts, finally praying to Venus that it be given life. His prayer granted, Pygmalion's lips 'pressed real lips, and she, his girl,/Felt every kiss, and blushed, and shyly raised/Her eyes to his and saw the world and him'. Venus further 'graced the union she had made,/And when nine times the crescent moon had filled/Her silver orb, an infant girl was born . . .'.[62] It is an engaging story, particularly from a male point of view. Shaw was not interested in catering to male sexual fantasies, but once he had decided to call the play *Pygmalion* he was, as it were, hoist by his own petard. While Shaw wanted readers and audiences to make the obvious connection with the myth, his aim was then to *subvert* rather than to *fulfil* their expectations. What he discovered, however, is that they preferred fulfilment to subversion and interpreted the play accordingly – i.e., Higgins (Pygmalion) wins his Galatea (Eliza).[63]

Such an outcome runs entirely contrary to perhaps the most important influence of all on *Pygmalion* (and on much else that Shaw wrote) – the plays of Norwegian playwright Henrik Ibsen, whose work (as mentioned above, p. xv) Shaw had celebrated in 1891 in *The Quintessence of Ibsenism*, which he was revising while writing *Pygmalion*.[64]

---

61 *The Observer*, 11 January 1914. Shaw identified Shakespeare, Dickens, Conan Doyle, Oscar Wilde, and Granville Barker as some of the fish in his net. The statement from *The Observer* is reprinted in BH IV, 799.

62 Ovid, *Metamorphoses*. Trans. A.D. Melville (Oxford, 1986), pp. 232–4. Ovid does not give a name to Pygmalion's statue.

63 J. Ellen Gainor has suggested that it is as if Shaw was relying on 'an informed, thoughtful audience's "self-alienation" from the expected outcome' (*Shaw's Daughters: Dramatic and Narrative Constructions of Gender* [Ann Arbor, MI, 1991], p. 227).

64 The revised edition of *Quintessence* was published on 28 August 1913 (LB, A12c), just a few weeks before the Vienna première of *Pygmalion*.

An 'Intensely and Deliberately Didactic' Play

While closely associated with issues of social reform, including women's rights, Ibsen shunned the role of public advocacy that Shaw so effectively and enthusiastically embraced. Thus, as well as describing *Pygmalion* in his 1916 Preface (below, p. 2) as an 'intensely and deliberately didactic' play, Shaw provocatively added – *pace* Oscar Wilde – that 'great art can never be anything else'. The remark would have puzzled some of the early critics of the play who would probably have quickly dismissed Shaw's theoretical declaration as perverse and then made the point that in any case didacticism implies clarity of purpose and meaning. And their experience of *Pygmalion* was anything but that. The anonymous critic of the *Westminster Gazette* (14 April 1914) was 'curious as to what is the foundation idea' of the play, in which he found 'plenty of ideas', but none 'predominant'. H.W. Massingham in *The Nation* (18 April 1914) was more blunt when he charged that 'Mr Shaw has failed to show his audience precisely what he meant'. One can hardly expect first-night reviewers to fathom everything at one sitting, especially the kind of opening-night *Pygmalion* that Beerbohm Tree gave them, and since then, aided by Shaw's changes to the ending, his 1916 Preface and Sequel, thousands of productions, and voluminous critical commentary, the 'predominant' ideas have become clearer.

Shaw doesn't do himself any favours by describing the play as 'didactic' – and 'intensely and deliberately' didactic at that. The term implies heavy moralizing and stuffy pedagogy, but *Pygmalion* – especially the *Pygmalion* we experience in the theatre – is far from that. It is a comfortably accessible play for audiences and readers alike, with an uncomplicated and 'singularly elegant'[65] structure (exposition in Act I; development of situation in Acts II, III, and IV; discussion and resolution in Act V), naturalistic dialogue, easily distinguishable characters, and a good deal of humour in language, situation, and character. But Shaw is neither joking nor being ironic when he says *Pygmalion* is didactic. Amid all of the laughter (including that generated by the wonderful Doolittle in Acts II and V) there is indeed a point being made, one about which Shaw felt passionately. It is best appreciated through the character of Eliza and her relationship to one of Ibsen's most famous characters.

Shaw's Nora

The title of Ibsen's *A Doll's House*, which Shaw reviewed for the *Manchester Guardian* on 8 June 1889, and again for the *Saturday Review*

---

65 Eric Bentley's term, 'A Personal Play', in Harold Bloom, ed., *George Bernard Shaw's Pygmalion* (New York, 1988), p. 16.

on 15 May 1897,[66] is indicative of the way in which Nora Helmer, married with three young children, is perceived and treated in the play by her bank manager husband. After a series of incidents that shock Nora into recognizing that she is merely a doll, a plaything, for her husband's amusement, she dramatically and courageously leaves him, in obedience, as Shaw put it in his 1897 review, 'to an impulse of duty to herself', famously slamming the door as she quits his house – a moment that Shaw described as 'the end of a chapter of human history ... more momentous than the cannon of Waterloo or Sedan'.[67] The image of a woman being treated as a doll occurs in *Pygmalion* when Mrs Higgins accuses her son and Colonel Pickering of being 'a pretty pair of babies, playing with your live doll' (Act III, lines 573–4). Higgins promptly rejects the notion that he's 'playing' with Eliza – 'It's the hardest job I ever tackled', he protests, and goes on to explain to his mother that she has 'no idea how frightfully interesting it is to take a human being and change her into a quite different human being by creating a new speech for her'. It is, Higgins says, 'filling up the deepest gulf that separates class from class and soul from soul' (Act III, lines 576–80). While Higgins myopically overlooks the importance of money and education in class divisions, he does recognize for the first time in the play what he is doing to and for Eliza. Far from simply amusing himself with a little experiment to win a bet with Pickering (Act II, lines 263–4), he is actually embarked on transforming a human being – not, like Pygmalion, from death to life, but from a life of abject and humiliating poverty[68] to one that opens up viable options for her, one of which – marrying Freddy and opening a flower shop – Shaw tells us in his Sequel, she chooses. Eliza, then, by the end of the play, is very much in the tradition of independent Shavian women – Vivie in *Mrs Warren's Profession*, Candida in *Candida*,[69] Barbara in *Major Barbara*, for example – who make their own decisions about their future, as does Nora. Eliza's transformation is not as breathtaking as Nora's, and Nora must achieve her transformation and independence in spite of her oppressive husband, but Eliza's departure

---

66 The reviews are in Dukore, *Drama Observed*, I, 106–7, and III, 847–50.

67 Dukore, *Drama Observed*, III, 848. Shaw is referring to the Battle of Waterloo (1815) and the Battle of Sedan (1870).

68 For Shaw, poverty was the 'worst of all crimes'. 'Poverty', continues Andrew Undershaft in *Major Barbara* (Act III), 'blights whole cities; spreads horrible pestilences; strikes dead the very souls of all who come within sight, sound, or smell of it'.

69 Candida's decision at the end of *Candida* is particularly interesting in that, unlike, Nora, she decides to *stay* with her husband – but it is a marriage in which Candida is the dominant partner.

from Higgins at the end of the play is in its way just as emphatic as Nora's slamming the door.[70] Eliza's parting words – 'What you are to do without me, I cannot imagine', might well have been Nora's. Transformation is not easy for either woman (they both contemplate suicide), though Eliza's future, it might be argued, is more predictable and secure than Nora's. Eliza is also – outwardly, at least – more anxious about her transformation, worrying, understandably enough, that although Higgins claims that he has made her 'free' (Act IV, line 201) she doesn't now know what she is 'fit for': 'Where am I to go? What am I to do? Whats to become of me?' (Act IV, lines 204–5). 'I wish youd left me where you found me', she says (Act IV, lines 238–9), but Higgins had found her in the gutter, and we know from the scene added by Shaw at the end of Act I that she is living in Angel Court in circumstances that are far from angelic – with *the irreducible minimum of poverty's needs*. Her transformation from Angel Court to a Kensington flower shop is, as one critic has put it, Eliza's 'salvation as a social being', and she emerges from her conflicts with Higgins (in this 'genuinely Ibsenist play') as 'a fine and independent Galatea'.[71]

This reading of the play – as an Ibsen-inspired tale of a woman's escape from class and gender oppression to a position of economic and personal freedom – has been challenged by critics such as Margery Morgan and J. Ellen Gainor. Morgan describes the theme of *Pygmalion* as 'the degradation of women and wastage of life in patriarchal society',[72] and Gainor cites the Sequel as evidence of Shaw's wish to deprive Eliza of the 'power she *seems* [my emphasis] to gain in her fight for independence'[73] – that is,

---

70 Eliza does get to slam the door on Higgins as she quits his house towards the end of Act IV (line 358).

71 Errol Durbach, '*Pygmalion*: Myth and Anti-Myth in the Plays of Ibsen and Shaw' in Bloom, *George Bernard Shaw's Pygmalion*, pp. 95–8. See also Harold F. Brooks, '*Pygmalion* and *When We Dead Awaken*', *Notes and Queries*, 205 (1960), 469–71 for further Ibsen parallels. Bernard Dukore and others have likened Eliza to Nora; see, e.g., Dukore's *Bernard Shaw, Playwright* (Columbia, 1973), pp. 60–4. In his introduction to *Quintessence*, J.L. Wisenthal notes the similarities between *Pygmalion* and Ibsen's play *When We Dead Awaken*, which also depicts a sculptor–model relationship in the characters of Rubek and Irene. See J.L. Wisenthal, ed., *Shaw and Ibsen: Bernard Shaw's 'The Quintessence of Ibsenism' and Related Writings* (Toronto, 1979), p. 58.

72 'Margery M. Morgan on Shaw and the Social System' in Harold Bloom, ed., *George Bernard Shaw* (2000), p. 78. Elsewhere, however, Morgan has recognized that 'the possibilities of life are open to the New Woman at the end of the play' (*The Shavian Playground: An Exploration of the Art of George Bernard Shaw* [2000], p. 175).

73 Gainor, *Shaw's Daughters*, p. 239. Arnold Silver has also warned against allowing 'Shaw's standing as a good Fabian' to obscure other dimensions of the play, which, in Silver's case, encompass an extensive psychoanalytical reading in which, for example, Higgins's habit of jingling (Silver calls it 'fingering') coins and keys in his pocket is equated with masturbation. (Arnold Silver, *Bernard Shaw: The Darker Side* [Stanford, CA, 1982], pp. 182, 211.)

Eliza is shown to be still dependent on Higgins and Pickering as she struggles to make a success of her flower shop. It is certainly true that the Eliza of the Sequel never gains the independence of, say, Vivie in *Mrs Warren's Profession*, but any degradation we see in the play applies much more to the vulnerable and poverty-stricken Eliza in the gutters of Covent Garden and the slums of Angel Court than in the feisty and self-confident woman in Mrs Higgins's drawing room in Act V (the one who tells Higgins 'Now I don't care that [*snapping her fingers*] for your bullying and your big talk') or the flower shop that Shaw describes in the Sequel.[74]

Pygmalion-Higgins

Shaw speaks at some length in his Preface (below, p. 2) of the work of British phonetician Henry Sweet, and while Shaw denies that Higgins is a portrait of Sweet, he acknowledges that 'there are touches of Sweet in the play' and that phoneticians such as Sweet 'are among the most important people in England at present' (below, pp. 5, 6).[75] That is, Shaw believed that a major barrier to social mobility in Britain's rigid Edwardian class system was elocution (encompassing accent and pronunciation, as well as delivery) and that phoneticians, by teaching elocution, could at least put some dents in the system and thus enable talented people like Eliza

---

74 Some of the divergence of opinion about *Pygmalion* relates directly to the various endings of the play discussed above, some interpretations in the 1950s, for example, resting on the invalid assumption that Shaw wrote *all* of the screenplay used in the 1938 film version and must, therefore, have had no problem with the audience gaining the impression that Higgins and Eliza had been 'more than reconciled' (Milton Crane, '*Pygmalion*: Bernard Shaw's Dramatic Theory and Practice', *PMLA* 66.6 [1951], 883). And Myron Matlaw later expressed the view that there is a 'dramatically inevitable' ending to the play – i.e., 'the "happy ending" Shaw himself wrote for Pascal's film' ('The Denoument of *Pygmalion*', *Modern Drama* 1 [1958–9], 29).

75 For appreciations of Sweet, see Bertrand M. Wainger, 'Henry Sweet – Shaw's Pygmalion', *Studies in Philology*, 27 (1930), 558–72, and M. Cummings, 'Sweet, Henry (1845–1912)', *Encyclopedia of Language & Lingusitics* (2006), 315–16. An interesting case is made by Beverley Collins and Inger M. Mees in *The Real Professor Higgins. The Life and Career of Daniel Jones* (Berlin and New York, 1999), pp. 97–103, that Higgins was based not on Henry Sweet, but on Daniel Jones, whom Shaw knew well, and who taught phonetics at University College London from 1907 to 1949. American actress Molly Tompkins, who took elocution lessons from Jones (arranged by Shaw), believed that Jones was 'one of the real persons from whom [Shaw] had drawn the character of Higgins in *Pygmalion*' (Peter Tompkins, ed., *Shaw and Molly Tompkins in their Own Words* [New York, 1961], p. 23). Jones makes no mention of this, however, in a short piece he wrote on 'G.B.S. and Phonetics' for a volume honouring Shaw on his 90th birthday (Stephen Winsten, ed., *G.B.S. at 90. Aspects of Bernard Shaw's Life and Works* [1946], pp. 158–60).

Doolittle to achieve some otherwise suppressed potential.[76] Thus, he says, with unusual modesty, if *Pygmalion* 'makes the public aware that there are such people as phoneticians, and that they are among the most important people in England at present, it will serve its turn' (Preface, below, p. 6). The relationship between elocution and class structure had been recognized in England since the early nineteenth century, one linguist, W.H. Savage, defining pronunciation in his 1833 book *The Vulgarisms and Improprieties of the English Language* as 'the talisman that will enforce admiration or beget contempt; that will produce esteem or preclude friendship; that will bar the door or make portals fly open'.[77] An 1839 exemplar, *Etiquette for Ladies and Gentlemen*, anticipated Eliza's predicament: 'The moment a Woman speaks, you can tell whether you are listening to a lady or not. The tone of the voice, the accent, the use of peculiar phrases, at once determine whether she is only an educated woman, but unused to good society; or a (perhaps) low educated person, but still used to associat[ing] with well-bred people'.[78] An outsider, with a Dublin accent that he used to his advantage, Shaw nonetheless knew of young people in London who were being held back professionally and socially by their accents. He told Sweet in a letter written on 2 February 1911 (the year before he began work on *Pygmalion*) of young men he had met through the Fabian Society, 'ambitious and clever young men of the elementary school teacher class', who 'generally make their first appearance at some political conference or other, and invariably announce themselves as "d'yollagytes", by which they mean delegates'. 'It takes these poor devils ten years of precarious intercourse with the professional and upper middle classes before they become presentable, and

---

76 Shaw wanted much more attention paid to elocution in Britain's schools. In an interview with the *Daily Chronicle* on 11 October 1921 he said that 'I attach great importance to *Pygmalion* as a means of calling public attention to the fact that poor people in this country are imprisoned in elementary schools for periods of from seven to nine years under pretence of educating them, at a cost for the ratepayers which is very far from being a pretence, with the net result that they are released at 13 unable to form or utter a single sentence properly, although a phonetic expert could make them perfectly presentable in six months'. Shaw gave private elocution lessons to actress Florence Farr in 1891 (CL I, 306). And many years later (1926) Shaw joined the BBC's Pronunciation Committee (succeeding Robert Bridges as Chair in 1930), which had the mandate of determining approved pronunciation for BBC announcers and news readers. See Vivian Ducat, 'Bernard Shaw and the King's English', *SHAW: The Annual of Bernard Shaw Studies* 9 (1989), 185–97, and L.W. Conolly, 'Shaw and BBC English', *The Independent Shavian*, 42.3 (2004), 59–63.

77 Qtd in Lynda Mugglestone, 'Shaw, Subjective Inequality, and the Social Meanings of Language in *Pygmalion*', *Review of English Studies*, 44 (1993), 375.

78 Qtd in Lynda Mugglestone, 'Ladylike Accents: Female Pronunciation and Perceptions of Prestige in Nineteenth-Century England', *Notes and Queries* 37.4 (1990), 51.

even then they betray themselves repeatedly. Most of them know this as well as a man can know a thing without being able to remedy it; and they would sell their souls for a book that would teach them to speak in a high class manner'.[79] Higgins makes much the same point when he tells Pickering in Act I [lines 380–1] of men who 'want to drop Kentish Town: but they give themselves away every time they open their mouths' – an anxiety sensitively captured by H.G. Wells in Kipps, his 1905 novel about a young shop assistant with social aspirations. And Shaw's wife was so convinced of the problems faced by the (Irish) Elizas and Kipps of the world that she left money in her will for 'the promotion and encouragement in Ireland' of elocution 'and the other arts of public, private, professional and business life'.[80]

Eliza can rely on much more than a book for her elocution lessons. Primarily – a consideration too often overlooked in discussions of Eliza – she can draw on her own determination, talent, and courage (especially in the face of Higgins's bullying). And, as Arnold Silver reminds us, Eliza is possessed of 'an extraordinary quickness of ear, an aptitude for learning, [and] a talent for music which Pickering declares amounts to genius'.[81] Her 'Professor' (an informal designation for Higgins – he doesn't hold a University post) develops Eliza's skills with the help of his well-equipped laboratory – described in some detail by Shaw at the

79 BL, Add Ms 50549, f. 244. In the same letter Shaw told Sweet that 'There is no such thing as a standard pronunciation. There is no such thing as an ideal pronunciation'. What you have to do, he said, 'is to write down the best practicable phonetic representation of the part of Hamlet as spoken by [actor] Forbes Robertson, and publish it with a certificate signed by half a dozen persons of satisfactory social standing, NOT that the pronunciation represented is the standard pronunciation, or correct pronunciation, or in any way binding on any human being or morally superior to Hackney cockney or Idaho american, but solely that if a man pronounces in that way he will be eligible as far as speech is concerned for the post of Lord Chief Justice, Chancellor of Oxford, Archbishop of Canterbury, Emperor, President, or Toast Master at the Mansion House'.

One popular (and inexpensive) way to improve elocution and to practice public speaking in Victorian London was to join a Public Reading Society, groups that organized so-called 'Penny Readings'; see Evelyn M. Sivier, 'Penny Readings: Popular Elocution in Late Nineteenth-Century England' in David W. Thompson, ed., Performance of Literature in Historical Perspectives (Lanham, MD, 1983), pp. 223–30. See also Lynda Mugglestone, 'Talking Proper': The Rise of Accent as Social Symbol (Oxford, 1995).

80 Holroyd IV, 101. Charlotte Shaw's will is reproduced in full by Holroyd (IV, 95–104). Charlotte's elocution support became known (jestingly) as 'Eliza Doolittle's bequest'. In his own will (Holroyd IV, 105–19), Shaw left funds for reform of the alphabet, proposing an expanded alphabet of 'at least 40 letters' that would remove the need for using unsounded letters in words such as 'though'. Shaw's wishes were never carried out, except for the publication (in 1962) of a phonetic 'Shaw Alphabet Edition' of Androcles and the Lion. (See Gibbs, Bernard Shaw: A Life, pp. 452–3.)

81 Silver, Bernard Shaw, p. 183. Pickering's praise of Eliza's musical ability is in Act III, lines 606–26.

beginning of Act II, though it is only in the film version of the play that we really get to see Higgins aggressively at work with his pupil. We do see in the play, however (in Act III, Mrs Higgins's at-home), some evidence of Eliza's progress, and then (also in Act III, at the Embassy) her triumph. The importance of the at-home scene is that while it shows Eliza's impressive progress in elocution, it also reveals that although she can speak well (with occasional sanguinary lapses) she doesn't have anything of substance to *say*.[82] The mechanical repetition of a weather forecast and an account of some dodgy family history might captivate Freddy, but the scene shows that Eliza has a long way to go before Higgins can declare his work done. He needs not only to keep improving Eliza's elocution, but also to attend to other necessary aspects of her transformation. But that is where this socially inept Higgins-Pygmalion is deficient. He needs help, and the help he gets has no equivalent in the Pygmalion myth. Shaw adds it in the shape of Colonel Pickering.

Pickering is no mean linguist (Higgins says in Act I that he was planning to go to the trouble of travelling to India to meet him), but he can't match Higgins's skills (Pickering is rather proud of his ability to pronounce twenty-four distinct vowel sounds, but Higgins can do a hundred and thirty). What Pickering *can* do, however, is provide Eliza with essential social manners and courtesies – for which she graciously thanks him in Act V – and money.[83] Having lost his bet with Higgins about passing off Eliza as a lady, Pickering pays the cost of her elocution lessons, and he also foots the bill for Eliza's clothes. More importantly, it is Pickering (we learn from the Sequel) who provides the financial backing for Eliza's flower shop business, without which it would have collapsed.

But there is still another component needed for Eliza's successful transformation, and that is some degree of cultural exposure. Here Higgins and Pickering seem to combine their efforts and interests. Higgins fancies himself as a student of Milton, a little of whose poetry Eliza perhaps absorbs during her stay with him, and Higgins and Pickering take her off to a Shakespeare exhibition after Mrs Higgins's at-home (Act III, line 676). It is clear as well (as previously noted) that Eliza has a natural musical talent, having learned to 'play the piano quite

---

82 Higgins has been worried about this, giving Eliza 'strict orders' he assures his mother, 'to keep to two subjects: the weather and everybody's health – Fine day and How do you do, you know – and not to let herself go on things in general' (Act III, lines 110–12).

83 Bernard Dukore has noted how central money is to almost every scene of the play, beginning with the coins requested by Eliza for her flowers in the opening scene (*Money & Politics in Ibsen, Shaw, and Brecht* [Columbia, MO, 1980], p. 11).

beautifully . . . though six months ago, she'd never as much as touched' one, Pickering tells Mrs Higgins (Act III, lines 625–6). She has been with her mentors to concerts and musical halls (Beethoven, Brahms, Lehar, Lionel Monckton) – and in an earlier version of the play Shaw had Higgins, Pickering, and Eliza attending a Puccini opera after the ambassadorial reception (Act IV, notes to lines 38 and 60).

It should be noted as well that Eliza is not taught exclusively by men. Mrs Pearce provides some valuable guidance on good manners (hoping, no doubt, that Eliza will surpass Higgins in this regard), and she is instrumental in introducing Eliza to other important practicalities – the conveniences of a modern bathroom, for example (in Act II). Mrs Higgins, on the other hand, provides Eliza with models of social decorum, as well as a refuge (from Higgins) when she needs it, and, what's more, a refuge of considerable artistic refinement (see Shaw's description of Mrs Higgins's drawing room at the beginning of Act III – and compare it to the description of Higgins's utilitarian laboratory-cum-drawing room at the beginning of Act II).

It is tempting to be critical of Higgins, for there is much to dislike about him. He is arrogant, patronizing, abusive, bullying, and insensitive – indeed, something of a Petruchio, though Eliza's relationship to her mentor at the end of *Pygmalion* is scarcely the same as Kate's to Petruchio at the end of *The Taming of the Shrew*.[84] But some critics have been forgiving of Higgins, even adulatory. It is hard to accept that Higgins is a '*victim* [my emphasis] of his own creation,'[85] though in his 2007 production of the play (referred to above, p. xxix) Peter Hall clearly saw it this way as a despondent, almost tearful Higgins at the end of the play – a dejected and rejected lover – faces the prospect of a future without Eliza, who has unfeelingly rebuffed him.[86] Myron Matlaw, more accurately, I think, in view of what Higgins says in the play about his attitude towards women – 'Oh, I cant be bothered with young women', he tells his mother. 'My idea of a lovable woman is somebody as like you as

---

84 See Lise Pedersen, 'Shakespeare's *The Taming of the Shrew* vs. Shaw's *Pygmalion*: Male Chauvinism vs. Women's Lib', in Rodelle Weintraub, ed., *Fabian Feminist: Bernard Shaw and Woman* (University Park, PA, 1977), pp. 14–22.

85 Crane, '*Pygmalion*: Bernard Shaw's Dramatic Theory and Practice', 882. Rodelle Weintraub has argued that much of Higgins's behaviour can be explained by the medical condition known as Asperger's Syndrome. See 'Bernard Shaw's Henry Higgins: A Classic Aspergen', *ELT: English Literature in Transition 1880–1920*, 49.4 (2006), 388–97.

86 In his programme note for the production Hall states that 'the play ends in heartbreak' – by which he means *Higgins's* heartbreak. (Private collection of L.W. Conolly.)

possible. I shall never get into the way of seriously liking young women: some habits lie too deep to be changed' (Act III, lines 79–82) – sees Higgins as 'divorced from human social and sensual drives'. But Matlaw's generosity gets the better of him when he adulates Higgins as a 'Shavian hero, standing alone, a superman ... representative of the vitality and creative evolution in which, in Shaw's philosophy, lies the ultimate hope of mankind'.[87] And it is hard to find evidence in the play that Higgins, as one critic has claimed, uses his 'linguistic knowledge and skills ... to defeat evil and [to] improve society'.[88] Higgins, like Henry Sweet, is a useful agent of social change, even, occasionally, an inspiring presence – as in his speech to Eliza about a 'Heaven where there are no third-class carriages' (Act V, lines 651–2). But if the 'ultimate hope of mankind' rests with Higgins's vision of 'three old bachelors' (i.e., himself, Pickering, and Eliza) in Wimpole Street (Act V, lines 916–7), then the future is bleak indeed.

J.L. Wisenthal doesn't see the ending of the play in terms of winners or losers – it 'does not take one side or the other'[89] – but audiences are not likely to remain neutral. Beerbohm Tree and Peter Hall (coming at it from diametrically opposed points of view) certainly didn't want them to, nor, I suggest, did Shaw. As A.M. Gibbs has pointed out, Higgins experiments on Eliza for his own sake, not Eliza's: 'it is an experiment carried out without regard to its human implications and consequences', says Gibbs,[90] and Higgins really has no idea what he's talking about when he triumphantly (and presumptuously) proclaims (Act V, lines 908–9) 'By George, Eliza, I said I'd make a woman of you; and I have'. Gibbs also usefully points out that Shaw's other Pygmalion character – in Part V of *Back to Methuselah* (*As Far as Thought Can Reach*) – dies after being bitten by a figure he has created, a Cleopatra–Semiramis hybrid. While Higgins-Pygmalion hardly deserves the same fate, and while Eliza achieves nothing like the power and status of a Cleopatra or Semiramis, the ending of *Pygmalion* has some of the same resonance as the circumstances in *As Far as Thought Can Reach* – Higgins has served his purpose and is dispensable; Eliza regally abandons him.

87 Matlaw, 'The Denouement of *Pygmalion*', p. 34.

88 Timothy G. Vesonder, 'Eliza's Choice: Transforming Myth and the Ending of *Pygmalion*' in Weintraub, *Fabian Feminist*, p. 42.

89 J.L. Wisenthal, *The Marriage of Contraries: Bernard Shaw's Middle Plays* (Cambridge, MA, 1974), p. 126.

90 A.M. Gibbs, *The Art and Mind of Shaw* (New York, 1983), p. 74. Like other commentators, Gibbs also links Higgins-Pygmalion to Mary Shelley's *Frankenstein* (1818). Unlike Victor Frankensein, however, Higgins neither creates a monster nor abandons it.

The 'Undeserving Poor' – and Rich

Eliza, then, gets a good deal further than Galatea, and not solely with the help of her Pygmalion. If Shaw is modest in his ambitions for Eliza – managing a small business, married to a loving nincompoop – her transformation is nonetheless profound: a relatively small step of Fabian progress for women and for social equality, but a huge leap for Eliza.[91] And if Freddy's sister Clara (as presented in the Sequel) takes a bigger intellectual step than Eliza in her pursuit of writers such as H.G. Wells and John Galsworthy it is only because she starts from a singularly more advantaged position. J. Ellen Gainor, again drawing on the Sequel for support, sees Clara as 'another princess locked away', but accuses Shaw of imposing 'masculine qualities' on her achievements.[92] Clara's suppressed independence has already been strongly intimated in Act III, not just by her repetition (twice) of Eliza's 'Not bloody likely', but by her protests against the 'old-fashioned' values of her family and its social circle. It is, however, essential to Shaw's point about the artificiality of class barriers that the upper classes in *Pygmalion* be seen in some instances to be Eliza's intellectual inferiors. Thus we have the Eynsford-Hills and some of those in attendance at the Embassy reception at the end of Act III, including the gormless Nepommuck and the vacuous Host and Hostess. '[N]othing can make me the same as these people', says Eliza (Act III, line 910), and the audience thankfully agrees.

The less amusing aspects of the values and behaviour of Doolittle, the play's representative of the 'undeserving poor', are often overlooked in performance. He and Eliza's 'sixth stepmother' turned Eliza out of home as soon as she was 'big enough to earn [her] own living' (Act II, line 384), and he denies playing any role in her upbringing, 'except to give her a lick of a strap now and again' (Act II, line 1180). Eliza, Doolittle says, is 'a fine handsome girl', but '[a]s a daughter she's not worth her keep', so he is willing to transfer his 'rights as a father' to Higgins for five pounds (Act II, lines 1005–8). Kitty Warren in Shaw's *Mrs Warren's Profession* has had a similarly crippling upbringing, and she turns to prostitution to survive. Eliza struggles against this option, insisting throughout that's she's a 'good girl'. Doolittle couldn't care less whether she's a good girl or not, but his

---

91 Mugglestone, in 'Shaw, Subjective Inequality, and the Social Meaning of Language in *Pygmalion*', does Eliza a disservice, I think, when she speaks of her 'minor transition' from gutter to flower shop (376), but is surely right in arguing that 'Fabianism and phonetics . . . achieve parallel aims in *Pygmalion*' (377).

92 Gainor, *Shaw's Daughters*, p. 233.

asking price of five pounds for her would have indicated to many audience members that he had no qualms about selling her to Higgins for his sexual indulgences, five pounds being the amount that journalist William T. Stead infamously paid the parents of a working-class girl for their daughter in 1885 as an exposé of child prostitution in London. Stead's article in the *Pall Mall Gazette* about the purchase – 'A Child of Thirteen Bought for £5' – caused an unremitting sensation, especially after it was revealed as a hoax.[93] And Doolittle's determination to get drunk on his £5 ('one good spree for myself and the missus' [Act II, line 1081]) is only one side of the coin of alcohol in working-class life: 'Theres lots of women has to make their husbands drunk to make them fit to live with', Eliza reveals to Mrs Higgins and her circle (Act III, lines 389–90).

Doolittle usually escapes opprobrium because of his wit and his disarming self-knowledge, and that is how Shaw intended it to be. Nicholas Grene, for example, has likened Doolittle to Falstaff, both of whom 'speak from a fulness of comic personality which is so purely itself that it leaves no room for ordinary moral judgement'.[94] *Pygmalion* is not as serious a play as *Major Barbara*, which, to be sure, has its undeserving poor as well (i.e., the spongers off the Salvation Army), but which also shows the sordidness of poverty and the degradation suffered by the deserving poor (i.e., those who, like Eliza, strive against all odds to be financially self-sufficient). Doolittle provides both comedy and romance, including the traditional ending to a romantic comedy – marriage. In this case the marriage is forced on him by 'middle class morality', a status imposed by his newfound wealth as a beneficiary of Ezra D. Wannafeller, provided Doolittle lecture several times a year for the Wannafeller Moral Reform World League. Doolittle has achieved this unlikely distinction at the instigation of Higgins who recommended him to Wannafeller as 'the most original moralist at present in England' (Act V, line 162). Doolittle's accidental and unearned social transformation stands in firm contrast to Eliza's conscious and studied determination to escape poverty.[95]

93 See Celia Marshik, 'Parodying the £5 Virgin: Bernard Shaw and the Playing of *Pygmalion*', *Yale Journal of Criticism*, 13.2 (2000), 324–41. Shaw initially supported Stead and his campaign, but after the hoax became known he distanced himself from him. Marshik interprets *Pygmalion* as a parody of the excessive zeal of moral campaigners such as Stead.

94 Nicholas Grene, *Bernard Shaw: A Critical View* (New York, 1984), p. 108.

95 Shaw says in the Sequel (below, p. 133) that Doolittle was eventually rejected by the middle class, 'which he loathed', but 'shot up at once into the highest circles by his wit, his dustmanship (which he carried like a banner), and his Nietzschean transcendence of good and evil' – further evidence of the irrelevance of moral and intellectual discrimination to social standing.

The Stage History of *Pygmalion*[96]

The next production of *Pygmalion* after its English and American pre-
mières in London and on Broadway in April and October 1914
respectively (and a North American tour that lasted until March 1916)
was a London revival at the Aldwych Theatre, again starring Mrs Patrick
Campbell (now in her mid-fifties) as Eliza. Higgins was played by C.
Aubrey-Smith, who was acted off the stage by a Mrs Pat who was, said
The Times (11 February 1920) not only still 'intact' but 'gave as much
delight as ever – the same wilful, petulant, repellent-attractive child of
nature'. But even Mrs Pat couldn't last for ever, and other Elizas suc-
ceeded her. Among the more notable early ones was British-born Lynn
Fontanne, who became a leading actress on the American stage (fre-
quently starring with her husband Alfred Lunt) from the late 1920s on.
One of Fontanne's earliest American performances was as Eliza in a
Theatre Guild production of *Pygmalion* in New York in November 1926,
which then toured the United States through 1927. Tours of *Pygmalion* in
England in the 1920s and 1930s were generally under the auspices of the
Macdona Players, a company formed by Charles Macdona in 1921. Many
Macdona productions were directed by Esmé Percy, who also played
Higgins on several occasions (including in brief runs at the Kingsway
Theatre in London in January 1927 and May 1931, at the Royal Court
Theatre in December 1929 and April 1931, and at the Cambridge Theatre
in London in September 1935; he also directed all these productions).

Another notable director attracted to *Pygmalion* was Tyrone Guthrie,
one of the leading figures of twentieth-century British and North
American theatre. He directed Diana Wynyard as Eliza and Robert
Morley as Higgins in a 'fresh and inventive' 1937 production at the Old
Vic, even if, according to *The Times* (22 September 1937) Diana Wynyard
(subsequently a leading Shakespearean actor at Stratford and in the West
End – and a film star) though 'charming, witty, and extremely entertain-
ing' was 'not born' to the part, and Morley (who also went on to a
distinguished stage and film career, including the role of Undershaft in
the 1941 film of Shaw's *Major Barbara*) played Higgins 'a trifle slowly'.
Pace seems not to have been a problem with the next major London production of *Pygmalion*, this one at the Haymarket Theatre in June 1939,

---

96 Unless otherwise stated, sources for information about the stage history of *Pygmalion* are J.P.
Wearing, ed., *The London Stage: A Calendar of Plays and Players* [1910–1959] (1982–93);
Raymond Mander and Joe Mitchenson, *Theatrical Companion to Shaw* (New York, 1955);
IBDB: Internet Broadway Database (www.ibdb.com); and L.W. Conolly and Ellen
Pearson, eds., *Papers from the 1989 International Shaw Conference* (Guelph, ON, 1991).

directed by Campbell Gullan, with Basil Sydney as Higgins and Margaret Rawlings as Eliza. The intensity of the Higgins–Eliza relationship reminded *The Times* reviewer (14 June 1939) of *The Taming of the Shrew*, but the reviewer was puzzled by the ending – as well he might have been – for some new staging and a new line had appeared from somewhere. After exiting, Eliza returned to the stage 'to ask what shall be the colour of the tie', thus creating a 'romantical clinch' that 'diverts the audience from the grim Shavian probability of Eliza's marrying Freddy Eynsford-Hill'. Presumably, the reviewer thought, 'Mr Shaw approved this odd amendment of the text'. Not bloody likely.

The Second World War slowed down British productions (though there was a December 1944 production at the Lyric Theatre, Hammersmith), but *Pygmalion* remained prominent in the United States and Canada through touring productions such as the one featuring Ruth Chatterton (better known as a film actress) as Eliza in 1941. There is again some evidence that the ending of the play in this production was romanticized. A plot outline in the programme describes Eliza as returning to the stage 'sheepishly' after telling Higgins to buy his own gloves and sweeping out: 'She looks at Higgins. He looks at her and laughs delightedly as she asks, "What size?" – and the curtain falls'.[97]

The first major post-war production of *Pygmalion* in the United States brought two star actors together – British-born Gertrude Lawrence and Canadian-born Raymond Massey – in a production, directed by Cedric Hardwicke, that ran on Broadway (at the Ethel Barrymore Theatre) for nearly 200 performances, from December 1945 to June 1946. The production subsequently went on tour, but with a new Higgins, Dennis King replacing Raymond Massey. The first major post-war British revival was in 1947 at the Lyric, Hammersmith, directed by Peter Ashmore, with Alec Clunes as Higgins and Brenda Bruce as Eliza. The first post-war West End revival was a 1953 production at the St James's Theatre. Director John

---

97 Private collection of L.W. Conolly. The 'What size?' line appears to have been another innovation by Tree (CL III, 253), willingly endorsed by Mrs Campbell. When the Minneapolis Civic Theatre cabled Shaw in February 1948 to ask if they could use 'Mrs Pat Campbell's line' Shaw responded 'I absolutely forbid the Campbell interpolation or any suggestion that the middleaged bully and the girl of eighteen are lovers' (CL IV, 815, 23 February 1948). The theatre used the line anyway, causing Shaw to cut them off from receiving further licences for any of his plays without his direct approval (BL Add Ms 56632, f. 70, 15 March 1948). According to Emil Davies (who interviewed Shaw at a Fabian gathering at the home of Sidney and Beatrice Webb in May 1914) Shaw had, however, apparently allowed a change to the ending of the Vienna and Berlin productions that allowed Eliza, 'as she goes out', to 'ask the Professor what size or colour gloves he requires – something which showed her devotion to him' (A.M. Gibbs, ed., *Shaw: Interviews and Recollections* [Iowa City, IA, 1990], p. 154).

Clements (he also played Higgins) again contrived, it seems, to 'defy the author' by romanticizing the ending. *The Times* (20 November 1953) defended Clements (and Kay Hammond, who played Eliza) by arguing that they enjoyed 'the spiritual connivance of their audiences' and that they could 'even plead that they are sustained by the logic of the comedy itself'.

British director John Dexter was having none of that for his 1974 production of *Pygmalion* at the Albery Theatre. In an interview with *The Times* (11 May 1974) Dexter adamantly declared that 'I have never seen [*Pygmalion*] done properly, although goodness knows I've watched it often enough and have acted in it three times myself in repertory'. 'Quite a lot of people', Dexter continued, 'have made quite a lot of money out of doing it wrongly, but I've never seen it fairly treated'. The theme of *Pygmalion*, Dexter insisted, is 'the creation of a woman of independence', and Shaw 'is saying just how unacceptable it is for a woman to go on being someone else's doormat'. Dexter chose to use Shaw's 1916 text, and interpreted the ending (as in Appendix III.1, below) as a 'final and conclusive statement' of Eliza's independence – 'it is Nora slamming the door at the end of *A Doll's House*'. (According to *Punch* reviewer Jeremy Kingston [29 May 1974], Dexter also had Eliza slam the door firmly as she left the stage at the end of the play.) To present this refreshingly respectful (and unusual) approach to the text, Dexter had two leading British actors – Diana Rigg and Alec McCowen (with an 'earth-shaking' performance as well from Bob Hoskins as Doolittle). Even so, critic Irving Wardle (*The Times*, 17 May 1974) still couldn't accept the Eliza-Nora analogy (the ending is *not*, he declared 'an echo' of *A Doll's House*), preferring to see Eliza and Higgins at the end as 'perfectly matched partners'.

The Albery production of *Pygmalion* was the first that Wardle had seen, and he blamed the scarcity of *Pygmalion* revivals on *My Fair Lady*, the Lerner & Loewe musical adaptation of the play that had premièred at the Mark Hellinger Theatre in New York on 15 March 1956 (2,717 performances) and at Drury Lane Theatre in London on 30 April 1958 (2,281 performances). The release in 1964 of the movie version of *My Fair Lady* also seemed to dampen rather than stimulate interest in the original play. Theatr Clwyd in North Wales got things back on track with a production in 1991 (directed by Michael McCaffery) that featured Cathy Tyson as Eliza, and then *Pygmalion* finally made it onto the stage of Britain's National Theatre.

Director Howard Davies used the full text of *Pygmalion* for his 1992 production (opening 9 April 1992), exploiting the sophisticated technical resources of the Olivier Theatre at the National in a design by William Dudley. As described in the *Daily Mail* (10 April 1992), Dudley's design comprised a 'series of hugely detailed, deceptively solid sets, from a towering Covent Garden colonnade to a ballroom complete with Palm Court orchestra – throwing in a vintage taxi for Eliza to ride in triumph'. And as performed by Alan Howard (whose uncle, Leslie, played Higgins in the 1938 film) and Frances Barber, the 'notoriously "unsatisfactory" ending' made 'complete sense', according to *Daily Telegraph* critic Charles Spencer (13 April 1992). 'For once', Spencer said, 'you don't want Eliza to settle down with Higgins – she has achieved an emotional maturity he will never be able to match'.

As in Britain, the success of *My Fair Lady* had deadened American interest in *Pygmalion* for a decade or two, and it needed the star power of Peter O'Toole and Amanda Plummer (not to mention Dora Bryan, Lionel Jeffries, John Mills, and Joyce Redman) to get it back on Broadway, where a revival opened, directed by Val May, on 26 April 1987 at the Plymouth Theatre, where it ran for a modest 113 performances. It took another twenty years for a return of *Pygmalion* to Broadway, this time with television and film star Claire Danes (in her Broadway début) paired with the more experienced Jefferson Mays. This Roundabout Theatre production opened at the American Airlines Theatre on 18 October 2007.

The most recent major British productions have been at the Chichester Festival in 1994 with Peter Bowles as Higgins and Fiona Fullerton as Eliza, supported by Michael Denison (Pickering) and Freddie Jones (Doolittle), directed by Patrick Garland; at the Albery Theatre in London in 1997 (in a heavily cut version directed by Ray Cooney); at the Glasgow Citizens' Theatre in 1999, directed by Philip Prowse (with contemporary profanity replacing Eliza's 'Not bloody likely' – unlike in the Citizens' previous production in 1979 directed by Giles Havergal); and in Bath (and on tour) by the Peter Hall Company in 2007, before transferring to the Old Vic in May 2008. A rare Dublin production was mounted at the Gate Theatre in 2004, directed by Robin Lefevre.

The Shaw Festival in Niagara-on-the-Lake, Ontario, has staged *Pygmalion* five times, most recently in 2004, directed by Jackie Maxwell and using the full text. (Previous Shaw Festival productions were in 1965, 1975, 1982, and 1992.) The 1982 Shaw Festival production was directed by Denise Coffey, who had previously (in 1981) done a stripped-down version at the Young Vic in London, bringing Shaw himself on stage (played by Donald Eccles) as narrator (a device Coffey retained for Niagara-on-the-Lake, Shaw being played by Herb Foster).

In addition to the 1913 Austrian and German productions mentioned above (p. xxi), there have been numerous foreign-language productions of *Pygmalion*. Notable ones include those at the Royal Dramatic Theatre in Stockholm in 1914, starring Harriet Bosse as Eliza; at the Alexandrinsky Theatre in St Petersburg in 1915 directed by Vsevolod Meyerhold; and three in Japan (1929, 1966, and 1974). There was a remarkable Swedish production at the avant-garde Orion Theatre in Stockholm in 1985, directed by Lars Rudolfsson, with an ending that would have surpassed even Shaw's imagination – Higgins, furious at Eliza's leaving him, fired shots at her as she left. In France, the première (Théâtre des Arts, Paris, 28 September 1923), handicapped by an inadequate translation by Augustin Hamon, failed,[98] but a 1955 French production, directed by Claude-André Puget, was more successful,[99] as was a widely acclaimed production by Nicolas Briançon in 2006, which went on a national tour after a run at the Théâtre Comedia in Paris.

Note on the Text

The original text of *Pygmalion*, as published by Constable in London and Brentano's in New York in 1916 with the original ending (as given below in Appendix III.1) and without the film scenes added by Shaw for the 1941 Constable and Penguin editions, is still considered by some scholars and directors to be superior to later versions. It was described, for example, in 1967 as 'still the most satisfactory version for any reader interested in stagecraft and good theatre rather than in Shaw's afterthoughts about his characters'.[100] Arnold Silver has judged the earlier text to be 'superior in all respects to the later version',[101] and, more recently, A.M. Gibbs has criticized the 1941 text for its 'structural and artistic flaws', and has expressed regret that this version 'has been widely circulated'.[102]

The fact remains, however, that the 1941 film-influenced text of *Pygmalion* is the one that Shaw – after considerable thought about the revisions – approved and authorized.[103] The 1941 text, to be sure, leaves

---

98 'Paris can now boast of being the only city in the world where [*Pygmalion*] has failed', Shaw wrote to Hamon (CL III, 857, 7 December 1923).

99 See Michel Pharand, *Bernard Shaw and the French* (Gainesville, FL, 2000), pp. 142–3.

100 Diderik Roll-Hansen, 'Shaw's *Pygmalion*: The Two Versions of 1916 and 1941', *Review of English Studies*, 8.3 (1967), 82.

101 *Bernard Shaw: The Darker Side*, p. 180n.

102 Gibbs, *Bernard Shaw: A Life*, p. 333.

103 It was also Shaw's clear directive to his Trustee and to 'all others under whose eyes any of my literary works and documents may pass not to publish or quote or suffer to be published or quoted any edition or extracts from my works in which any earlier text shall be substituted either wholly or partly for the text as contained in the printed volumes finally passed by me for press' (i.e., in the case of *Pygmalion*, Constable's Standard Edition of 1941). See Holroyd IV, 105–19 for the full text of Shaw's will. In incorporating the film scenes into the text Shaw was guilty, however, of an occasional oversight; see note to Act IV line 60.

less to the imagination – it *shows*, for example, Eliza's lodging at the end of Act I, her being bathed by Mrs Pearce in Act II, the Embassy scene in Act III, her courtship with Freddy at the end of Act IV, and it provides an emphatic conclusion about Eliza's plans to marry Freddy. Shaw was well aware (see his 'Note for Technicians', below, p. 8) that many theatres would not (and will not) have the mechanical and technical capabilities to mount the film scenes effectively on stage – in which case, Shaw says, they are 'to be omitted'. But some of the changes do considerably more than exploit the technical facilities of screen and stage; their purpose is, rather, to enhance and reinforce the play's thematic imperatives – *seeing* the poverty (at the end of Act I) in which Eliza lives in Angel Court, Drury Lane, for example, emphasizes the economic and social gap between her circumstances at the beginning and at the end of the play, and the courtship scene between Eliza and Freddy at the end of Act IV gives the audience some sense of the development of their relationship (which is barely touched upon in the 1916 text of the play) and greater credibility to Eliza's decision to marry him.

The text of *Pygmalion* given in this edition is, therefore, Shaw's final definitive text. A line of asterisks separates the scenes incorporated from the film script from the earlier theatrical script. Footnotes identify significant differences between the several editions (1914 onwards) of the play, and Appendix III gives the texts of various stage and film endings of *Pygmalion*. Appendix I publishes for the first time sections of dialogue from Shaw's original manuscript of the play, subsequently discarded. Notes to the text also identify Shaw's views on how certain scenes or lines should be played, as expressed in rehearsal copies, correspondence, or other sources. (For a more detailed analysis of Shaw's own directing of the play, see Dukore, *Shaw's Theater*.)

The texts of the play and appendices in this edition retain most of Shaw's idiosyncratic punctuation and spelling practices. For example, Shaw preferred to use the apostrophe only when absolutely necessary (believing it to be redundant in most cases, and always typographically ugly), so he eliminated it whenever he could – e.g., *Ive, youve, thats, werent, wont*. He had to retain the apostrophe, however, in instances where its omission might cause confusion – e.g., *I'll, it's, he'll*. Shaw also retained a few archaic spellings (e.g., *shew* for *show*) and dropped the 'u' in 'our' spellings (e.g., *honor*).

Shaw's practice was also to use spacing between letters to indicate emphasis of a word (e.g., h i s rather than *his*), reserving the use of italics for stage directions. This practice has, however, caused considerable confusion over the years, since the variant spacing between letters of a word has not always been immediately apparent to editors, typesetters, and proofreaders. Thus, different editions of any particular Shaw play provide different readings, sometimes indicating emphasis of a word, sometimes not. In order to avoid prolonging the confusion, and to restore and confirm Shaw's intentions for emphasizing words (as reflected in manuscript versions and in editions prepared under Shaw's supervision), this edition of *Pygmalion*, in common with other Shaw plays published by Methuen/ New Mermaids, uses italics in the conventional way for dramatic texts – i.e., both for stage directions and to indicate emphasis of particular words or phrases in the dialogue.

A Note on Places and Money in *Pygmalion*

Shaw lived in London from 1876, initially with his mother in Victoria Grove, Kensington, then at several other addresses, before taking in 1927 a spacious flat in Whitehall Court about half a mile north of the Houses of Parliament, which he kept until 1949–though by then he was living permanently in Ayot St Lawrence in Hertfordshire, where he and Charlotte had bought a large house (a former rectory) in 1906. Shaw was an enthusiastic walker, and he got to know the geography of London very well. The action of *Pygmalion* is carefully located in actual and distinct socio-economic areas of the city and its environs, beginning in Act I in Covent Garden, site then of London's major flower market, but also close to fashionable theatres, and not far–though a long walk for Freddy in the rain–from busy thoroughfares (Southampton Street, Charing Cross, the Strand, Ludgate Circus, Trafalgar Square) where Freddy tries to find a taxi. A two-minute taxi ride from Covent Garden takes Eliza to her slum lodging in Angel Court, Drury Lane, though she would normally walk from there to Covent Garden and (a longer walk, further west) to Tottenham Court Road where she also sold flowers (and encountered, she tells Higgins, women selling themselves). The walk to Covent Garden from her previous lodgings in Lisson Grove ('wasnt fit for a pig to live in') two miles northwest would have taken much longer. People in the crowd that gathers around Eliza and Higgins in the opening scene are identified by Higgins as having originated in districts close to central London, such as Hoxton, a mile or so northeast of Covent Garden, or much further away in towns such as Selsey (seventy miles south, on the coast of West Sussex) or Hanwell, a few miles west of Covent Garden. Mrs Eynsford Hill's accent locates her as from affluent Epsom, fifteen miles south of London, while Higgins himself lives on Wimpole Street (Acts II and IV), a short taxi ride west of Covent Garden, and Pickering is staying at the Carlton Hotel, in the Haymarket, close to Trafalgar Square.

Higgins also draws a contrast in Act I between working class Kentish Town (two miles north of Covent Garden) and upscale Park Lane (running down the east side of Hyde Park). Mrs Higgins's expensively furnished home (Acts III and V) is on the Chelsea Embankment, with a view of the Thames, three miles southwest of the hustle and bustle of Covent Garden. The nocturnal perambulations of Eliza and Freddy at the end of Act IV take them from Wimpole Street to nearby Cavendish Square, then south across Oxford Street to Hanover Square (where they return for Doolittle's wedding at St George's Church at the end of Act V), and then (by taxi) a few miles southwest to Wimbledon Common.

The locations in *Pygmalion* are often specifically linked with economic indicators. Shaw was, of course, working with the pre-decimal system (introduced in 1971) of British currency, based on pounds, shillings, and pence (twenty shillings to a pound, twelve pence to a shilling). Other currency terms are also used by Shaw's characters: a sovereign is one pound (£1); half-a-crown is two shillings and sixpence; a florin is two shillings; a tanner is sixpence; and a farthing is one quarter of one pence. It is important to understand the currency structure and terminology in order to appreciate the economic status of different characters and locations. It is nothing for Pickering to have a sovereign in his pocket (Act I, line 159), but that amount represents five times the weekly rent Eliza pays (four shillings) for her Drury Lane slum, and eight times the amount that Higgins reckons is Eliza's daily income (half-a-crown, Act II, line 215). Eliza is grateful for tuppence (two pence) for a bunch of flowers, and the handful of change that Higgins tosses into her basket at the end of Act I is a veritable fortune for her. The wage earners in Kentish Town with an income, Higgins says (Act I, line 379), of £80 a year are further up the economic scale, but there is still a huge gulf between that and the hundred thousand a year the better-spoken men of Park Lane can earn, according to Higgins. The £5 Doolittle asks for Eliza in Act II is enough for a weekend of revelry for Doolittle, his wife, and friends; and while the £3,000 a year he gets from the Ezra D. Wannafeller bequest (Act V) doesn't put him in the Park Lane bracket, it is enough to make relatives, solicitors, and doctors far more attentive to him than they were when he earned a lowly dustman's wage.

FURTHER READING

(Unless otherwise noted, the place of publication for books listed
here is London.)

Works by Shaw

Bernard Shaw, *The Bodley Head Bernard Shaw. Collected Plays with Their Prefaces*. Under the editorial supervision of Dan H. Laurence. 7 vols. (1970–4).

——. *The Drama Observed*, ed. Bernard Dukore. 4 vols. (University Park, PA, 1993).

J.L. Wisenthal, ed., *Shaw and Ibsen. Bernard Shaw's 'The Quintessence of Ibsenism' and Related Writings* (Toronto, 1979).

Bibliography and Reference

T.F. Evans, ed., *Shaw: The Critical Heritage* (1976).

A.M. Gibbs, *A Bernard Shaw Chronology* (Basingstoke, 2001).

Dan H. Laurence, *Bernard Shaw: A Bibliography*. 2 vols. (Oxford, 1983).

Raymond Mander and Joe Mitchenson, *Theatrical Companion to Shaw* (New York, 1955).

Biography

St John Ervine, *Bernard Shaw: His Life, Work and Friends* (New York, 1956).

A.M. Gibbs, *Bernard Shaw: A Life* (Gainesville, FL, 2005).

Michael Holroyd, *Bernard Shaw*. 5 vols. (1988–92).

Correspondence

Alan Dent, ed., *Bernard Shaw and Mrs Patrick Campbell: Their Correspondence* (New York, 1952).

Dan H. Laurence, ed., *Bernard Shaw. Collected Letters*. 4 vols. (New York, 1985–8).

Collections of Criticism

Harold Bloom, ed., *George Bernard Shaw's Pygmalion* (New York, 1988).

Christopher Innes, ed., *The Cambridge Companion to George Bernard Shaw* (Cambridge, 1998).

Rodelle Weintraub, ed., *Fabian Feminist: Bernard Shaw and Woman* (University Park, PA, 1977).

Gary Wiener, ed., *Readings on Pygmalion* (San Diego, CA, 2002).

Criticism

Charles A. Berst, *Pygmalion: Shaw's Spin on Myth and Cinderella* (New York, 1995).

John A. Bertolini, *The Playwrighting Self of Bernard Shaw* (Carbondale, IL, 1991).

Milton Crane, '*Pygmalion*: Bernard Shaw's Dramatic Theory and Practice', *PMLA* 66.6 (1951), 879–85.

Bernard F. Dukore, *Bernard Shaw, Playwright* (Columbia, MO, 1973).

——, *Shaw's Theater* (Gainesville, FL, 2000).

Errol Durbach, '*Pygmalion*: Myth and Anti-Myth in the Plays of Ibsen and Shaw', in Bloom, *Bernard Shaw's Pygmalion*, pp. 87–98.

J. Ellen Gainor, *Shaw's Daughters: Dramatic and Narrative Construction of Gender* (Ann Arbor, MI, 1991).

Arthur Ganz, *George Bernard Shaw* (New York, 1983).

A.M. Gibbs, *The Art and Mind of Shaw* (New York, 1983).

Nicholas Grene, *Bernard Shaw: A Critical View* (New York, 1984).

Diderik Roll-Hansen, 'Shaw's *Pygmalion*: The two Versions of 1916 and 1941', *Review of English Literature*, 8.3 (1967), 81–90.

Richard Huggett, *The Truth About 'Pygmalion'* (New York, 1969).

Essaka Joshua, *Pygmalion and Galatea. The History of a Narrative in English Literature* (Aldershot, 2001).

Myron Matlaw, 'The Denouement of *Pygmalion*', *Modern Drama*, 1 (1958–9), 29–34.

Margery M. Morgan, *The Shavian Playground: An Exploration of the Art of George Bernard Shaw* (1972).

Lynda Mugglestone, 'Shaw, Subjective Inequality, and the Social Meaning of Language in *Pygmalion*', *Review of English Studies*, 44 (1993), 373–85.

Lise Pedersen, 'Shakespeare's *The Taming of the Shrew* vs. Shaw's *Pygmalion*: Male Chauvinism vs. Women's Lib', in Rodelle Weintraub, ed., *Fabian Feminist: Bernard Shaw and Woman* (University Park, PA, 1977), pp.14–22.

Michel Pharand, *Bernard Shaw and the French* (Gainesville, FL, 2000).

Jean Reynolds, *Pygmalion's Wordplay. The Postmodern Shaw* (Gainesville, FL, 1999).

Arnold Silver, *Bernard Shaw: The Darker Side* (Stanford, CA, 1982).

Maurice Valency, *The Cart and the Trumpet: The Plays of George Bernard Shaw* (New York, 1973).

Timothy G. Vesonder, 'Eliza's Choice: Transforming Myth and the Ending of *Pygmalion*' in Rodelle Weintraub, ed., *Fabian Feminist: Bernard Shaw and Woman* (University Park, PA, 1977), pp. 38–45.

J.L. Wisenthal, *The Marriage of Contraries: Bernard Shaw's Middle Plays* (Cambridge, MA, 1974).

BERNARD SHAW

PYGMALION

A Romance in Five Acts

PREFACE[1]

A Professor of Phonetics

As will be seen later on, Pygmalion needs, not a preface, but a sequel, which I have supplied in its due place.

The English have no respect for their language, and will not teach their children to speak it.[2] They cannot spell it because they have nothing to spell it with but an old foreign alphabet of which only the consonants – and not all of them – have any agreed speech value. Consequently no man can teach himself what it should sound like from reading it; and it is impossible for an Englishman to open his mouth without making some other Englishman despise him. Most European languages are now accessible in black and white to foreigners: English and French are not thus accessible even to Englishmen and Frenchmen. The reformer we need most today is an energetic phonetic enthusiast: that is why I have made such a one the hero of a popular play.

There have been heroes of that kind crying in the wilderness for many years past. When I became interested in the subject towards the end of the eighteen-seventies, the illustrious Alexander Melville Bell, the inventor of Visible Speech,[3] had emigrated to Canada, where his son invented the telephone; but Alexander J. Ellis[4] was still a London patriarch, with an impressive head always covered by a velvet skull cap, for which he would apologize to public meetings in a very courtly manner. He and Tito Pagliardini,[5] another phonetic veteran, were men whom it was impossible

---

1   The Preface was first published in C1916 and revised for C1941. Significant variations between the two versions are recorded in these notes.

2   From here to the end of the paragraph originally read (C1916, C1931) 'They spell it so abominably that no man can teach himself what it sounds like. It is impossible for an Englishman to open his mouth without making some other Englishman hate or despise him. German and Spanish are accessible to foreigners: English is not accessible even to Englishmen. The reformer England needs today is an energetic phonetic enthusiast: that is why I have made such a one the hero of a popular play'.

3   Visible Speech is a phonetic alphabet created by Alexander Melville Bell (1819–1905). Born in Edinburgh, Bell emigrated to Canada in 1870. His son, Alexander Graham Bell (1847–1922), patented the telephone in the United Sates in 1876.

4   Alexander John Ellis (1814–90) was a leading British philologist and phonetician. His major work was the multi-volume *On Early English Pronunciation* (1869–89).

5   Tito Pagliardini (1817–95) was a London-based Italian singer and teacher. His *National Education and the English Language* was published in 1868.

to dislike. Henry Sweet,[6] then a young man, lacked their sweetness of character: he was about as conciliatory to conventional mortals as Ibsen[7] or Samuel Butler.[8] His great ability as a phonetician (he was, I think, the best of them all at his job) would have entitled him to high official recognition, and perhaps enabled him to popularize his subject, but for his Satanic contempt for all academic dignitaries and persons in general who thought more of Greek than of phonetics. Once, in the days when the Imperial Institute rose in South Kensington,[9] and Joseph Chamberlain[10] was booming the Empire, I induced the editor of a leading monthly review to commission an article from Sweet on the imperial importance of his subject. When it arrived, it contained nothing but a savagely derisive attack on a professor of language and literature whose chair Sweet regarded as proper to a phonetic expert only. The article, being libellous, had to be returned as impossible; and I had to renounce my dream of dragging its author into the limelight. When I met him afterwards, for the first time for many years, I found to my astonishment that he, who had been a quite tolerably presentable young man, had actually managed by sheer scorn to alter his personal appearance until he had become a sort of walking repudiation of Oxford and all its traditions. It must have been largely in his own despite that he was squeezed into something called a Readership of phonetics there.[11] The future of phonetics rests probably with his pupils, who all swore by him; but nothing could bring the man himself into any sort of compliance with the university to which he nevertheless clung by divine right in an intensely Oxonian way. I daresay his papers, if he has left any, include some satires that may be published without too destructive results fifty years hence. He was, I believe, not in the least an ill-natured man: very much the opposite, I should say; but he would not suffer fools gladly; and to him all scholars who were not rabid phoneticians were fools.[12]

---

6 For the influence of Henry Sweet (1845–1912) on *Pygmalion* see Shaw's subsequent remarks in this Preface, and Introduction, above, pp. xxxvii.

7 Norwegian playwright Henrik Ibsen (1828–1906) was a major influence on Shaw's career, especially on his early plays. Shaw wrote a major study of Ibsen, *The Quintessence of Ibsenism*, first published in 1891 and updated and revised for a second edition in 1913. See Introduction, above, pp. xv, xxxiv–xxxvi.

8 English writer and musician Samuel Butler (1835–1902) was another major influence on Shaw. Shaw said he 'swore by' Butler's 1872 Utopian satire, *Erewhon* (Holroyd III, 39).

9 The Imperial Institute was built between 1887 and 1893 in South Kensington to celebrate Queen Victoria's Golden Jubilee and to promote the interests of the British Empire. With the exception of the Queen's Tower (now part of Imperial College), it was demolished in the 1960s.

10 Joseph Chamberlain (1836–1914), a passionate imperialist, served as Colonial Secretary in the British Government from 1895 to 1903.

11 Sweet was appointed Reader in Phonetics at Oxford in 1901.

12 The final part of the sentence (after 'gladly') was added in C1941.

Those who knew him will recognize in my third act the allusion to the Current Shorthand[13] in which he used to write postcards. It may be acquired from a four and sixpenny manual published by the Clarendon Press.[14] The postcards which Mrs Higgins describes are such as I have received from Sweet. I would decipher a sound which a cockney would represent by *zerr*, and a Frenchman by *seu*, and then write demanding with some heat what on earth it meant. Sweet, with boundless contempt for my stupidity, would reply that it not only meant but obviously was the word Result, as no other word containing that sound, and capable of making sense with the context, existed in any language spoken on earth. That less expert mortals should require fuller indications was beyond Sweet's patience. Therefore, though the whole point of his Current Shorthand is that it can express every sound in the language perfectly, vowels as well as consonants, and that your hand has to make no stroke except the easy and current ones with which you write m, n, and u, l, p, and q, scribbling them at whatever angle comes easiest to you, his unfortunate determination to make this remarkable and quite legible script serve also as a shorthand reduced it in his own practice to the most inscrutable of cryptograms. His true objective was the provision of a full, accurate, legible script for our language;[15] but he was led past that by his contempt for the popular Pitman system of shorthand,[16] which he called the Pitfall system. The triumph of Pitman was a triumph of business organization: there was a weekly paper to persuade you to learn Pitman: there were cheap textbooks and exercise books and transcripts of speeches for you to copy, and schools where experienced teachers coached you up to the necessary proficiency. Sweet could not organize his market in that fashion. He might as well have been the Sybil who tore up the leaves of prophecy that nobody would attend to.[17] The four and sixpenny manual, mostly in his lithographed handwriting, that was never vulgarly advertized, may perhaps some day be taken up by a syndicate and pushed upon the public as *The Times* pushed the *Encyclopaedia Britannica*; but until then it will certainly not prevail against Pitman. I

---

13 'patent shorthand' in all editions prior to C1941.

14 At the beginning of Act III Mrs Higgins tells Higgins that 'though I like to get pretty postcards in your patent shorthand, I always have to read the copies in ordinary writing you so thoughtfully send me' (Act III, lines 57–9, this edition). The 'four and sixpenny manual' is Sweet's *Manual of Current Shorthand, Orthographic and Phonetic* (1892).

15 In C1916 and C1931 'noble but ill-dressed' appears before 'language'.

16 Devised by Sir Isaac Pitman (1813–97).

17 Of the several mythological Sybils, Shaw probably has in mind the Erythraean Sybil, who wrote her prophecies on leaves.

have bought three copies of it during my lifetime; and I am informed by the publishers that its cloistered existence is still a steady and healthy one. I actually learned the system two several times; and yet the shorthand in which I am writing these lines is Pitman's. And the reason is, that my secretary cannot transcribe Sweet, having been perforce taught in the schools of Pitman.[18] In America I could use the commercially organized Gregg shorthand,[19] which has taken a hint from Sweet by making its letters writable (current, Sweet would have called them) instead of having to be geometrically drawn like Pitman's; but all these systems, including Sweet's, are spoilt by making them available for verbatim reporting, in which complete and exact spelling and word division are impossible. A complete and exact phonetic script is neither practicable nor necessary for ordinary use; but if we enlarge our alphabet to the Russian size, and make our spelling as phonetic as Spanish, the advance will be prodigious.

Pygmalion Higgins is not a portrait of Sweet, to whom the adventure of Eliza Doolittle would have been impossible; still, as will be seen, there are touches of Sweet in the play. With Higgins's physique and temperament Sweet might have set the Thames on fire. As it was, he impressed himself professionally on Europe to an extent that made his comparative personal obscurity, and the failure of Oxford to do justice to his eminence, a puzzle to foreign specialists in his subject. I do not blame Oxford, because I think Oxford is quite right in demanding a certain social amenity from its nurslings (heaven knows it is not exorbitant in its requirements!); for although I well know how hard it is for a man of genius with a seriously underrated subject to maintain serene and kindly relations with the men who underrate it, and who keep all the best places for less important subjects which they profess without originality and sometimes without much capacity for them, still, if he overwhelms them with wrath and disdain, he cannot expect them to heap honors on him.

Of the later generations of phoneticians I know little. Among them towered Robert Bridges, to whom perhaps Higgins may owe his Miltonic sympathies,[20] though here again I must disclaim all portraiture. But if the

---

18 In C1916 and C1931 the remainder of this paragraph reads 'Therefore, Sweet railed at Pitman as vainly as Thersites railed at Ajax: his raillery, however it may have eased his soul, gave no popular vogue to Current Shorthand'. (Shaw is referring to Act II, Scene I of Shakespeare's *Troilus and Cressida*.)

19 Devised by John Robert Gregg (1867–1948).

20 Robert Bridges (1844–1930) was appointed Poet Laureate in 1913, the year in which he also co-founded the Society for Pure English. In 1926 he became the founding chair of the BBC's Pronunciation Committee, which Shaw joined (and succeeded Bridges as chair in 1930). Bridges published *Milton's Prosody* in 1893.

play makes the public aware that there are such people as phoneticians, and that they are among the most important people in England at present, it will serve its turn.

I wish to boast that Pygmalion has been an extremely successful play, both on stage and screen,[21] all over Europe and North America as well as at home. It is so intensely and deliberately didactic, and its subject is esteemed so dry, that I delight in throwing it at the heads of the wiseacres who repeat the parrot cry that art should never be didactic. It goes to prove my contention that great art can never be anything else.[22]

Finally, and for the encouragement of people troubled with accents that cut them off from all high employment, I may add that the change wrought by Professor Higgins in the flower-girl is neither impossible nor uncommon. The modern concierge daughter who fulfils her ambition by playing the Queen of Spain in *Ruy Blas*[23] at the Théâtre Français is only one of many thousands of men and women who have sloughed off their native dialects and acquired a new tongue. Our West End shop assistants and domestic servants are bi-lingual.[24] But the thing has to be done scientifically, or the last state of the aspirant may be worse than the first. An honest slum dialect is more tolerable than the attempts of phonetically untaught persons to imitate the plutocracy. Ambitious flower-girls who read this play must not imagine that they can pass themselves off as fine ladies by untutored imitation. They must learn their alphabet over again, and different, from a phonetic expert. Imitation will only make them ridiculous.[25]

21 'on stage and screen' was added in C1941 (to take into account the success of the 1938 film version of *Pygmalion*).

22 'great art *should* [my emphasis] never be anything else' in all editions prior to C1941.

23 A melodrama by Victor Hugo, first performed in 1838.

24 This sentence was added in C1941.

25 There is a different ending to the Preface in editions prior to C1941. Instead of 'An honest slum dialect . . . make them ridiculous' the text reads 'An honest and natural slum dialect is more tolerable than the attempt of a phonetically untaught person to imitate the vulgar dialect of the golf club; and I am sorry to say that in spite of the efforts of our Royal Academy of Dramatic Art, there is still too much sham golfing English on our stage, and too little of the noble English of Forbes Robertson'. (The Royal Academy of Dramatic Art [RADA] was and is one of England's leading theatre schools, founded in 1904 by Herbert Beerbohm Tree, Higgins in the English première of *Pygmalion*. Shaw served on RADA's Governing Council from 1911 to 1941. English actor and producer Johnston Forbes Roberston [1853–1937] was also a member of RADA's Council.)

THE PERSONS OF THE PLAY

[His Majesty's Theatre, London, 11 April 1914]

CLARA EYNSFORD HILL	*Margaret Bussé*
MRS EYNSFORD HILL	*Carlotta Addison*
A BYSTANDER	*Roy Byford*
FREDDY EYNSFORD HILL	*Algernon Greig*
ELIZA DOOLITTLE	*Mrs Patrick Campbell*
COLONEL PICKERING	*Philip Merivale*
HENRY HIGGINS	*Herbert Beerbohm Tree*
A SARCASTIC BYSTANDER	*Alexander Sarner*
MRS PEARCE	*Geraldine Olliffe*
ALFRED DOOLITTLE	*Edmund Gurney*
MRS HIGGINS	*Rosamund Mayne-Young*
PARLORMAID	*Irene Delisse*

THE SCENES OF THE PLAY

Act I	*The Portico of St Paul's, Covent Garden, 11.15 p.m.*
Act II	*Professor Higgins's Phonetic Laboratory, Wimpole Street. Next Day. 11 a.m.*
Act III	*The Drawing Room in Mrs Higgins's Flat on Chelsea Embankment. Several Months Later. At-home Day.*
Act IV	*The Same as Act II. Several Months Later. Midnight.*
Act V	*The Same as Act III. The Following Morning.*

NOTE FOR TECHNICIANS[1]

A complete representation of the play as printed for the first time in this edition is technically possible only on the cinema screen or on stages furnished with exceptionally elaborate machinery. For ordinary theatrical use the scenes separated by rows of asterisks are to be omitted.

In the dialogue an e upside down indicates the indefinite vowel,[2] sometimes called obscure or neutral, for which, though it is one of the commonest sounds in English speech, our wretched alphabet has no letter.

---

1 This note first appeared in C1941, the edition in which Shaw first included scenes and dialogue from the film script of *Pygmalion*.
2 The 'e upside down' is not used in editions prior to C1941.

ACT I

London at 11.15 p.m. Torrents of heavy summer rain. Cab whistles blowing frantically in all directions. Pedestrians running for shelter into the portico of St Paul's church (not Wren's cathedral but Inigo Jones's church in Covent Garden vegetable market), among them A LADY *and her* DAUGHTER *in evening dress. All are peering out gloomily at the rain, except one man with his back turned to the rest, wholly preoccupied with a notebook in which he is writing.*

   The church clock strikes the first quarter.

THE DAUGHTER [*in the space between the central pillars, close to the one on her left*]
   I'm getting chilled to the bone. What can Freddy be doing all this time? He's been gone twenty minutes.

THE MOTHER [*on her* DAUGHTER*'s right*]
   Not so long. But he ought to have got us a cab by this.

A BYSTANDER [*on the* LADY*'s right*]
   He wont get no cab not until half-past eleven, missus, when they come back after dropping their theatre fares.

THE MOTHER
   But we must have a cab. We cant stand here until half-past eleven. It's too bad.

THE BYSTANDER
   Well it aint my fault, missus.

THE DAUGHTER
   If Freddy had a bit of gumption, he would have got one at the theatre door.

5
10
15
20
25

3–4   *Wren's cathedral . . . Inigo Jones's church* Shaw did not add the distinction between the two St Paul's until the 1941 revised text of the play (C1941). At the world première of *Pygmalion* at the Hofburg Theatre, Vienna, on 16 October 1913, the set showed 'the wrong church', Shaw said (CL III, 835). Wren's St Paul's was built between 1675 and 1710, Jones's ('The Actors' Church') between 1631 and 1633.

16   *wont* For Shaw's reasons for frequently omitting the apostrophe in contractions see the Note on the Text, above, p. xlix. EM does not follow Shaw's practice; apostrophes are used in contractions. NASH *does* follow Shaw's practice.

THE MOTHER

What could he have done, poor boy?

THE DAUGHTER

Other people get cabs. Why couldnt he?

FREDDY *rushes in out of the rain from the Southampton Street*   30
side, and comes between them closing a dripping umbrella. He
is a young man of twenty, in evening dress, very wet round the
ankles.

THE DAUGHTER

Well, havnt you got a cab?   35

FREDDY

Theres not one to be had for love or money.

THE MOTHER

Oh, Freddy, there must be one. You cant have tried.

THE DAUGHTER   40

It's too tiresome. Do you expect us to go and get one ourselves?

FREDDY

I tell you theyre all engaged. The rain was so sudden: nobody
was prepared; and everybody had to take a cab. Ive been to
Charing Cross one way and nearly to Ludgate Circus the other;   45
and they were all engaged.

THE MOTHER

Did you try Trafalgar Square?

FREDDY

There wasnt one at Trafalgar Square.   50

THE DAUGHTER

Did you try?

FREDDY

I tried as far as Charing Cross Station. Did you expect me to
walk to Hammersmith?   55

THE DAUGHTER

You havnt tried at all.

THE MOTHER

You really are very helpless, Freddy. Go again; and dont come
back until you have found a cab.   60

FREDDY

I shall simply get soaked for nothing.

THE DAUGHTER

And what about us? Are we to stay here all night in this draught,
with next to nothing on? You selfish pig–   65

FREDDY

Oh, very well: I'll go, I'll go. [*He opens his umbrella and dashes off Strandwards, but comes into collision with a flower girl who is hurrying in for shelter, knocking her basket out of her hands. A blinding flash of lightning, followed instantly by a rattling peal of thunder, orchestrates the incident*] 70

THE FLOWER GIRL

Nah then, Freddy: look wh' y' gowin, deah.

FREDDY

Sorry [*he rushes off*]. 75

THE FLOWER GIRL [*picking up her scattered flowers and replacing them in the basket*]

Theres menners f' yer! Tə-oo banches o voylets trod into the mad. [*She sits down on the plinth of the column, sorting her flowers, on the* LADY's *right. She is not at all a romantic figure.* 80 *She is perhaps eighteen, perhaps twenty, hardly older. She wears a little sailor hat of black straw that has long been exposed to the dust and soot of London and has seldom if ever been brushed. Her hair needs washing rather badly: its mousy color can hardly be natural. She wears a shoddy black coat that reaches nearly to her* 85 *knees and is shaped to her waist. She has a brown skirt with a coarse apron. Her boots are much the worse for wear. She is no doubt as clean as she can afford to be: but compared to the ladies she is very dirty. Her features are no worse than theirs; but their condition leaves something to be desired; and she needs the* 90 *services of a dentist*]

THE MOTHER

How do you know that my son's name is Freddy, pray?

THE FLOWER GIRL

Ow, eez yə-ooa san, is e? Wal, fewd dan y' d-ooty bawmz a 95 mather should, eed now bettern to spawl a pore gel's flahrzn than ran awy athaht pyin. Will ye-oo py me f'them? [*Here, with apologies, this desperate attempt to represent her dialect without a phonetic alphabet must be abandoned as unintelligible outside London*] 100

80 *She is not at all a romantic figure* Originally (EM/NASH, C1916, C1931) 'She is not at all an attractive person'.

99 *must be abandoned* Shaw leaves us with a particularly challenging piece of phonetic dialect: 'Oh, he's your son, is he? Well, if you'd done your duty by him as a mother should, he'd know better than to spoil a poor girl's flowers then run away without paying. Will you pay me for them?' Shaw had previously used London dialect extensively in *Major Barbara* (1905).

THE DAUGHTER
Do nothing of the sort, mother. The idea!

THE MOTHER
Please allow me, Clara. Have you any pennies?

THE DAUGHTER   105
No. Ive nothing smaller than sixpence.

THE FLOWER GIRL [*hopefully*]
I can give you change for a tanner, kind lady.

THE MOTHER [*to* CLARA]
Give it to me. [CLARA *parts reluctantly*] Now [*to* THE GIRL] This   110
is for your flowers.

THE FLOWER GIRL
Thank you kindly, lady.

THE DAUGHTER
Make her give you the change. These things are only a penny a   115
bunch.

THE MOTHER
Do hold your tongue, Clara. [*To* THE GIRL] You can keep the
change.

THE FLOWER GIRL   120
Oh, thank you, lady.

THE MOTHER
Now tell me how you know that young gentleman's name.

THE FLOWER GIRL
I didnt.   125

THE MOTHER
I heard you call him by it. Dont try to deceive me.

THE FLOWER GIRL [*protesting*]
Who's trying to deceive you? I called him Freddy or Charlie
same as you might yourself if you was talking to a stranger and   130
wished to be pleasant.

THE DAUGHTER
Sixpence thrown away! Really, mamma, you might have spared
Freddy that. [*She retreats in disgust behind the pillar*]

An elderly GENTLEMAN *of the amiable military type rushes*   135
into the shelter, and closes a dripping umbrella. He is in the same
plight as FREDDY, *very wet about the ankles. He is in evening*

108 *tanner* sixpence

dress, with a light overcoat. He takes the place left vacant by THE
DAUGHTER.

THE GENTLEMAN   140
Phew!

THE MOTHER [*to* THE GENTLEMAN]
Oh, sir, is there any sign of its stopping?

THE GENTLEMAN
I'm afraid not. It started worse than ever about two minutes   145
ago. [*He goes to the plinth beside* THE FLOWER GIRL; *puts up his
foot on it; and stoops to turn down his trouser ends*]

THE MOTHER
Oh dear! [*She retires sadly and joins her* DAUGHTER]

THE FLOWER GIRL [*taking advantage of the military* GENTLE-   150
MAN's *proximity to establish friendly relations with him*]
If it's worse, it's a sign it's nearly over. So cheer up, Captain: and
buy a flower off a poor girl.

THE GENTLEMAN
I'm sorry. I havnt any change.   155

THE FLOWER GIRL
I can give you change, Captain.

THE GENTLEMAN
For a sovereign? Ive nothing less.

THE FLOWER GIRL   160
Garn! Oh do buy a flower off me, Captain. I can change half-a-
crown. Take this for tuppence.

THE GENTLEMAN
Now dont be troublesome: theres a good girl. [*Trying his
pockets*] I really havnt any change – Stop: heres three hapence, if   165
thats any use to you [*he retreats to the other pillar*].

THE FLOWER GIRL [*disappointed, but thinking three half-pence
better than nothing*]
Thank you, sir.

THE BYSTANDER [*to* THE GIRL]   170
You be careful: give him a flower for it. Theres a bloke here
behind taking down every blessed word youre saying. [*All turn
to the man who is taking notes*]

THE FLOWER GIRL [*springing up terrified*]
I aint done nothing wrong by speaking to the gentleman. Ive a   175

---

161   *do buy a flower off me, Captain* 'Try to put the flower into his buttonhole', Shaw
      urged Eliza at this point (Dukore 147).

right to sell flowers if I keep off the kerb. [*Hysterically*] I'm a
respectable girl: so help me, I never spoke to him except to ask
him to buy a flower off me.

[*General hubbub, mostly sympathetic to* THE FLOWER GIRL,
but deprecating her excessive sensibility. Cries of Dont start hol-   180
lerin. Who's hurting you? Nobody's going to touch you. Whats
the good of fussing? Steady on. Easy easy, etc., *come from the
elderly staid spectators, who pat her comfortingly. Less patient ones
bid her shut her head, or ask her roughly what is wrong with her. A
remoter group, not knowing what the matter is, crowd in and*   185
increase the noise with question and answer]: Whats the row?
What-she-do? Where is he? A tec taking her down. What! him?
Yes: him over there: Took money off the gentleman, etc.

THE FLOWER GIRL [*breaking through them to* THE GENTLEMAN,
crying wildly]   190
Oh, sir, dont let him charge me. You dunno what it means to
me. Theyll take away my character and drive me on the streets
for speakin to gentlemen. They—

THE NOTE TAKER [*coming forward on her right, the rest crowding
after him*]   195
There! there! there! there! who's hurting you, you silly girl?
What do you take me for?

THE BYSTANDER
It's aw rawt: e's a genleman: look at his bə-oots. [*Explaining to
THE NOTE TAKER*] She thought you was a copper's nark, sir.   200

THE NOTE TAKER [*with quick interest*]
Whats a copper's nark?

THE BYSTANDER [*inapt at definition*]
It's a — well, it's a copper's nark, as you might say. What else
would you call it? A sort of informer.   205

THE FLOWER GIRL [*still hysterical*]
I take my Bible oath I never said a word—

THE NOTE TAKER [*overbearing but good-humored*]
Oh, shut up, shut up. Do I look like a policeman?

THE FLOWER GIRL [*far from reassured*]   210
Then what did you take down my words for? How do I know
whether you took me down right? You just shew me what youve

187 *tec* detective

14

wrote about me. [THE NOTE TAKER *opens his book and holds it steadily under her nose, though the pressure of the mob trying to read it over his shoulders would upset a weaker man*] Whats that? 215
That aint proper writing. I cant read that.

THE NOTE TAKER

I can. [*Reads, reproducing her pronunciation exactly*] 'Cheer ap, Keptin; n' baw ya flahr orf a pore gel.'

THE FLOWER GIRL [*much distressed*] 220

It's because I called him Captain. I meant no harm. [*To* THE GENTLEMAN] Oh, sir, dont let him lay a charge agen me for a word like that. You—

THE GENTLEMAN

Charge! I make no charge. [*To* THE NOTE TAKER] Really, sir, if 225
you are a detective, you need not begin protecting me against molestation by young women until I ask you. Anybody could see that the girl meant no harm.

THE BYSTANDERS GENERALLY [*demonstrating against police espionage*] 230
Course they could. What business is it of yours? You mind your own affairs. He wants promotion, he does. Taking down people's words! Girl never said a word to him. What harm if she did? Nice thing a girl cant shelter from the rain without being insulted, etc., etc., etc. [*She is conducted by the more sympathetic* 235
demonstrators back to her plinth, where she resumes her seat and struggles with her emotion]

THE BYSTANDER

He aint a tec. He's a blooming busy-body: thats what he is. I tell you, look at his bə-oots. 240

THE NOTE TAKER [*turning on him genially*]

And how are all your people down at Selsey?

THE BYSTANDER [*suspiciously*]

Who told you my people come from Selsey?

THE NOTE TAKER 245

Never you mind. They did. [*To* THE GIRL] How do you come to be up so far east? You were born in Lisson Grove.

THE FLOWER GIRL [*appalled*]

Oh, what harm is there in my leaving Lisson Grove? It wasnt fit for a pig to live in; and I had to pay four-and-six a week. [*In* 250
tears] Oh, boo – hoo – oo–

THE NOTE TAKER
　Live where you like; but stop that noise.

THE GENTLEMAN [*to* THE GIRL]
　Come, come! he cant touch you: you have a right to live where　255
　you please.

A SARCASTIC BYSTANDER [*thrusting himself between* THE NOTE
TAKER *and* THE GENTLEMAN]
　Park Lane, for instance. I'd like to go into the Housing Question
　with you, I would.　　　　　　　　　　　　　　　　　　　　260

THE FLOWER GIRL [*subsiding into a brooding melancholy over her
basket, and talking very low-spiritedly to herself*]
　I'm a good girl, I am.

THE SARCASTIC BYSTANDER [*not attending to her*]
　Do you know where *I* come from?　　　　　　　　　　　　　265

THE NOTE TAKER [*promptly*]
　Hoxton.
　　　Titterings. Popular interest in THE NOTE TAKER'*s perform-*
　ance increases.

THE SARCASTIC ONE [*amazed*]　　　　　　　　　　　　　　270
　Well, who said I didnt? Bly me! you know everything, you do.

THE FLOWER GIRL [*still nursing her sense of injury*]
　Aint no call to meddle with me, he aint.

THE BYSTANDER [*to her*]
　Of course he aint. Dont you stand it from him. [*To* THE NOTE　275
　TAKER] See here: what call have you to know about people what
　never offered to meddle with you?

THE FLOWER GIRL
　Let him say what he likes. I dont want to have no truck with him.

THE BYSTANDER　　　　　　　　　　　　　　　　　　　　280
　You take us for dirt under your feet, dont you? Catch you
　taking liberties with a gentleman!

259　*Housing Question* Shaw's first play, *Widowers' Houses* (1892), had dealt with the
　　　issue of slum housing in London.
263　*I'm a good girl, I am* Marked in RC2 to be spoken 'slowly'.
271　*Bly me* 'Blimey,' an expresion of surprise or alarm, more fully expressed as
　　　'gorblimey' (from 'God blind me' or 'God blame me').
279　*have no truck with* have nothing to do with

THE SARCASTIC BYSTANDER

Yes: tell *him* where he come from if you want to go fortune-
telling.   285

THE NOTE TAKER

Cheltenham, Harrow, Cambridge, and India.

THE GENTLEMAN

Quite right. [*Great laughter. Reaction in* THE NOTE TAKER's
favor. Exclamations of] He knows all about it. Told him proper.   290
Hear him tell the toff where he come from? etc.

THE GENTLEMAN

May I ask, sir, do you do this for your living at a music hall?

THE NOTE TAKER

I've thought of that. Perhaps I shall some day.   295
    *The rain has stopped: and the persons on the outside of the
    crowd begin to drop off.*

THE FLOWER GIRL [*resenting the reaction*]

He's no gentleman, he aint, to interfere with a poor girl.

THE DAUGHTER [*out of patience, pushing her way rudely to the front   300
and displacing* THE GENTLEMAN, *who politely retires to the other
side of the pillar*]

What on earth is Freddy doing? I shall get pneumownia if I stay
in this draught any longer.

THE NOTE TAKER [*to himself, hastily making a note of her pronun-*   305
ciation of 'monia']

Earlscourt.

THE DAUGHTER [*violently*]

Will you please keep your impertinent remarks to yourself.

THE NOTE TAKER   310

Did I say that out loud? I didnt mean to. I beg your pardon. Your
mother's Epsom, unmistakeably.

---

287 *Cheltenham, Harrow, Cambridge* Respectively a spa town about 80 miles northwest
     of London, a borough of London about 12 miles west of central London, and a
     university city about 50 miles north of London. Pickering attended Harrow
     School, one of England's leading independent schools, and Cambridge University.
303 *pneumownia* Originally (EM/NASH, C1916, C1931) 'pneumonia'.
307 *Earlscourt* Bayswater in RC1; Earlscourt from EM/NASH onwards.

THE MOTHER [*advancing between* THE DAUGHTER *and* THE NOTE
TAKER]

How very curious! I was brought up in Largelady Park, near   315
Epsom.

THE NOTE TAKER [*uproariously amused*]

Ha! ha! what a devil of a name! Excuse me. [*To* THE DAUGHTER]
You want a cab, do you?

THE DAUGHTER   320

Dont dare speak to me.

THE MOTHER

Oh, please, please, Clara. [*Her* DAUGHTER *repudiates her with
an angry shrug and retires haughtily*] We should be so grateful
to you, sir, if you found us a cab. [THE NOTE TAKER *produces a*   325
whistle] Oh, thank you. [*She joins her* DAUGHTER]

THE NOTE TAKER *blows a piercing blast.*

THE SARCASTIC BYSTANDER

There! I knowed he was a plainclothes copper.

THE BYSTANDER   330

That aint a police whistle: thats a sporting whistle.

THE FLOWER GIRL [*still preoccupied with her wounded feelings*]

He's no right to take away my character. My character is the
same to me as any lady.

THE NOTE TAKER   335

I dont know whether youve noticed it; but the rain stopped
about two minutes ago.

THE BYSTANDER

So it has. Why didnt you say so before? and us losing our time
listening to your silliness! [*He walks off towards the Strand*]   340

THE SARCASTIC BYSTANDER

I can tell where you come from. You come from Anwell. Go
back there.

THE NOTE TAKER [*helpfully*]

Hanwell.   345

THE SARCASTIC BYSTANDER [*affecting great distinction of speech*]

Thenk you, teacher. Haw haw! So long. [*He touches his hat with
mock respect and strolls off*]

THE FLOWER GIRL

Frightening people like that! How would he like it himself?   350

THE MOTHER

It's quite fine now, Clara. We can walk to a motor bus. Come.

[*She gathers her skirts above her ankles and hurries off towards the Strand*]

THE DAUGHTER 355

But the cab— [*her* MOTHER *is out of hearing*] Oh, how tiresome! [*She follows angrily*]

    All the rest have gone except THE NOTE TAKER, THE GENTLEMAN, *and* THE FLOWER GIRL, *who sits arranging her basket, and still pitying herself in murmurs.* 360

THE FLOWER GIRL

Poor girl! Hard enough for her to live without being worrited and chivied.

THE GENTLEMAN [*returning to his former place on* THE NOTE TAKER's *left*] 365

How do you do it, if I may ask?

THE NOTE TAKER

Simply phonetics. The science of speech. Thats my profession: also my hobby. Happy is the man who can make a living by his hobby! You can spot an Irishman or a Yorkshireman by his 370 brogue. I can place any man within six miles. I can place him within two miles in London. Sometimes within two streets.

THE FLOWER GIRL

Ought to be ashamed of himself, unmanly coward!

THE GENTLEMAN 375

But is there a living in that?

THE NOTE TAKER

Oh, yes, Quite a fat one. This is an age of upstarts. Men begin in Kentish Town with £80 a year, and end in Park Lane with a hundred thousand. They want to drop Kentish Town: but they 380 give themselves away every time they open their mouths. Now I can teach them—

THE FLOWER GIRL

Let him mind his own business and leave a poor girl—

THE NOTE TAKER [*explosively*] 385

Woman: cease this detestable boohooing instantly; or else seek the shelter of some other place of worship.

THE FLOWER GIRL [*with feeble defiance*]

Ive a right to be here if I like, same as you.

386 *boohooing instantly* 'Dont holler' this, Shaw instructed Beerbohm Tree (RN2).

THE NOTE TAKER   390

A woman who utters such depressing and disgusting sounds has
no right to be anywhere – no right to live. Remember that you
are a human being with a soul and the divine gift of articulate
speech: that your native language is the language of Shakespear
and Milton and The Bible: and dont sit there crooning like a   395
bilious pigeon.

THE FLOWER GIRL [*quite overwhelmed, looking up at him in
mingled wonder and deprecation without daring to raise her head*]
Ah-ah-ah-ow-ow-ow-oo!

THE NOTE TAKER [*whipping out his book*]   400
Heavens! what a sound! [*He writes; then holds out the book and
reads, reproducing her vowels exactly*] Ah-ah-ah-ow-ow-ow-oo!

THE FLOWER GIRL [*tickled by the performance, and laughing in
spite of herself*]
Garn!   405

THE NOTE TAKER

You see this creature with her kerbstone English: the English
that will keep her in the gutter to the end of her days. Well, sir,
in three months I could pass that girl off as a duchess at an
ambassador's garden party. I could even get her a place as lady's   410
maid or shop assistant, which requires better English.

THE FLOWER GIRL

What's that you say?

THE NOTE TAKER

Yes, you squashed cabbage leaf, you disgrace to the noble   415
architecture of these columns, you incarnate insult to the English
language: I could pass you off as the Queen of Sheba. [*To* THE
GENTLEMAN] Can you believe that?

---

394 *Shakespear* Shaw's usual spelling of Shakespeare.
411 *requires better English* EM/NASH, C1916, and C1931 contain two additional sen-
     tences for Higgins: 'Thats the sort of thing I do for commercial millionaires. And
     on the profits of it I do genuine scientific work in phonetics, and a little as a poet
     on Miltonic lines'. Higgins's interest in Milton is referred to by Shaw in the Sequel,
     below, p. 131, and is also reflected in some of Higgins's language (see, for example,
     Act II, line 909).
417 *Queen of Sheba* Biblical monarch, whose visit to Jerusalem – 'with a very great
     train, with camels that bare spices, and very much gold, and precious stones' – to
     test the wisdom of Solomon is described in 1 *Kings* 10. This speech by Higgins
     (beginning with 'Yes, you squashed cabbage leaf') does not appear in editions prior
     to C1941.

THE GENTLEMAN
   Of course I can. I am myself a student of Indian dialects; and–   420
THE NOTE TAKER [eagerly]
   Are you? Do you know Colonel Pickering, the author of
   Spoken Sanscrit?
THE GENTLEMAN
   I *am* Colonel Pickering. Who are you?   425
THE NOTE TAKER
   Henry Higgins, author of Higgins's Universal Alphabet.
PICKERING [with enthusiasm]
   I came from India to meet you.
HIGGINS   430
   I was going to India to meet you.
PICKERING
   Where do you live?
HIGGINS
   27A Wimpole Street. Come and see me tomorrow.   435
PICKERING
   I'm at the Carlton. Come with me now and lets have a jaw over
   some supper.
HIGGINS
   Right you are.   440
THE FLOWER GIRL [to PICKERING, as he passes her]
   Buy a flower, kind gentleman. I'm short for my lodging.
PICKERING
   I really havnt any change. I'm sorry. [He goes away]
HIGGINS [shocked at THE GIRL's mendacity]   445
   Liar. You said you could change half-a-crown.
THE FLOWER GIRL [rising in desperation]
   You ought to be stuffed with nails, you ought. [Flinging
   the basket at his feet] Take the whole blooming basket for
   sixpence.   450
      The church clock strikes the second quarter.

---

427 *Higgins's Universal Alphabet* Fictitious, but similarly titled to several contemporary
     works, such as, for example, *Phonetic Spelling. A Proposed Universal Alphabet*, by
     Harry Hamilton Johnson (1913).
437 *the Carlton* the Carlton Hotel, in the Haymarket, adjacent to His Majesty's Theatre
     where *Pygmalion* had its English-language première.

HIGGINS [*hearing in it the voice of God, rebuking him for his Pharisaic want of charity to the poor girl*]

A reminder. [*He raises his hat solemnly: then throws a handful of money into the basket and follows* PICKERING] 455

THE FLOWER GIRL [*picking up a half-crown*]

Ah-ow-ooh! [*Picking up a couple of florins*] Aaah-ow-ooh! [*Picking up several coins*] Aaaaaah-ow-ooh! [*Picking up a half-sovereign*] Aaaaaaaaaaaah-ow-ooh!!!

FREDDY [*springing out of a taxicab*] 460

Got one at last. Hallo! [*To* THE GIRL] Where are the two ladies that were here?

THE FLOWER GIRL

They walked to the bus when the rain stopped.

FREDDY 465

And left me with a cab on my hands! Damnation!

THE FLOWER GIRL [*with grandeur*]

Never mind, young man. *I'm* going home in a taxi. [*She sails off to the cab. The driver puts his hand behind him and holds the door firmly shut against her. Quite understanding his mistrust,* 470 *she shews him her handful of money*] A taxi fare aint no object to me, Charlie. [*He grins and opens the door*] Here. What about the basket?

THE TAXIMAN

Give it here. Tuppence extra. 475

LIZA

No: I dont want nobody to see it. [*She crushes it into the cab and gets in, continuing the conversation through the window*] Goodbye, Freddy.

---

453 *Pharisaic want of charity* A reference to an ancient Jewish sect known for its strict adherence to spiritual law, but also for its self-righteousness and hypocrisy.

471 *A taxi fare aint no object to me, Charlie* The line in EM/NASH, C1916, and C1931 is 'Eightpence aint no object to me, Charlie'. Eliza then tells the taxi driver to take her to 'Angel Court, Drury Lane, round the corner of Micklejohn's oil shop. Lets see how fast you can make her hop it'. The stage direction then reads '*She gets in and pulls the door to with a slam as the taxicab starts*', leaving Freddy alone on the stage to bring the act to a close with 'Well, I'm dashed!' There is no trace in the early text of the seeds of a romantic attachment between Eliza and Freddy as potentially reflected in the stage direction for Freddy to 'dazedly' raise his hat as he says 'Goodbye' to Eliza.

FREDDY [*dazedly raising his hat*]   480
  Goodbye.
TAXIMAN
  Where to?
LIZA
  Bucknam Pellis [Buckingham Palace].   485
TAXIMAN
  What d'ye mean – Bucknam Pellis?
LIZA
  Dont you know where it is? In the Green Park, where the King
  lives. Goodbye, Freddy. Dont let me keep you standing there.   490
  Goodbye.
FREDDY
  Goodbye. [*He goes*]
TAXIMAN
  Here? Whats this about Bucknam Pellis? What business have   495
  you at Bucknam Pellis?
LIZA
  Of course I havnt none. But I wasnt going to let him know that.
  You drive me home.
TAXIMAN   500
  And wheres home?
LIZA
  Angel Court, Drury Lane, next Meiklejohn's oil shop.
TAXIMAN
  That sounds more like it, Judy. [*He drives off*]   505

                              *   *   *

  Let us follow the taxi to the entrance to Angel Court, a narrow
little archway between two shops, one of them Meiklejohn's oil
shop. When it stops there, Eliza gets out, dragging her basket
with her.

LIZA   510
  How much?

485 *Buckingham Palace* The square-bracketed insertion is Shaw's.
505 The line of asterisks was adopted by Shaw in C1941 to indicate where scenes from
     the 1938 film were incorporated into the text.

TAXIMAN [*indicating the taximeter*]
Cant you read? A shilling.

LIZA
A shilling for two minutes!! 515

TAXIMAN
Two minutes or ten: it's all the same.

LIZA
Well, I dont call it right. 520

TAXIMAN
Ever been in a taxi before?

LIZA [*with dignity*]
Hundreds and thousands of times, young man.

TAXIMAN [*laughing at her*]
Good for you, Judy. Keep the shilling, darling, with best love 525
from all at home. Good luck! [*He drives off*]

LIZA [*humiliated*]
Impidence!

[*She picks up the basket and trudges up the alley with it to her
lodging: a small room with very old wall paper hanging loose in* 530
*the damp places. A broken pane in the window is mended with
paper. A portrait of a popular actor and a fashion plate of ladies'
dresses, all wildly beyond poor* ELIZA's *means, both torn from
newspapers, are pinned up on the wall. A birdcage hangs in the
window; but its tenant died long ago: it remains as a memorial* 535
only.

*These are the only visible luxuries: the rest is the irreducible
minimum of poverty's needs: a wretched bed heaped with all sorts
of coverings that have any warmth in them, a draped packing case
with a basin and jug on it and a little looking glass over it, a chair* 540
*and table, the refuse of some suburban kitchen, and an American
alarum clock on the shelf above the unused fireplace: the whole
lighted with a gas lamp with a penny in the slot meter. Rent: four
shillings a week*]

Here Eliza, chronically weary, but too excited to go to bed, 545
sits, counting her new riches and dreaming and planning what
to do with them, until the gas goes out, when she enjoys for the
first time the sensation of being able to put in another penny
without grudging it. This prodigal mood does not extinguish
her gnawing sense of the need for economy sufficiently to 550

prevent her from calculating that she can dream and plan in bed more cheaply and warmly than sitting up without a fire. So she takes off her shawl and skirt and adds them to the miscellaneous bedclothes. Then she kicks off her shoes and gets into bed without any further change.

555

ACT II

Next day at 11 a.m. HIGGINS*'s laboratory in Wimpole Street. It is a room on the first floor, looking on the street, and was meant for the drawing room. The double doors are in the middle of the back wall; and persons entering find in the corner to their right two tall file cabinets at right angles to one another against the wall. In this* 5
corner stands a flat writing-table, on which are a phonograph, a laryngoscope, a row of tiny organ pipes with a bellows, a set of lamp chimneys for singing flames with burners attached to a gas plug in the wall by an indiarubber tube, several tuning-forks of different sizes, a life-size image of half a human head, shewing in section the 10
vocal organs, and a box containing a supply of wax cylinders for the phonograph.

Further down the room, on the same side, is a fireplace, with a comfortable leather-covered easy-chair at the side of the hearth nearest the door, and a coal-scuttle. There is a clock on the mantelpiece. 15
Between the fireplace and the phonograph table is a stand for newspapers.

On the other side of the central door, to the left of the visitor, is a cabinet of shallow drawers. On it is a telephone and the telephone directory. The corner beyond, and most of the side wall, is occupied 20
by a grand piano, with the keyboard at the end furthest from the door, and a bench for the player extending the full length of the keyboard. On the piano is a dessert dish heaped with fruit and sweets, mostly chocolates.

The middle of the room is clear. Besides the easy-chair, the piano 25
bench, and two chairs at the phonograph table, there is one stray chair. It stands near the fireplace. On the walls, engravings: mostly Piranesis and mezzotint portraits. No paintings.

PICKERING *is seated at the table, putting down some cards and a tuning-fork which he has been using.* HIGGINS *is standing up near* 30
him, closing two or three file drawers which are hanging out. He appears in the morning light as a robust, vital, appetizing sort of man

---

8   *singing flames* Part of Higgins's laboratory apparatus for creating and experimenting with sounds by covering the flame with various shapes of glass 'chimneys'.

28   *Piranesis* Giambattista Piranesi (1720–78), Italian architect and engraver, particularly of Roman antiquities.

of forty or thereabouts, dressed in a professional-looking black frock-coat with a white linen collar and black silk tie. He is of the energetic scientific type, heartily, even violently interested in everything that can be studied as a scientific subject, and careless about himself and other people, including their feelings. He is, in fact, but for his years and size, rather like a very impetuous baby 'taking notice' eagerly and loudly, and requiring almost as much watching to keep him out of unintended mischief. His manner varies from genial bullying when he is in a good humor to stormy petulance when anything goes wrong: but he is so entirely frank and void of malice that he remains likeable even in his least reasonable moments.

HIGGINS [*as he shuts the last drawer*]
Well, I think thats the whole show.

PICKERING
It's really amazing. I havnt taken half of it in, you know.

HIGGINS
Would you like to go over any of it again?

PICKERING [*rising and coming to the fireplace, where he plants himself with his back to the fire*]
No, thank you: not now. I'm quite done up for this morning.

HIGGINS [*following him, and standing beside him on his left*]
Tired of listening to sounds?

PICKERING
Yes. It's a fearful strain. I rather fancied myself because I can pronounce twenty-four distinct vowel sounds; but your hundred and thirty beat me. I cant hear a bit of difference between most of them.

HIGGINS [*chuckling, and going over to the piano to eat sweets*]
Oh, that comes with practice. You hear no difference at first; but you keep on listening, and presently you find theyre all as different as A from B. [MRS PEARCE *looks in: she is* HIGGINS's *housekeeper*] Whats the matter?

MRS PEARCE [*hesitating, evidently perplexed*]
A young woman asks to see you, sir.

HIGGINS
A young woman! What does she want?

MRS PEARCE
Well, sir, she says youll be glad to see her when you know what she's come about. She's quite a common girl, sir. Very common indeed. I should have sent her away, only I thought perhaps you

27

wanted her to talk into your machines. I hope Ive not done
wrong; but really you see such queer people sometimes – youll
excuse me, I'm sure, sir– 75

HIGGINS

Oh, thats all right, Mrs Pearce. Has she an interesting accent?

MRS PEARCE

Oh, something dreadful, sir, really. I dont know how you can
take an interest in it. 80

HIGGINS [*to* PICKERING]

Lets have her up. Shew her up, Mrs Pearce [*he rushes across to
his working table and picks out a cylinder to use on the
phonograph*]

MRS PEARCE [*only half resigned to it*] 85

Very well, sir. It's for you to say. [*She goes downstairs*]

HIGGINS

This is rather a bit of luck. I'll shew you how I make records.
We'll set her talking: and I'll take it down first in Bell's Visible
Speech; then in broad Romic; and then we'll get her on the 90
phonograph so that you can turn her on as often as you like with
the written transcript before you.

MRS PEARCE [*returning*]

This is the young woman, sir.

THE FLOWER GIRL *enters in state. She has a hat with three* 95
*ostrich feathers, orange, sky-blue, and red. She has a nearly clean
apron and the shoddy coat has been tidied a little. The pathos of
this deplorable figure, with its innocent vanity and consequential
air, touches* PICKERING, *who has already straightened himself in
the presence of* MRS PEARCE. *But as to* HIGGINS, *the only distinc-* 100
*tion he makes between men and women is that when he is neither
bullying nor exclaiming to the heavens against some featherweight
cross, he coaxes women as a child coaxes its nurse when it wants to
get anything out of her.*

HIGGINS [*brusquely, recognizing her with unconcealed disappoint-* 105
ment, and at once, babylike, making an intolerable grievance of it]

Why, this is the girl I jotted down last night. She's no use: Ive got

---

89–90   *Bell's Visible Speech* See Preface, note 3, above, p. 2.
  90   *broad Romic* A phonetic alphabet created by Henry Sweet, the precursor of the
International Phonetic Alphabet.

all the records I want of the Lisson Grove lingo; and I'm not
going to waste another cylinder on it. [*To* THE GIRL] Be off with
you: I dont want you.   110

THE FLOWER GIRL

Dont you be so saucy. You aint heard what I come for yet. [*To*
MRS PEARCE, *who is waiting at the door for further instructions*]
Did you tell him I come in a taxi?   115

MRS PEARCE

Nonsense, girl! what do you think a gentleman like Mr Higgins
cares what you came in?

THE FLOWER GIRL

Oh, we *are* proud! He aint above giving lessons, not him: I heard
him say so. Well, I aint come here to ask for any compliment;   120
and if my money's not good enough I can go elsewhere.

HIGGINS

Good enough for what?

THE FLOWER GIRL

Good enough for yə-oo. Now you know, dont you? I'm coming   125
to have lessons, I am. And to pay for em tə-oo: make no
mistake.

HIGGINS [*stupent*]

Well!!! [*Recovering his breath with a gasp*] What do you expect
me to say to you?   130

THE FLOWER GIRL

Well, if you was a gentleman, you might ask me to sit down, I
think. Dont I tell you I'm bringing you business?

HIGGINS

Pickering: shall we ask this baggage to sit down, or shall we   135
throw her out of the window?

THE FLOWER GIRL [*running away in terror to the piano, where she
turns at bay*]

Ah-ah-oh-ow-ow-ow-oo! [*Wounded and whimpering*] I wont
be called a baggage when Ive offered to pay like any lady.   140

    *Motionless, the two men stare at her from the other side of the
room, amazed.*

PICKERING [*gently*]

But what is it you want?

128   *stupent* 'he is astounded' (Latin)

THE FLOWER GIRL   145

I want to be a lady in a flower shop stead of sellin at the corner of
Tottenham Court Road. But they wont take me unless I can talk
more genteel. He said he could teach me. Well, here I am ready to
pay him – not asking any favor – and he treats me zif I was dirt.

MRS PEARCE   150

How can you be such a foolish ignorant girl as to think you
could afford to pay Mr Higgins?

THE FLOWER GIRL

Why shouldnt I? I know what lessons cost as well as you do;
and I'm ready to pay.   155

HIGGINS

How much?

THE FLOWER GIRL [*coming back to him, triumphant*]

Now youre talking! I thought youd come off it when you saw a
chance of getting back a bit of what you chucked at me last   160
night. [*Confidentially*] Youd had a drop in, hadnt you?

HIGGINS [*peremptorily*]

Sit down.

THE FLOWER GIRL

Oh, if youre going to make a compliment of it–   165

HIGGINS [*thundering at her*]

Sit down.

MRS PEARCE [*severely*]

Sit down, girl. Do as youre told.

THE FLOWER GIRL   170

Ah-ah-ah-ow-ow-oo! [*She stands, half rebellious, half-bewildered*]

PICKERING [*very courteous*]

Wont you sit down? [*He places the stray chair near the hearthrug
between himself and* HIGGINS]

THE FLOWER GIRL [*coyly*]   175

Dont mind if I do. [*She sits down.* PICKERING *returns to the
hearthrug*]

HIGGINS

Whats your name?

---

149   *zif* 'as if' in EM/NASH, C1916, and C1931.

159   *Now youre talking* Shaw notes here in RC1, 'The sun breaks through the clouds'
      (for Eliza).

174   *between himself and* HIGGINS In EM/NASH, C1916, and C1931 the chair is moved
      (to the same location) by Mrs Pearce, not Pickering.

THE FLOWER GIRL 180
    Liza Doolittle.
HIGGINS [*declaiming gravely*]
        Eliza, Elizabeth, Betsy and Bess,
        They went to the woods to get a bird's nes':
PICKERING 185
        They found a nest with four eggs in it:
HIGGINS
        They took one apiece, and left three in it.
        They laugh heartily at their own fun.
LIZA 190
    Oh, dont be silly.
MRS PEARCE [*placing herself behind* ELIZA*'s chair*]
    You mustnt speak to the gentleman like that.
LIZA
    Well, why wont he speak sensible to me? 195
HIGGINS
    Come back to business. How much do you propose to pay me
    for the lessons?
LIZA
    Oh, I know whats right. A lady friend of mine gets French 200
    lessons for eighteenpence an hour from a real French gentleman.
    Well, you wouldnt have the face to ask me the same for teaching
    me my own language as you would for French; so I wont give
    more than a shilling. Take it or leave it.
HIGGINS [*walking up and down the room, rattling his keys and his* 205
    cash in his pockets]
    You know, Pickering, if you consider a shilling, not as a simple
    shilling, but as a percentage of this girl's income, it works
    out as fully equivalent to sixty or seventy guineas from a
    millionaire. 210
PICKERING
    How so?
HIGGINS
    Figure it out. A millionaire has about £150 a day. She earns about
    half-a-crown. 215

---

192 *behind* ELIZA*'s chair* The stage direction does not appear in editions prior to
    C1941.

LIZA [*haughtily*]

Who told you I only–

HIGGINS [*continuing*]

She offers me two-fifths of her day's income for a lesson. Two-fifths of a millionaire's income for a day would be somewhere about £60. It's handsome. By George, it's enormous! it's the biggest offer I ever had. 220

LIZA [*rising, terrified*]

Sixty pounds! What are you talking about? I never offered you sixty pounds. Where would I get– 225

HIGGINS

Hold your tongue.

LIZA [*weeping*]

But I aint got sixty pounds. Oh–

MRS PEARCE 230

Dont cry, you silly girl. Sit down. Nobody is going to touch your money.

HIGGINS

Somebody is going to touch you, with a broomstick, if you dont stop snivelling. Sit down. 235

LIZA [*obeying slowly*]

Ah-ah-ah-ow-oo-o! One would think you was my father.

HIGGINS

If I decide to teach you, I'll be worse than two fathers to you. Here! [*He offers her his silk handkerchief*] 240

LIZA

Whats this for?

HIGGINS

To wipe your eyes. To wipe any part of your face that feels moist. Remember: thats your handkerchief; and thats your sleeve. Dont mistake the one for the other if you wish to become a lady in a shop. 245

LIZA, *utterly bewildered, stares helplessly at him.*

MRS PEARCE

It's no use talking to her like that, Mr Higgins: she doesnt 250 understand you. Besides, youre quite wrong: she doesnt do it that way at all. [*She takes the handkerchief*]

LIZA [*snatching it*]

Here! You give me that handkerchief. He gev it to me, not to you. 255

PICKERING [*laughing*]

He did. I think it must be regarded as her property, Mrs Pearce.

MRS PEARCE [*resigning herself*]

Serve you right, Mr Higgins.

PICKERING   260

Higgins: I'm interested. What about the ambassador's garden party? I'll say youre the greatest teacher alive if you make that good. I'll bet you all the expenses of the experiment you cant do it. And I'll pay for the lessons.

LIZA   265

Oh, you are real good. Thank you, Captain.

HIGGINS [*tempted, looking at her*]

It's almost irresistible. She's so deliciously low – so horribly dirty–

LIZA [*protesting extremely*]   270

Ah-ah-ah-ah-ow-ow-oo-oo!!! I aint dirty: I washed my face and hands afore I come, I did.

PICKERING

Youre certainly not going to turn her head with flattery, Higgins.   275

MRS PEARCE [*uneasy*]

Oh, dont say that, sir: theres more ways than one of turning a girl's head; and nobody can do it better than Mr Higgins, though he may not always mean it. I do hope, sir, you wont encourage him to do anything foolish.   280

HIGGINS [*becoming excited as the idea grows on him*]

What is life but a series of inspired follies? The difficulty is to find them to do. Never lose a chance: it doesnt come every day. I shall make a duchess of this draggletailed guttersnipe.

LIZA [*strongly deprecating this view of her*]   285

Ah-ah-ah-ow-ow-oo!

HIGGINS [*carried away*]

Yes: in six months – in three if she has a good ear and a quick tongue – I'll take her anywhere and pass her off as anything. We'll start today: now! this moment! Take her away and clean   290

---

257 *her property, Mrs Pearce* RC1 has Liza giving Pickering '*an appreciative wink*' at this point.

her, Mrs Pearce. Monkey Brand, if it wont come off any other
way. Is there a good fire in the kitchen?

MRS PEARCE [*protesting*]

Yes; but—

HIGGINS [*storming on*]   295

Take all her clothes off and burn them. Ring up Whiteley or
somebody for new ones. Wrap her up in brown paper til they
come.

LIZA

Youre no gentleman, youre not, to talk of such things. I'm a   300
good girl, I am; and I know what the like of you are, I do.

HIGGINS

We want none of your Lisson Grove prudery here, young
woman. Youve got to learn to behave like a duchess. Take her
away, Mrs Pearce. If she gives you any trouble, wallop her.   305

LIZA [*springing up and running between* PICKERING *and* MRS
PEARCE *for protection*]

No! I'll call the police, I will.

MRS PEARCE

But Ive no place to put her.   310

HIGGINS

Put her in the dustbin.

LIZA

Ah-ah-ah-ow-ow-oo!

PICKERING   315

Oh come, Higgins! be reasonable.

MRS PEARCE [*resolutely*]

You *must* be reasonable, Mr Higgins: really you *must*. You cant
walk over everybody like this.

> HIGGINS, *thus scolded, subsides. The hurricane is succeeded by*   320
> *a zephyr of amiable surprise.*

HIGGINS [*with professional exquisiteness of modulation*]

I walk over everybody! My dear Mrs Pearce, my dear Pickering, I
never had the slightest intention of walking over anyone. All I
propose is that we should be kind to this poor girl. We must help   325

---

291 *Monkey Brand* A scouring soap (e.g., for kitchen utensils) manufactured by Lever
     Brothers and sold under the 'Monkey Brand' label (depicted by a monkey looking
     at its reflection in a mirror).

296 *Whiteley* A department store established in 1863 in Bayswater (less than a mile
     from Higgins's home on Wimpole Street) by William Whiteley (1831–1907).

her to prepare and fit herself for her new station in life. If I did
not express myself clearly it was because I did not wish to hurt
her delicacy, or yours.

    LIZA, *reassured, steals back to her chair.*

MRS PEARCE [*to* PICKERING]

    Well, did you ever hear anything like that, sir?   330

PICKERING [*laughing heartily*]

    Never, Mrs Pearce: never.

HIGGINS [*patiently*]

    Whats the matter?   335

MRS PEARCE

    Well, the matter is, sir, that you cant take a girl up like that as if
you were picking up a pebble on the beach.

HIGGINS

    Why not?   340

MRS PEARCE

    Why not! But you dont know anything about her. What about
her parents? She may be married.

LIZA

    Garn!   345

HIGGINS

    There! As the girl very properly says, Garn! Married indeed!
Dont you know that a woman of that class looks a worn out
drudge of fifty a year after she's married?

LIZA

    Whood marry me?   350

HIGGINS [*suddenly resorting to the most thrillingly beautiful low
tones in his best elocutionary style*]

    By George, Eliza, the streets will be strewn with the bodies
of men shooting themselves for your sake before Ive done   355
with you.

MRS PEARCE

    Nonsense, sir. You mustnt talk like that to her.

LIZA [*rising and squaring herself determinedly*]

    I'm going away. He's off his chump, he is. I dont want no balmies   360
teaching me.

HIGGINS [*wounded in his tenderest point by her insensibility to his
elocution*]

    Oh, indeed! I'm mad, am I? Very well, Mrs Pearce: you neednt
order the new clothes for her. Throw her out.   365

LIZA [whimpering]

Nah-ow. You got no right to touch me.

MRS PEARCE

You see now what comes of being saucy. [Indicating the door]
This way, please.   370

LIZA [almost in tears]

I didnt want no clothes. I wouldnt have taken them. [She
throws away the handkerchief] I can buy my own clothes.

HIGGINS [deftly retrieving the handkerchief and intercepting her on
her reluctant way to the door]   375

Youre an ungrateful wicked girl. This is my return for offering
to take you out of the gutter and dress you beautifully and make
a lady of you.

MRS PEARCE

Stop, Mr Higgins. I wont allow it. It's you that are wicked.   380
Go home to your parents, girl; and tell them to take better care
of you.

LIZA

I aint got no parents. They told me I was big enough to earn
my own living and turned me out.   385

MRS PEARCE

Wheres your mother?

LIZA

I aint got no mother. Her that turned me out was my sixth
stepmother. But I done without them. And I'm a good girl,   390
I am.

HIGGINS

Very well, then, what on earth is all this fuss about? The girl
doesnt belong to anybody – is no use to anybody but me. [He
goes to MRS PEARCE and begins coaxing] You can adopt her,   395
Mrs Pearce: I'm sure a daughter would be a great amusement to
you. Now dont make any more fuss. Take her downstairs; and–

380   I wont allow it During a rehearsal for a revival of Pygmalion at the Aldwych Theatre
      in February 1920 (directed by Shaw), Mrs Pearce (played by Agnes Thomas) 'went
      angry' on this line, but Shaw advised Mrs Campbell (playing Eliza) that 'this was a
      slip'. 'She will say it steadily and quietly' in the future (Theatrics 153).

390–1 I'm a good girl, I am Eliza, said Shaw, 'should be rather shy and naïve under their
      scrutiny and enquiries' (Theatrics 153).

MRS PEARCE

But whats to become of her? Is she to be paid anything? Do be
sensible, sir.   400

HIGGINS

Oh, pay her whatever is necessary: put it down in the
housekeeping book. [*Impatiently*] What on earth will she want
with money? She'll have her food and her clothes. She'll only
drink if you give her money.   405

LIZA [*turning on him*]

Oh you are a brute. It's a lie: nobody ever saw the sign of liquor
on me. [*To* PICKERING] Oh, sir: youre a gentleman: dont let him
speak to me like that.

PICKERING [*in good-humored remonstrance*]   410

Does it occur to you, Higgins, that the girl has some feelings?

HIGGINS [*looking critically at her*]

Oh no, I dont think so. Not any feelings that we need bother
about. [*Cheerily*] Have you, Eliza?

LIZA   415

I got my feelings same as anyone else.

HIGGINS [*to* PICKERING, *reflectively*]

You see the difficulty?

PICKERING

Eh? What difficulty?   420

HIGGINS

To get her to talk grammar. The mere pronunciation is easy
enough.

LIZA

I dont want to talk grammar. I want to talk like a lady in a   425
flower-shop.

MRS PEARCE

Will you please keep to the point, Mr Higgins. I want to know on
what terms the girl is to be here. Is she to have any wages? And
what is to become of her when youve finished your teaching?   430
You must look ahead a little.

---

409   *speak to me like that* This sentence does not appear in EM/NASH, C1916, C1931.
      Rather, Eliza '*goes back to her chair and plants herself there defiantly*'.
425–6 *in a flower-shop* Added in C1941.

HIGGINS [*impatiently*]

Whats to become of her if I leave her in the gutter? Tell me that, Mrs Pearce.

MRS PEARCE   435

Thats her own business, not yours, Mr Higgins.

HIGGINS

Well, when Ive done with her, we can throw her back into the gutter; and then it will be her own business again; so thats all right.

LIZA   440

Oh, youve no feeling heart in you: you dont care for nothing but yourself. [*She rises and takes the floor resolutely*] Here! Ive had enough of this. I'm going [*making for the door*]. You ought to be ashamed of yourself, you ought.

HIGGINS [*snatching a chocolate cream from the piano, his eyes*   445
suddenly beginning to twinkle with mischief]

Have some chocolates, Eliza.

LIZA [*halting, tempted*]

How do I know what might be in them? Ive heard of girls being drugged by the like of you.   450

    HIGGINS *whips out his penknife; cuts a chocolate in two; puts one half into his mouth and bolts it; and offers her the other half.*

HIGGINS Pledge of good faith, Eliza. I eat one half: you eat the other. [LIZA *opens her mouth to retort: he pops the half choco-late into it*] You shall have boxes of them, barrels of them, every   455
day. You shall live on them. Eh?

LIZA [*who has disposed of the chocolate after being nearly choked by it*]

I wouldnt have ate it, only I'm too ladylike to take it out of my mouth.   460

HIGGINS

Listen, Eliza. I think you said you came in a taxi.

LIZA

Well, what if I did? Ive as good a right to take a taxi as anyone else.

---

450   *the like of you* Eliza's suspicion of Higgins's intentions would not have surprised contemporary audiences. It was commonly assumed that sexual predators used drugged drinks and candies to snare their victims. See Marshik, 'Parodying the £5 Virgin', p. 329.

HIGGINS   465

You have, Eliza; and in future you shall have as many taxis as
you want. You shall go up and down and round the town in a
taxi every day. Think of that, Eliza.

MRS PEARCE

Mr Higgins: youre tempting the girl. It's not right. She should   470
think of the future.

HIGGINS

At her age! Nonsense! Time enough to think of the future when
you havnt any future to think of. No, Eliza: do as this lady does:
think of other people's futures; but never think of your own.   475
Think of chocolates, and taxis, and gold, and diamonds.

LIZA

No: I dont want no gold and no diamonds. I'm a good girl, I
am. [*She sits down again, with an attempt at dignity*]

HIGGINS   480

You shall remain so, Eliza, under the care of Mrs Pearce. And you
shall marry an officer in the Guards, with a beautiful moustache:
the son of a marquis, who will disinherit him for marrying you,
but will relent when he sees your beauty and goodness–

PICKERING   485

Excuse me, Higgins; but I really must interfere. Mrs Pearce is
quite right. If this girl is to put herself in your hands for six
months for an experiment in teaching, she must understand
thoroughly what she's doing.

HIGGINS   490

How can she? She's incapable of understanding anything.
Besides, do any of us understand what we are doing? If we did,
would we ever do it?

PICKERING

Very clever, Higgins; but not to the present point. [*To* ELIZA]   495
Miss Doolittle–

LIZA [*overwhelmed*]

Ah-ah-ow-oo!

HIGGINS

There! Thats all youll get out of Eliza. Ah-ah-ow-oo! No use   500
explaining. As a military man you ought to know that. Give her

---

495   *but not to the present point* Replaces 'but not sound sense' in EM/NASH, C1916,
       C1931.

her orders: thats enough for her. Eliza: you are to live here for the next six months, learning how to speak beautifully, like a lady in a florist's shop. If youre good and do whatever youre told, you shall sleep in a proper bedroom, and have lots to eat, 505 and money to buy chocolates and take rides in taxis. If youre naughty and idle you will sleep in the back kitchen among the black beetles, and be walloped by Mrs Pearce with a broomstick. At the end of six months you shall go to Buckingham Palace in a carriage, beautifully dressed. If the King finds out youre not a 510 lady, you will be taken by the police to the Tower of London, where your head will be cut off as a warning to other presumptuous flower girls. If you are not found out, you shall have a present of seven-and-sixpence to start life with as a lady in a shop. If you refuse this offer you will be a most ungrateful 515 wicked girl; and the angels will weep for you. [*To* PICKERING] Now are you satisfied, Pickering? [*To* MRS PEARCE] Can I put it more plainly and fairly, Mrs Pearce?

MRS PEARCE [*patiently*]

I think youd better let me speak to the girl properly in private. I 520 dont know that I can take charge of her or consent to the arrangement at all. Of course I know you dont mean her any harm; but when you get what you call interested in people's accents, you never think or care what may happen to them or you. Come with me, Eliza. 525

HIGGINS

Thats all right. Thank you, Mrs Pearce. Bundle her off to the bathroom.

LIZA [*rising reluctantly and suspiciously*]

Youre a great bully, you are. I wont stay here if I dont like. I 530 wont let nobody wallop me. I never asked to go to Bucknam Palace, I didnt. I was never in trouble with the police, not me. I'm a good girl—

MRS PEARCE

Dont answer back, girl. You dont understand the gentleman. 535 Come with me. [*She leads the way to the door, and holds it open for* ELIZA]

---

508   *with a broomstick* Shaw directed Eliza to 'catch the chair' on this line (RN2). And in the same note he said she shouldn't delay her approaching exit 'to get all your lines out – get off the stage'.

LIZA [*as she goes out*]

Well, what I say is right. I wont go near the King, not if I'm
going to have my head cut off. If I'd known what I was letting   540
myself in for, I wouldn't have come here. I always been a good
girl; and I never offered to say a word to him; and I dont owe
him nothing; and I dont care; and I wont be put upon; and I
have my feelings the same as anyone else—

MRS PEARCE *shuts the door; and* ELIZA's *plaints are no*   545
longer audible.

* * *

Eliza is taken upstairs to the third floor greatly to her
surprise; for she expected to be taken down to the scullery.
There Mrs Pearce opens a door and takes her into a spare bedroom.   550

MRS PEARCE

I will have to put you here. This will be your bedroom.

LIZA.

O-h, I couldnt sleep here, missus. It's too good for the likes of
me. I should be afraid to touch anything. I aint a duchess yet,   555
you know.

MRS PEARCE

You have got to make yourself as clean as the room: then you
wont be afraid of it. And you must call me Mrs Pearce, not
missus. [*She throws open the door of the dressing-room, now*   560
modernized as a bathroom]

LIZA

Gawd! whats this? Is this where you wash clothes? Funny sort of
copper I call it.

545–6   *no longer audible* In all pre-C1941 editions the stage direction at this point continues, 'PICKERING *comes from the hearth to the chair and sits astride it with his*
arms on the back'. The dialogue then continues with Pickering's 'Excuse the straight
question, Higgins. Are you a man of good character where women are concerned?'
(lines 659–60 in this edition). The bathroom scene (lines 547–653) was not published until C1941, and had to be submitted for a licence for performance. It is
included with LC (on two separate typed pages, undated). There was some concern
about the propriety of the stage direction that has Mrs Pearce '*deftly snatching the*
gown away and throwing ELIZA *down on her back*' (lines 650–1), but an official
noted that 'As long as this is done off [stage] – I suppose the whole bath is just
off – I think it would make a nice scene'.

564   *copper* Eliza mistakes the bathtub for a container for boiling laundry.

MRS PEARCE   565

It is not a copper. This is where we wash ourselves, Eliza, and
where I am going to wash you.

LIZA

You expect me to get into that and wet myself all over! Not me.
I should catch my death. I knew a woman did it every Saturday   570
night; and she died of it.

MRS PEARCE

Mr Higgins has the gentlemen's bathroom downstairs; and he
has a bath every morning, in cold water.

                                                                          575
LIZA

Ugh! He's made of iron, that man.

MRS PEARCE

If you are to sit with him and the Colonel and be taught you will
have to do the same. They wont like the smell of you if you dont.
But you can have the water as hot as you like. There are two taps: 580
hot and cold.

LIZA [weeping]

I couldnt. I dursnt. It's not natural: it would kill me. Ive never
had a bath in my life: not what youd call a proper one.

                                                                          585
MRS PEARCE

Well, dont you want to be clean and sweet and decent, like a
lady? You know you cant be a nice girl inside if youre a dirty slut
outside.

LIZA
                                                                          590
Boohoo!!!!

MRS PEARCE

Now stop crying and go back into your room and take off all
your clothes. Then wrap yourself in this [taking down a gown
from its peg and handing it to her] and come back to me. I will
get the bath ready.   595

LIZA [all tears]

I cant. I wont. I'm not used to it. Ive never took off all my
clothes before. It's not right: it's not decent.

MRS PEARCE

Nonsense, child. Dont you take off all your clothes every night   600
when you go to bed?

LIZA [amazed]

No. Why should I? I should catch my death. Of course I take off
my skirt.

MRS PEARCE 605

Do you mean that you sleep in the underclothes you wear in the daytime?

LIZA

What else have I to sleep in?

MRS PEARCE 610

You will never do that again as long as you live here. I will get you a proper nightdress.

LIZA

Do you mean change into cold things and lie awake shivering half the night? You want to kill me, you do. 615

MRS PEARCE

I want to change you from a frowzy slut to a clean respectable girl fit to sit with the gentlemen in the study. Are you going to trust me and do what I tell you or be thrown out and sent back to your flower basket? 620

LIZA

But you dont know what the cold is to me. You dont know how I dread it.

MRS PEARCE

Your bed wont be cold here: I will put a hot water bottle in it. 625 [*Pushing her into the bedroom*] Off with you and undress.

LIZA

Oh, if only I'd a known what a dreadful thing it is to be clean I'd never have come. I didnt know when I was well off. I– [MRS PEARCE *pushes her through the door, but leaves it partly* 630 *open lest her prisoner should take to flight*]

MRS PEARCE *puts on a pair of white rubber sleeves, and fills the bath, mixing hot and cold, and testing the result with the bath thermometer. She perfumes it with a handful of bath salts and adds a palmful of mustard. She then takes a formidable looking* 635 *long handled scrubbing brush and soaps it profusely with a ball of scented soap.*

ELIZA *comes back with nothing on but the bath gown huddled tightly round her, a piteous spectacle of abject terror.*

MRS PEARCE 640

Now come along. Take that thing off.

LIZA

Oh I couldnt, Mrs Pearce: I reely couldnt. I never done such a thing.

43

MRS PEARCE   645

Nonsense. Here: step in and tell me whether it's hot enough
for you.

LIZA

Ah-oo! Ah-oo! It's too hot.

MRS PEARCE [*deftly snatching the gown away and throwing* ELIZA   650
down on her back]

It wont hurt you. [*She sets to work with the scrubbing brush*]
ELIZA's *screams are heartrending.*

* * *

Meanwhile THE COLONEL has been having it out with
HIGGINS about ELIZA. PICKERING has come from the hearth to   655
the chair and seated himself astride of it with his arms on the
back to cross-examine him.

PICKERING

Excuse the straight question, Higgins. Are you a man of good
character where women are concerned?   660

HIGGINS [*moodily*]

Have you ever met a man of good character where women are
concerned?

PICKERING

Yes: very frequently.   665

HIGGINS [*dogmatically, lifting himself on his hands to the level of
the piano, and sitting on it with a bounce*]

Well, I havnt. I find that the moment I let a woman make
friends with me, she becomes jealous, exacting, suspicious, and a
damned nuisance. I find that the moment I let myself make   670
friends with a woman, I become selfish and tyrannical. Women
upset everything. When you let them into your life, you find
that the woman is driving at one thing and youre driving at
another.

670 *damned nuisance* 'dashed nuisance' in EM, but 'damned nuisance' in all other
editions. The change in EM presumably reflects editorial censorship practices
at *Everybody's Magazine*, though 'bloody' in Act III is spared the censorship,
as is Higgins's 'Such damned nonsense!' leading into Clara's 'Such bloody
nonsense!'

PICKERING 675

At what, for example?

HIGGINS [*coming off the piano restlessly*]

Oh, Lord knows! I suppose the woman wants to live her own life; and the man wants to live his; and each tries to drag the other on to the wrong track. One wants to go north and the 680 other south; and the result is that both have to go east, though they both hate the east wind. [*He sits down on the bench at the keyboard*] So here I am, a confirmed old bachelor, and likely to remain so.

PICKERING [*rising and standing over him gravely*] 685

Come, Higgins! You know what I mean. If I'm to be in this business I shall feel responsible for that girl. I hope it's understood that no advantage is to be taken of her position.

HIGGINS

What! That thing! Sacred, I assure you. [*Rising to explain*] You 690 see, she'll be a pupil; and teaching would be impossible unless pupils were sacred. Ive taught scores of American millionairesses how to speak English: the best looking women in the world. I'm seasoned. They might as well be blocks of wood. *I* might as well be a block of wood. It's– 695

MRS PEARCE *opens the door. She has* ELIZA*'s hat in her hand.*
PICKERING *retires to the easy-chair at the hearth and sits down.*

HIGGINS [*eagerly*]

Well, Mrs Pearce: is it all right?

MRS PEARCE [*at the door*] 700

I just wish to trouble you with a word, if I may, Mr Higgins.

HIGGINS

Yes, certainly. Come in. [*She comes forward*] Dont burn that, Mrs Pearce. I'll keep it as a curiosity. [*He takes the hat*]

MRS PEARCE 705

Handle it carefully, sir, please. I had to promise her not to burn it; but I had better put it in the oven for a while.

HIGGINS [*putting it down hastily on the piano*]

Oh! thank you. Well, what have you to say to me?

PICKERING 710

Am I in the way?

MRS PEARCE

Not at all, sir. Mr Higgins: will you please be very particular what you say before the girl?

45

HIGGINS [*sternly*]   715

Of course. I'm always particular about what I say. Why do you say this to me?

MRS PEARCE [*unmoved*]

No sir: youre not at all particular when youve mislaid anything or when you get a little impatient. Now it doesnt matter before   720 me: I'm used to it. But you really must not swear before the girl.

HIGGINS [*indignantly*]

I swear! [*Most emphatically*] I never swear. I detest the habit. What the devil do you mean?   725

MRS PEARCE [*stolidly*]

Thats what I mean, sir. You swear a great deal too much. I dont mind your damning and blasting, and what the devil and where the devil and who the devil—

HIGGINS   730

Mrs Pearce: this language from your lips! Really!

MRS PEARCE [*not to be put off*]

—but there is a certain word I must ask you not to use. The girl used it herself when she began to enjoy the bath. It begins with the same letter as bath. *She* knows no better: she learnt   735 it at her mother's knee. But she must not hear it from your lips.

HIGGINS [*loftily*]

I cannot charge myself with having ever uttered it, Mrs Pearce. [*She looks at him steadfastly. He adds, hiding an uneasy conscience*   740 *with a judicial air*] Except perhaps in a moment of extreme and justifiable excitement.

MRS PEARCE

Only this morning, sir, you applied it to your boots, to the butter, and to the brown bread.   745

HIGGINS

Oh, that! Mere alliteration, Mrs Pearce, natural to a poet.

MRS PEARCE

Well, sir, whatever you choose to call it, I beg you not to let the girl hear you repeat it.   750

HIGGINS

Oh, very well, very well. Is that all?

MRS PEARCE

No, sir. We shall have to be very particular with this girl as to personal cleanliness.   755

HIGGINS
Certainly. Quite right. Most important.
MRS PEARCE
I mean not to be slovenly about her dress or untidy in leaving
things about.   760
HIGGINS [*going to her solemnly*]
Just so. I intended to call your attention to that. [*He passes on to*
PICKERING, *who is enjoying the conversation immensely*] It is
these little things that matter, Pickering. Take care of the pence
and the pounds will take care of themselves is as true of personal   765
habits as of money. [*He comes to anchor on the hearthrug, with
the air of a man in an unassailable position*]
MRS PEARCE
Yes, sir. Then might I ask you not to come down to breakfast
in your dressing-gown, or at any rate not to use it as a napkin   770
to the extent you do, sir. And if you would be so good as not
to eat everything off the same plate, and to remember not to
put the porridge saucepan out of your hand on the clean
tablecloth, it would be a better example to the girl. You know
you nearly choked yourself with a fishbone in the jam only last   775
week.
HIGGINS [*routed from the hearthrug and drifting back to the
piano*]
I may do these things sometimes in absence of mind; but surely
I dont do them habitually. [*Angrily*] By the way: my dressing-   780
gown smells most damnably of benzine.
MRS PEARCE
No doubt it does, Mr Higgins. But if you will wipe your fingers—
HIGGINS [*yelling*]
Oh very well, very well: I'll wipe them in my hair in future.   785
MRS PEARCE
I hope youre not offended, Mr Higgins.
HIGGINS [*shocked at finding himself thought capable of an unamiable
sentiment*]
Not at all, not at all. Youre quite right, Mrs Pearce: I shall be   790
particularly careful before the girl. Is that all?

---

781 *benzine* A petroleum-based cleaning fluid, probably used by Higgins for his laboratory equipment.

MRS PEARCE

No, sir. Might she use some of those Japanese dresses you
brought from abroad? I really cant put her back into her old
things.   795

HIGGINS

Certainly. Anything you like. Is *that* all?

MRS PEARCE

Thank you, sir. Thats all. [*She goes out*]

HIGGINS   800

You know, Pickering, that woman has the most extraordinary
ideas about me. Here I am, a shy, diffident sort of man. Ive never
been able to feel really grown-up and tremendous, like other
chaps. And yet she's firmly persuaded that I'm an arbitrary
overbearing bossing kind of person. I cant account for it.   805

MRS PEARCE *returns.*

MRS PEARCE

If you please, sir, the trouble's beginning already. Theres a
dustman downstairs, Alfred Doolittle, wants to see you. He says
you have his daughter here.   810

PICKERING [*rising*]

Phew! I say!

HIGGINS [*promptly*]

Send the blackguard up.

MRS PEARCE   815

Oh, very well, sir. [*She goes out*]

PICKERING

He may not be a blackguard, Higgins.

HIGGINS

Nonsense. Of course he's a blackguard.   820

PICKERING

Whether he is or not, I'm afraid we shall have some trouble
with him.

HIGGINS [*confidently*]

Oh no: I think not. If theres any trouble he shall have it with me,   825
not I with him. And we are sure to get something interesting out
of him.

PICKERING

About the girl?

809   *dustman* Or, in North America, garbage collector.

HIGGINS   830

No. I mean his dialect.

PICKERING

Oh!

MRS PEARCE [*at the door*]

Doolittle, sir. [*She admits* DOOLITTLE *and retires*]   835

ALFRED DOOLITTLE *is an elderly but vigorous dustman,
clad in the costume of his profession, including a hat with a back
brim covering his neck and shoulders. He has well marked and
rather interesting features, and seems equally free from fear and
conscience. He has a remarkably expressive voice, the result of a* 840
*habit of giving vent to his feelings without reserve. His present pose
is that of wounded honor and stern resolution.*

DOOLITTLE [*at the door, uncertain which of the two gentlemen is
his man*]

Professor Iggins?   845

HIGGINS

Here. Good morning. Sit down.

DOOLITTLE

Morning, Governor. [*He sits down magisterially*] I come about a
very serious matter, Governor.   850

HIGGINS [*to* PICKERING]

Brought up in Hounslow. Mother Welsh, I should think.
[DOOLITTLE *opens his mouth, amazed.* HIGGINS *continues*]
What do you want, Doolittle?

DOOLITTLE [*menacingly*]   855

I want my daughter: thats what I want. See?

HIGGINS

Of course you do. Youre her father, arnt you? You dont suppose
anyone else wants her, do you? I'm glad to see you have some
spark of family feeling left. She's upstairs. Take her away at   860
once.

DOOLITTLE [*rising, fearfully taken aback*]

What!

HIGGINS

Take her away. Do you suppose I'm going to keep your   865
daughter for you?

DOOLITTLE [*remonstrating*]

Now, now, look here, Governor. Is this reasonable? Is it fairity
to take advantage of a man like this? The girl belongs to me.
You got her. Where do I come in? [*He sits down again*]   870

HIGGINS

> Your daughter had the audacity to come to my house and ask me
> to teach her how to speak properly so that she could get a place
> in a flower-shop. This gentleman and my housekeeper have been
> here all the time. [*Bullying him*] How dare you come here and   875
> attempt to blackmail me? You sent her here on purpose.

DOOLITTLE [*protesting*]

> No, Governor.

HIGGINS

> You must have. How else could you possibly know that she is   880
> here?

DOOLITTLE

> Dont take a man up like that, Governor.

HIGGINS

> The police shall take you up. This is a plant – a plot to extort   885
> money by threats. I shall telephone for the police. [*He goes
> resolutely to the telephone and opens the directory*]

DOOLITTLE

> Have I asked you for a brass farthing? I leave it to the gentleman
> here: have I said a word about money?   890

HIGGINS [*throwing the book aside and marching down on* DOO-
LITTLE *with a poser*]

> What else did you come for?

DOOLITTLE [*sweetly*]

> Well, what *would* a man come for? Be human, Governor.   895

HIGGINS [*disarmed*]

> Alfred: did you put her up to it?

DOOLITTLE

> So help me, Governor, I never did. I take my Bible oath I aint
> seen the girl these two months past.   900

HIGGINS

> Then how did you know she was here?

DOOLITTLE [*'most musical, most melancholy'*]

> I'll tell you, Governor, if youll only let me get a word in. I'm
> willing to tell you. I'm wanting to tell you. I'm waiting to   905
> tell you.

---

903 '*most musical, most melancholy*' From Milton's *Il Penseroso* (1645), and quoted by
Coleridge in 'The Nightingale' (1798) – an intriguing and suggestive direction to
the actor playing Doolittle.

HIGGINS

Pickering: this chap has a certain natural gift of rhetoric. Observe the rhythm of his native woodnotes wild. 'I'm willing to tell you: I'm wanting to tell you: I'm waiting to tell you.' Sentimental   910 rhetoric! thats the Welsh strain in him. It also accounts for his mendacity and dishonesty.

PICKERING

Oh, please, Higgins: I'm west country myself. [*To* DOOLITTLE] How did you know the girl was here if you didnt send her?   915

DOOLITTLE

It was like this, Governor. The girl took a boy in the taxi to give him a jaunt. Son of her landlady, he is. He hung about on the chance of her giving him another ride home. Well, she sent him back for her luggage when she heard you was willing for her to   920 stop here. I met the boy at the corner of Long Acre and Endell Street.

HIGGINS

Public house. Yes?

DOOLITTLE   925

The poor man's club, Governor: why shouldnt I?

PICKERING

Do let him tell his story, Higgins.

DOOLITTLE

He told me what was up. And I ask you, what was my feelings   930 and my duty as a father? I says to the boy, 'You bring me the luggage,' I says—

PICKERING

Why didnt you go for it yourself?

DOOLITTLE   935

Landlady wouldnt have trusted me with it, Governor. She's that kind of woman: *you* know. I had to give the boy a penny afore he trusted me with it, the little swine. I brought it to her just to oblige you like, and make myself agreeable. Thats all.

HIGGINS   940

How much luggage?

DOOLITTLE

Musical instrument, Governor. A few pictures, a trifle of jewlery, and a bird-cage. She said she didn't want no clothes. What was I

---

909   *native woodnotes wild* Another Miltonic allusion, this one to Milton's depiction of Shakespeare's verse in *L'Allegro* (1645).

to think from that, Governor? I ask you as a parent what was 945
I to think?

HIGGINS

So you came to rescue her from worse than death eh?

DOOLITTLE [*appreciatively: relieved at being so well understood*]

Just so, Governor. Thats right. 950

PICKERING

But why did you bring her luggage if you intended to take her
away?

DOOLITTLE

Have I said a word about taking her away? Have I now? 955

HIGGINS [*determinedly*]

Youre going to take her away, double quick. [*He crosses to the
hearth and rings the bell*]

DOOLITTLE [*rising*]

No, Governor. Dont say that. I'm not the man to stand in my 960
girl's light. Heres a career opening for her as you might say;
and—

MRS PEARCE *opens the door and awaits orders.*

HIGGINS

Mrs Pearce: this is Eliza's father. He has come to take her away. 965
Give her to him. [*He goes back to the piano, with an air of
washing his hands of the whole affair*]

DOOLITTLE

No. This is a misunderstanding. Listen here—

MRS PEARCE 970

He cant take her away, Mr Higgins: how can he? You told me to
burn her clothes.

DOOLITTLE

Thats right. I cant carry the girl through the streets like a
blooming monkey, can I? I put it to you. 975

HIGGINS

You have put it to me that you want your daughter. Take your
daughter. If she has no clothes go out and buy her some.

DOOLITTLE [*desperate*]

Wheres the clothes she come in? Did I burn them or did your 980
missus here?

MRS PEARCE

I am the housekeeper, if you please. I have sent for some clothes
for the girl. When they come you can take her away. You can wait
in the kitchen. This way, please. 985

DOOLITTLE, *much troubled, accompanies her to the door;*
then hesitates: finally turns confidentially to HIGGINS.

DOOLITTLE

Listen here, Governor. You and me is men of the world,
aint we?   990

HIGGINS

Oh! Men of the world, are we? Youd better go, Mrs Pearce.

MRS PEARCE

I think so, indeed, sir. [*She goes, with dignity*]

PICKERING   995

The floor is yours, Mr Doolittle.

DOOLITTLE [*to* PICKERING]

I thank you, Governor. [*To* HIGGINS, *who takes refuge on the piano*
bench, a little overwhelmed by the proximity of his visitor; for
DOOLITTLE *has a professional flavor of dust about him*] Well, the   1000
truth is, Ive taken a sort of fancy to you, Governor; and if you
want the girl, I'm not so set on having her back home again but
what I might be open to an arrangement. Regarded in the light of
a young woman, she's a fine handsome girl. As a daughter she's
not worth her keep; and so I tell you straight. All I ask is my rights   1005
as a father; and youre the last man alive to expect me to let her go
for nothing; for I can see youre one of the straight sort, Governor.
Well, whats a five-pound note to you? and whats Eliza to me? [*He*
turns to his chair and sits down judicially]

PICKERING   1010

I think you ought to know, Doolittle, that Mr Higgins's intentions
are entirely honorable.

DOOLITTLE

Course they are, Governor. If I thought they wasn't, I'd ask fifty.

HIGGINS [*revolted*]   1015

Do you mean to say that you would sell your daughter for
£50?

998   *I thank you, Governor* 'D[oolittle] is intimate and confidential. Higgins finally sits
      down on the piano bench to escape his caressses' (Shaw's note in RC1).

1008 *five-pound* Doolittle's asking price for Eliza would have reminded some audience
      members of the notorious series of articles published in 1885 in the *Pall Mall*
      Gazette by William Stead exposing the child prostitution trade in London. One of
      Stead's articles, 'A Child of Thirteen Bought for £5', involved an Eliza – Eliza
      Armstrong – bought by Stead himself for publicity purposes (for which Stead was
      subsequently prosecuted). See Marshik, 'Parodying the £5 Virgin'.

1016 *mean to say* EM/NASH, C1916, and C1931 insert 'you callous rascal' at this point.

DOOLITTLE

Not in a general way I wouldnt; but to oblige a gentleman like
you I'd do a good deal, I do assure you.   1020

PICKERING

Have you no morals, man?

DOOLITTLE [*unabashed*]

Cant afford them, Governor. Neither could you if you was as
poor as me. Not that I mean any harm, you know. But if Liza is   1025
going to have a bit out of this, why not me too?

HIGGINS [*troubled*]

I dont know what to do, Pickering. There can be no question
that as a matter of morals it's a positive crime to give this chap
a farthing. And yet I feel a sort of rough justice in his claim.   1030

DOOLITTLE

Thats it, Governor. Thats all I say. A father's heart, as it were.

PICKERING

Well, I know the feeling; but really it seems hardly right—

                                                                      1035

DOOLITTLE

Dont say that, Governor. Dont look at it that way. What am I,
Governors both? I ask you, what am I? I'm one of the
undeserving poor: thats what I am. Think of what that means to
a man. It means that he's up agen middle class morality all the
time. If theres anything going, and I put in for a bit of it, it's   1040
always the same story: 'Youre undeserving; so you cant have it.'
But my needs is as great as the most deserving widow's that ever
got money out of six different charities in one week for the
death of the same husband. I dont need less than a deserving
man: I need more. I dont eat less hearty than him; and I drink   1045
a lot more. I want a bit of amusement, cause I'm a thinking
man. I want cheerfulness and a song and a band when I feel low.
Well, they charge me just the same for everything as they charge
the deserving. What is middle class morality? Just an excuse for
never giving me anything. Therefore, I ask you, as two gentle-   1050
men, not to play that game on me. I'm playing straight with
you. I aint pretending to be deserving. I'm undeserving; and I

1020   *good deal* 'great deal' in EM

54

mean to go on being undeserving. I like it; and thats the truth. Will you take advantage of a man's nature to do him out of the price of his own daughter.what he's brought up and fed and clothed/by the sweat of his brow/until she's growed big enough to be interesting to you two gentlemen? Is five pounds unreasonable? I put it to you; and I leave it to you.

HIGGINS [*rising, and going over to* PICKERING]

Pickering: if we were to take this man in hand for three months, he could choose between a seat in the Cabinet and a popular pulpit in Wales.

PICKERING

What do you say to that, Doolittle?

DOOLITTLE

Not me, Governor, thank you kindly. Ive heard all the preachers and all the prime ministers – for I'm a thinking man and game for politics or religion or social reform same as all the other amusements – and I tell you it's a dog's life any way you look at it. Undeserving poverty is my line. Taking one station in society with another, it's – it's – well, it's the only one that has any ginger in it, to my taste.

HIGGINS

I suppose we must give him a fiver.

PICKERING

He'll make a bad use of it, I'm afraid.

DOOLITTLE

Not me, Governor, so help me I wont. Dont you be afraid that I'll save it and spare it and live idle on it. There wont be a penny of it left by Monday: I'll have to go to work same as if I never had it. It wont pauperize me, you bet. Just one good spree for myself and the missus, giving pleasure to ourselves and employment to others, and satisfaction to you to think it's not been throwed away. You couldnt spend it better.

HIGGINS [*taking out his pocket book and coming between* DOO-LITTLE *and the piano*]

This is irresistible. Lets give him ten. [*He offers two notes to the dustman*]

DOOLITTLE

No, Governor. She wouldnt have the heart to spend ten; and perhaps I shouldnt neither. Ten pounds is a lot of money: it makes a man feel prudent like; and then goodbye to happiness.

You give me what I ask you, Governor: not a penny more, and not a penny less.

PICKERING 1095

Why dont you marry that missus of yours? I rather draw the line at encouraging that sort of immorality.

DOOLITTLE

Tell her so, Governor: tell her so. *I'm* willing. It's me that suffers by it. Ive no hold on her. I got to be agreeable to her. I got to give her 1100 presents. I got to buy her clothes something sinful. I'm a slave to that woman, Governor, just because I'm not her lawful husband. And she knows it too. Catch her marrying me! Take my advice, Governor – marry Eliza while she's young and dont know no better. If you dont youll be sorry for it after. If you do, *she'll* be 1105 sorry for it after; but better her than you, because youre a man, and she's only a woman and dont know how to be happy anyhow.

HIGGINS

Pickering: If we listen to this man another minute, we shall have no convictions left. [*To* DOOLITTLE] Five pounds I think you 1110 said.

DOOLITTLE

Thank you kindly, Governor.

HIGGINS 1115

Youre sure you wont take ten?

DOOLITTLE

Not now. Another time, Governor.

HIGGINS [*handing him a five-pound note*]

Here you are.

DOOLITTLE 1120

Thank you, Governor. Good morning. [*He hurries to the door, anxious to get away with his booty. When he opens it he is confronted with a dainty and exquisitely clean young Japanese lady in a simple blue cotton kimono printed cunningly with small white jasmine blossoms.* MRS PEARCE *is with her. He gets out of* 1125 *her way deferentially and apologizes*] Beg pardon, miss.

THE JAPANESE LADY

Garn! Dont you know your own daughter?

DOOLITTLE	} exclaiming	{ Bly me! it's Eliza!	
HIGGINS	} simul-	{ Whats that? This!	1130
PICKERING	} taneously	{ By Jove!	

LIZA

Dont I look silly?

HIGGINS

    Silly?   1135

MRS PEARCE [*at the door*]

    Now, Mr Higgins, please dont say anything to make the girl conceited about herself.

HIGGINS [*conscientiously*]

    Oh! Quite right, Mrs Pearce. [*To* ELIZA] Yes: damned silly.   1140

MRS PEARCE

    Please, sir.

HIGGINS [*correcting himself*]

    I mean extremely silly.

LIZA   1145

    I should look all right with my hat on. [*She takes up her hat; puts it on; and walks across the room to the fireplace with a fashionable air*]

HIGGINS

    A new fashion, by George! And it ought to look horrible!   1150

DOOLITTLE [*with fatherly pride*]

    Well, I never thought she'd clean up as good looking as that, Governor. She's a credit to me, aint she?

LIZA

    I tell you, it's easy to clean up here. Hot and cold water on tap, 1155
just as much as you like, there is. Woolly towels, there is; and a towel horse so hot, it burns your fingers. Soft brushes to scrub yourself, and a wooden bowl of soap smelling like primroses. Now I know why ladies is so clean. Washing's a treat for them. Wish they could see what it is for the like of me!   1160

HIGGINS

    I'm glad the bathroom met with your approval.

LIZA

    It didnt: not all of it; and I dont care who hears me say it. Mrs Pearce knows.   1165

HIGGINS

    What was wrong, Mrs Pearce?

MRS PEARCE [*blandly*]

    Oh, nothing, sir. It doesnt matter.

LIZA   1170

    I had a good mind to break it. I didn't know which way to look. But I hung a towel over it, I did.

HIGGINS

    Over what?

MRS PEARCE   1175

Over the looking-glass sir.

HIGGINS

Doolittle: you have brought your daughter up too strictly.

DOOLITTLE

Me! I never brought her up at all, except to give her a lick of a   1180
strap now and again. Dont put it on me, Governor. She aint
accustomed to it, you see: thats all. But she'll soon pick up your
free-and-easy ways.

LIZA

I'm a good girl, I am; and I wont pick up no free-and-easy   1185
ways.

HIGGINS

Eliza: if you say again that youre a good girl, your father shall
take you home.

LIZA   1190

Not him. You dont know my father. All he come here for was to
touch you for some money to get drunk on.

DOOLITTLE

Well, what else would I want money for? To put into the plate in
church, I suppose. [*She puts out her tongue at him. He is so*   1195
incensed by this that PICKERING *presently finds it necessary to*
step between them] Dont you give me none of your lip; and dont
let me hear you giving this gentleman any of it neither, or youll
hear from me about it. See?

HIGGINS   1200

Have you any further advice to give her before you go,
Doolittle? Your blessing, for instance.

DOOLITTLE

No, Governor: I aint such a mug as to put up my children to all
I know myself. Hard enough to hold them in without that. If   1205
you want Eliza's mind improved, Governor, you do it yourself
with a strap. So long, gentlemen. [*He turns to go*]

HIGGINS [*impressively*]

Stop. Youll come regularly to see your daughter. It's your duty,
you know. My brother is a clergyman; and he could help you in   1210
your talks with her.

DOOLITTLE [*evasively*]

Certainly, I'll come, Governor. Not just this week, because I have
a job at a distance. But later on you may depend on me.

Afternoon, gentlemen. Afternoon, maam. [*He touches his hat to* 1215
MRS PEARCE, *who disdains the salutation and goes out. He winks
at* HIGGINS, *thinking him probably a fellow-sufferer from* MRS
PEARCE'*s difficult disposition, and follows her*]

LIZA

Dont you believe the old liar. He'd as soon you set a bulldog on 1220
him as a clergyman. You wont see him again in a hurry.

HIGGINS

I dont want to, Eliza. Do you?

LIZA

Not me. I dont want never to see him again, I dont. He's a 1225
disgrace to me, he is, collecting dust, instead of working at his
trade.

PICKERING

What is his trade, Eliza?

LIZA

1230

Talking money out of other people's pockets into his own. His
proper trade's a navvy; and he works at it sometimes too – for
exercise – and earns good money at it. Aint you going to call
me Miss Doolittle any more?

PICKERING

1235

I beg your pardon, Miss Doolittle. It was a slip of the tongue.

LIZA

Oh, I dont mind; only it sounded so genteel. I *should* just like to
take a taxi to the corner of Tottenham Court Road and get out
there and tell it to wait for me, just to put the girls in their place 1240
a bit. I wouldnt speak to them, you know.

PICKERING

Better wait til we get you something really fashionable.

HIGGINS

Besides, you shouldnt cut your old friends now that you have 1245
risen in the world. Thats what we call snobbery.

LIZA

You dont call the like of them my friends now, I should hope.
Theyve took it out of me often enough with their ridicule when
they had the chance; and now I mean to get a bit of my own 1250
back. But if I'm to have fashionable clothes, I'll wait. I should like

---

1215 *touches his hat* 'takes off his hat' in EM/NASH, C1916, and C1931
1232 *navvy* labourer (initially in the construction of roads, railways, and canals)

to have some. Mrs Pearce says youre going to give me some to
wear in bed at night different to what I wear in the daytime; but
it do seem a waste of money when you could get something to
shew. Besides, I never could fancy changing into cold things on a   1255
winter night.

MRS PEARCE [coming back]
   Now, Eliza. The new things have come for you to try on.

LIZA
   Ah-ow-oo-oooh! [She rushes out]   1260

MRS PEARCE [following her]
   Oh, dont rush about like that, girl. [She shuts the door behind her]

HIGGINS
   Pickering: we have taken on a stiff job.

PICKERING [with conviction]   1265
   Higgins: we have.

* * *

   There seems to be some curiosity as to what Higgins's lessons
to Eliza were like. Well, here is a sample: the first one.
   Picture Eliza, in her new clothes, and feeling her inside put
out of step by a lunch, dinner, and breakfast of a kind to which   1270
it is unaccustomed, seated with Higgins and the Colonel in the
study, feeling like a hospital out-patient at a first encounter with
the doctors.
   Higgins, constitutionally unable to sit still, discomposes her
still more by striding restlessly about. But for the reassuring   1275
presence and quietude of her friend the Colonel she would run
for her life, even back to Drury Lane.

HIGGINS
   Say your alphabet.

LIZA   1280
   I know my alphabet. Do you think I know nothing? I dont need
   to be taught like a child.

HIGGINS [thundering]
   Say your alphabet.

1266   *Higgins: we have* The original Act II (EM/NASH, C1916, C1931) ended here.

PICKERING   1285

Say it, Miss Doolittle. You will understand presently. Do what
he tells you; and let him teach you in his own way.

LIZA

Oh well, if you put it like that – Ahyee, bəyee, cəyee, dəyee–

HIGGINS [*with the roar of a wounded lion*]   1290

Stop. Listen to this, Pickering. This is what we pay for as
elementary education. This unfortunate animal has been
locked up for nine years in school at our expense to teach her
to speak and read the language of Shakespear and Milton. And
the result is Ahyee, Bə-yee, Cə-yee, Də-yee. [*To* ELIZA] Say A, B,   1295
C, D.

LIZA [*almost in tears*]

But I'm saying it. Ahyee, Bə-yee, Cə-yee–

HIGGINS

Stop. Say a cup of tea.   1300

LIZA

A cappətə-ee.

HIGGINS

Put your tongue forward until it squeezes against the top of
your lower teeth. Now say cup.   1305

LIZA

C-c-c – I cant. C-Cup.

PICKERING

Good. Splendid, Miss Doolittle.

HIGGINS   1310

By Jupiter, she's done it at the first shot. Pickering: we shall make
a duchess of her. [*To* ELIZA] Now do you think you could
possibly say tea? Not tə-yee, mind: if you ever say bə-yee cə-yee
də-yee again you shall be dragged round the room three times by
the hair of your head. [*Fortissimo*] T, T, T, T.   1315

LIZA [*weeping*]

I cant hear no difference cep that it sounds more genteel-like
when you say it.

HIGGINS

Well, if you can hear that difference, what the devil are you   1320
crying for? Pickering: give her a chocolate.

PICKERING

No, no. Never mind crying a little, Miss Doolittle: you are
doing very well; and the lessons wont hurt. I promise you I
wont let him drag you round the room by your hair.   1325

HIGGINS

Be off with you to Mrs Pearce and tell her about it. Think about it. Try to do it by yourself: and keep your tongue well forward in your mouth instead of trying to roll it up and swallow it. Another lesson at half-past four this afternoon. Away with you.   1330

ELIZA, *still sobbing, rushes from the room.*

And that is the sort of ordeal poor Eliza has to go through for months before we meet her again on her first appearance in London society of the professional class.

ACT III

It is MRS HIGGINS's *at-home day. Nobody has yet arrived. Her
drawing room, in a flat on Chelsea Embankment, has three windows
looking on the river; and the ceiling is not so lofty as it would be in
an older house of the same pretension. The windows are open, giving
access to a balcony with flowers in pots. If you stand with your face to*   5
*the windows, you have the fireplace on your left and the door in the
right-hand wall close to the corner nearest the windows.*

MRS HIGGINS *was brought up on Morris and Burne Jones; and
her room, which is very unlike her son's room in Wimpole Street, is
not crowded with furniture and little tables and nick-nacks. In the*   10
*middle of the room there is a big ottoman; and this, with the carpet,
the Morris wallpapers, and the Morris chintz window curtains and
brocade covers of the ottoman and its cushions, supply all the orna-
ment, and are much too handsome to be hidden by odds and ends of
useless things. A few good oil-paintings from the exhibitions in the*   15
*Grosvenor Gallery thirty years ago (the Burne Jones, not the Whistler
side of them) are on the walls. The only landscape is a Cecil Lawson
on the scale of a Rubens. There is a portrait of* MRS HIGGINS *as she
was when she defied the fashion in her youth in one of the beautiful
Rossettian costumes which, when caricatured by people who did*   20
*not understand, led to the absurdities of popular estheticism in the
eighteen-seventies.*

  8 *Morris and Burne Jones* William Morris (1834–96) and Sir Edward Coley Burne-
       Jones (1833–98), leading Victorian artists and designers. The mystery and romance
       of their work are in marked contrast to the more cerebral values represented by
       Higgins's choice of Piranesis (Act II, line 28).
 16 *the Grosvenor Gallery* A private art gallery founded in London in 1877 by Sir Coutts
       Lindsay and his wife Blanche (née Rothschild) as a more progressive alternative to
       the conservative Royal Academy (founded in 1768). Works by Burne-Jones and the
       more controversial James Whistler (1834–1903) were exhibited at the Grosvenor.
17–18 *Cecil Lawson on the scale of a Rubens* The landscapes of English painter Cecil
       Lawson (1851–82) were on the large scale of those of the Flemish painter Peter
       Paul Rubens (1577–1640). Some of Lawson's early works were of Chelsea subjects,
       the area of London in which Mrs Higgins lives.
19–20 *beautiful Rossettian costumes* i.e., as in the paintings of Dante Gabriel Rossetti
       (1828–82), one of the founders of the Pre-Raphaelite movement in England, and
       friend of William Morris and Edward Coley Burne-Jones.

In the corner diagonally opposite the door MRS HIGGINS, *now over*
sixty and long past taking the trouble to dress out of the fashion, sits
writing at an elegantly simple writing-table with a bell button within 25
reach of her hand. There is a Chippendale chair further back in the
room between her and the window nearest her side. At the other side of
the room, further forward, is an Elizabethan chair roughly carved in the
taste of Inigo Jones. On the same side a piano in a decorated case. The
corner between the fireplace and the window is occupied by a divan 30
cushioned in Morris chintz.
     It is between four and five in the afternoon.
     The door is opened violently; and HIGGINS *enters with his hat on.*

MRS HIGGINS [*dismayed*]

     Henry! [*Scolding him*] What are you doing here today? It is my   35
     at-home day: you promised not to come. [*As he bends to kiss*
     her, she takes his hat off, and presents it to him]

HIGGINS

     Oh bother! [*He throws the hat down on the table*]

MRS HIGGINS   40

     Go home at once.

HIGGINS [*kissing her*]

     I know, mother. I came on purpose.

MRS HIGGINS

     But you mustnt. I'm serious, Henry. You offend all my friends: 45
     they stop coming whenever they meet you.

HIGGINS

     Nonsense! I know I have no small talk; but people dont mind.
     [*He sits on the settee*]

MRS HIGGINS   50

     Oh! dont they? Small talk indeed! What about your large talk?
     Really, dear, you mustnt stay.

HIGGINS

     I must. Ive a job for you. A phonetic job.

MRS HIGGINS   55

     No use, dear. I'm sorry; but I cant get round your vowels; and
     though I like to get pretty postcards in your patent shorthand,

---

26 *Chippendale chair* i.e., in the ornate style created by English furniture maker
     Thomas Chippendale (1718–79).
28–9 *in the taste of Inigo Jones* i.e., in the English classical style favoured by architect and
     designer Inigo Jones (1573–1652).

I always have to read the copies in ordinary writing you so thoughtfully send me.

HIGGINS   60

Well, this isnt a phonetic job.

MRS HIGGINS

You said it was.

HIGGINS

Not your part of it. Ive picked up a girl.   65

MRS HIGGINS

Does that mean that some girl has picked you up?

HIGGINS

Not at all. I dont mean a love affair.

MRS HIGGINS   70

What a pity!

HIGGINS

Why?

MRS HIGGINS

Well, you never fall in love with anyone under forty-five. When   75
will you discover that there are some rather nice-looking young
women about?

HIGGINS

Oh, I cant be bothered with young women. My idea of a lovable
woman is somebody as like you as possible. I shall never get into   80
the way of seriously liking young women: some habits lie too
deep to be changed. [*Rising abruptly and walking about, jingling
his money and his keys in his trouser pockets*] Besides, theyre all
idiots.

MRS HIGGINS   85

Do you know what you would do if you really loved me,
Henry?

HIGGINS

Oh bother! What? Marry, I suppose.

MRS HIGGINS   90

No. Stop fidgeting and take your hands out of your pockets.
[*With a gesture of despair, he obeys and sits down again*] Thats a
good boy. Now tell me about the girl.

HIGGINS

She's coming to see you.   95

79–80   *a lovable woman is somebody* 'a lovable woman' didn't become a 'somebody' until
         C1941; prior to that she was a 'something'.

65

MRS HIGGINS

I dont remember asking her.

HIGGINS

You didnt. *I* asked her. If youd known her you wouldnt have
asked her. 100

MRS HIGGINS

Indeed! Why?

HIGGINS

Well, it's like this. She's a common flower girl. I picked her off
the kerbstone. 105

MRS HIGGINS

And invited her to my at-home!

HIGGINS [*rising and coming to her to coax her*]

Oh, thatll be all right. Ive taught her to speak properly; and she
has strict orders as to her behavior. She's to keep to two subjects: 110
the weather and everybody's health – Fine day and How do you
do, you know – and not to let herself go on things in general.
That will be safe.

MRS HIGGINS

Safe! To talk about our health! about our insides! perhaps 115
about our outsides! How could you be so silly, Henry?

HIGGINS [*impatiently*]

Well, she must talk about something. [*He controls himself and
sits down again*] Oh, she'll be all right: dont you fuss. Pickering
is in it with me. Ive a sort of bet on that I'll pass her off as a 120
duchess in six months. I started on her some months ago; and
she's getting on like a house on fire. I shall win my bet. She has a
quick ear; and she's been easier to teach than my middle-class
pupils because she's had to learn a complete new language. She
talks English almost as you talk French. 125

MRS HIGGINS

Thats satisfactory, at all events.

HIGGINS

Well, it is and it isnt.

MRS HIGGINS 130

What does that mean?

HIGGINS

You see, Ive got her pronunciation all right; but you have to

---

105   *kerbstone* 'curbstone' in EM (reflecting American spelling).

consider not only *how* a girl pronounces, but *what* she pronounces; and thats where—   135

    They are interrupted by THE PARLORMAID, *announcing
guests.*

THE PARLORMAID

Mrs and Miss Eynsford Hill. [*She withdraws*]

HIGGINS   140

Oh Lord! [*He rises: snatches his hat from the table; and makes for
the door; but before he reaches it his mother introduces him*]

    MRS *and* MISS EYNSFORD HILL *are the mother and daughter
who sheltered from the rain in Covent Garden. The mother is well
bred, quiet, and has the habitual anxiety of straitened means. The*   145
*daughter has acquired a gay air of being very much at home in
society: the bravado of genteel poverty.*

MRS EYNSFORD HILL [*to* MRS HIGGINS]

How do you do? [*They shake hands*]

MISS EYNSFORD HILL   150

How d'you do? [*She shakes*]

MRS HIGGINS [*introducing*]

My son Henry.

MRS EYNSFORD HILL

Your celebrated son! I have so longed to meet you, Professor   155
Higgins.

HIGGINS [*glumly, making no movement in her direction*]

Delighted. [*He backs against the piano and bows brusquely*]

MISS EYNSFORD HILL [*going to him with confident familiarity*]

How do you do?   160

HIGGINS [*staring at her*]

Ive seen you before somewhere. I havnt the ghost of a notion
where; but Ive heard your voice. [*Drearily*] It doesnt matter.
Youd better sit down.

MRS HIGGINS   165

I'm sorry to say that my celebrated son has no manners. You
mustnt mind him.

MISS EYNSFORD HILL [*gaily*]

I dont. [*She sits in the Elizabethan chair*]

---

158   *brusquely* 'bruskly' in EM (reflecting American spelling).

MRS EYNSFORD HILL [*a little bewildered*]   170

Not at all. [*She sits on the ottoman between her* DAUGHTER *and*
MRS HIGGINS, *who has turned her chair away from the writing-table*]

HIGGINS

Oh, have I been rude? I didn't mean to be.

He goes to the central window, through which, with his back to   175
the company, he contemplates the river and the flowers in Battersea
Park on the opposite bank as if they were a frozen desert.

THE PARLORMAID *returns, ushering in* PICKERING.

THE PARLORMAID

Colonel Pickering. [*She withdraws*]   180

PICKERING

How do you do, Mrs Higgins?

MRS HIGGINS

So glad youve come. Do you know Mrs Eynsford Hill – Miss
Eynsford Hill? [*Exchange of bows.* THE COLONEL *brings the*   185
Chippendale chair a little forward between MRS HILL *and* MRS
HIGGINS, *and sits down*]

PICKERING

Has Henry told you what weve come for?

HIGGINS [*over his shoulder*]   190

We were interrupted: damn it!

MRS HIGGINS

Oh Henry, Henry, really!

MRS EYNSFORD HILL [*half rising*]

Are we in the way?   195

MRS HIGGINS [*rising and making her sit down again*]

No, no. You couldnt have come more fortunately: we want you
to meet a friend of ours.

HIGGINS [*turning hopefully*]

Yes, by George! We want two or three people. Youll do as well as   200
anybody else.

THE PARLORMAID *returns, ushering* FREDDY.

THE PARLORMAID

Mr Eynsford Hill.

HIGGINS [*almost audibly, past endurance*]   205

God of Heaven! another of them.

FREDDY [*shaking hands with* MRS HIGGINS]

Ahdedo?

MRS HIGGINS

    Very good of you to come. [*Introducing*] Colonel Pickering.   210

FREDDY [*bowing*]

    Ahdedo?

MRS HIGGINS

    I dont think you know my son, Professor Higgins.

FREDDY [*going to* HIGGINS]   215

    Ahdedo?

HIGGINS [*looking at him much as if he were a pickpocket*]

    I'll take my oath Ive met you before somewhere.
    Where was it?

FREDDY   220

    I dont think so.

HIGGINS [*resignedly*]

    It dont matter, anyhow. Sit down.

       He shakes FREDDY*'s hand and almost slings him on to the*
    ottoman with his face to the window; then comes round to the   225
    other side of it.

HIGGINS

    Well, here we are, anyhow! [*He sits down on the ottoman next*
    MRS EYNSFORD HILL, *on her left*] And now, what the devil are
    we going to talk about until Eliza comes?   230

MRS HIGGINS

    Henry: you are the life and soul of the Royal Society's soirées;
    but really youre rather trying on more commonplace occasions.

HIGGINS

    Am I? Very sorry. [*Beaming suddenly*] I suppose I am, you   235
    know. [*Uproariously*] Ha, ha!

MISS EYNSFORD HILL [*who considers* HIGGINS *quite eligible*
matrimonially]

    I sympathize. I havnt any small talk. If people would only be
    frank and say what they really think!   240

HIGGINS [*relapsing into gloom*]

    Lord forbid!

MRS EYNSFORD HILL [*taking up her daughter's cue*]

    But why?

---

232 *Royal Society soirées* Evening lecture and discussion sessions of the Royal Society, a
    prestigious scientific institution founded in 1666.

HIGGINS 245

What they think they ought to think is bad enough, Lord knows; but what they really think would break up the whole show. Do you suppose it would be really agreeable if I were to come out now with what *I* really think?

MISS EYNSFORD HILL [*gaily*] 250

Is it so very cynical?

HIGGINS

Cynical! Who the dickens said it was cynical? I mean it wouldnt be decent.

MRS EYNSFORD HILL [*seriously*] 255

Oh! I'm sure you dont mean that, Mr Higgins.

HIGGINS

You see, we're all savages, more or less. We're supposed to be civilized and cultured – to know all about poetry and philosophy and art and science, and so on; but how many of us 260 know even the meanings of these names? [*To* MISS HILL] What do *you* know of poetry? [*To* MRS HILL] What do *you* know of science? [*Indicating* FREDDY] What does *he* know of art or science or anything else? What the devil do you imagine I know of philosophy? 265

MRS HIGGINS [*warningly*]

Or of manners, Henry?

THE PARLORMAID [*opening the door*]

Miss Doolittle. [*She withdraws*]

HIGGINS [*rising hastily and running to* MRS HIGGINS] 270

Here she is, mother. [*He stands on tiptoe and makes signs over his mother's head to* ELIZA *to indicate to her which lady is her hostess*]

ELIZA, *who is exquisitely dressed, produces an impression of such remarkable distinction and beauty as she enters that they all* 275 *rise, quite fluttered. Guided by* HIGGINS's *signals, she comes to* MRS HIGGINS *with studied grace.*

LIZA [*speaking with pedantic correctness of pronunciation and great beauty of tone*]

How do you do, Mrs Higgins? [*She gasps slightly in making sure* 280 *of the H in Higgins, but is quite successful*] Mr Higgins told me I might come.

MRS HIGGINS [*cordially*]

Quite right: I'm very glad indeed to see you.

PICKERING   285
>How do you do, Miss Doolittle?

LIZA [*shaking hands with him*]
>Colonel Pickering, is it not?

MRS EYNSFORD HILL
>I feel sure we have met before, Miss Doolittle. I remember your   290
>eyes.

LIZA
>How do you do? [*She sits down on the ottoman gracefully in the
>place just left vacant by* HIGGINS]

MRS EYNSFORD HILL [*introducing*]   295
>My daughter Clara.

LIZA
>How do you do?

CLARA [*impulsively*]
>How do you do? [*She sits down on the ottoman beside* ELIZA,   300
>*devouring her with her eyes*]

FREDDY [*coming to their side of the ottoman*]
>Ive certainly had the pleasure.

MRS EYNSFORD HILL [*introducing*]
>My son Freddy.   305

LIZA
>How do you do?

>   FREDDY *bows and sits down in the Elizabethan chair, infatuated.*

HIGGINS [*suddenly*]
>By George, yes: it all comes back to me! [*They stare at him*]   310
>Covent Garden! [*Lamentably*] What a damned thing!

MRS HIGGINS
>Henry, please! [*He is about to sit on the edge of the table*] Dont
>sit on my writing-table: youll break it.

HIGGINS [*sulkily*]   315
>Sorry.

>   *He goes to the divan, stumbling into the fender and over the
>   fire-irons on his way; extricating himself with muttered impreca-
>   tions; and finishing his disastrous journey by throwing himself so
>   impatiently on the divan that he almost breaks it.* MRS HIGGINS   320
>   *looks at him, but controls herself and says nothing.*

321 *says nothing* Shaw notes in RC1 that Mrs Higgins '*flinches*' at this point.

A long and painful pause ensues.

MRS HIGGINS [*at last, conversationally*]

Will it rain, do you think?

LIZA   325

The shallow depression in the west of these islands is likely to
move slowly in an easterly direction. There are no indications
of any great change in the barometrical situation.

FREDDY

Ha! ha! how awfully funny!   330

LIZA

What is wrong with that, young man? I bet I got it right.

FREDDY

Killing!

MRS EYNSFORD HILL   335

I'm sure I hope it wont turn cold. Theres so much influenza
about. It runs right through our whole family regularly every
spring.

LIZA [*darkly*]

My aunt died of influenza: so they said.   340

MRS EYNSFORD HILL [*clicks her tongue sympathetically*]!!!

LIZA [*in the same tragic tone*]

But it's my belief they done the old woman in.

MRS HIGGINS [*puzzled*]

Done her in?   345

LIZA

Y-e-e-e-es, Lord love you! Why should she die of influenza?
She come through diphtheria right enough the year before.
I saw her with my own eyes. Fairly blue with it, she was. They
all thought she was dead; but my father he kept ladling gin   350
down her throat til she came to so sudden that she bit the bowl
off the spoon.

MRS EYNSFORD HILL [*startled*]

Dear me!

LIZA [*piling up the indictment*]   355

What call would a woman with that strength in her have to die
of influenza? What become of her new straw hat that should
have come to me? Somebody pinched it; and what I say is, them
as pinched it done her in.

MRS EYNSFORD HILL   360

What does doing her in mean?

HIGGINS [*hastily*]

Oh, thats the new small talk. To do a person in means to kill them.

MRS EYNSFORD HILL [*to* ELIZA, *horrified*]   365

You surely dont believe that your aunt was killed?

LIZA

Do I not! Them she lived with would have killed her for a hat-pin, let alone a hat.

MRS EYNSFORD HILL   370

But it cant have been right for your father to pour spirits down her throat like that. It might have killed her.

LIZA

Not her. Gin was mother's milk to her. Besides, he poured so much down his own throat that he knew the good of it.   375

MRS EYNSFORD HILL

Do you mean that he drank?

LIZA

Drank! My word! Something chronic.

MRS EYNSFORD HILL   380

How dreadful for you!

LIZA

Not a bit. It never did him no harm what I could see. But then he did not keep it up regular. [*Cheerfully*] On the burst, as you might say, from time to time. And always more agreeable   385
when he had a drop in. When he was out of work, my mother used to give him fourpence and tell him to go out and not come back until he'd drunk himself cheerful and loving-like. Theres lots of women has to make their husbands drunk to make them fit to live with. [*Now quite at her ease*] You see, it's   390
like this. If a man has a bit of a conscience, it always takes him when he's sober; and then it makes him low-spirited. A drop of booze just takes that off and makes him happy. [*To* FREDDY, *who is in convulsions of suppressed laughter*] Here! what are you sniggering at?
                                                              395
FREDDY

The new small talk. You do it so awfully well.

LIZA

If I was doing it proper, what was you laughing at? [*To* HIGGINS] Have I said anything I oughtnt?
                                                              400
MRS HIGGINS [*interposing*]

Not at all, Miss Doolittle.

LIZA

Well, thats a mercy, anyhow. [*Expansively*] What I always say is—

HIGGINS [*rising and looking at his watch*]   405

Ahem!

LIZA [*looking round at him; taking the hint; and rising*]

Well: I must go. [*They all rise.* FREDDY *goes to the door*] So pleased
to have met you. Goodbye. [*She shakes hands with* MRS HIGGINS]

MRS HIGGINS   410

Goodbye.

LIZA

Goodbye, Colonel Pickering.

PICKERING

Goodbye, Miss Doolittle. [*They shake hands*]   415

LIZA [*nodding to the others*]

Goodbye, all.

FREDDY [*opening the door for her*]

Are you walking across the Park, Miss Doolittle? If so –

LIZA [*with perfectly elegant diction*]   420

Walk! Not bloody likely. [*Sensation*] I am going in a taxi. [*She
goes out*]

> PICKERING *gasps and sits down.* FREDDY *goes out on the
> balcony to catch another glimpse of* ELIZA.

MRS EYNSFORD HILL [*suffering from shock*]   425

Well, I really cant get used to the new ways.

CLARA [*throwing herself discontentedly into the Elizabethan chair*]

Oh, it's all right, mamma, quite right. People will think we never
go anywhere or see anybody if you are so old-fashioned.

MRS EYNSFORD HILL   430

I daresay I am very old-fashioned; but I do hope you wont
begin using that expression, Clara. I have got accustomed to
hear you talking about men as rotters, and calling everything

---

420 *with perfectly elegant diction* Not added until C1941.
421 *Not bloody likely* 'No bloody fear' in both RC1 and RC2. 'No bloody fear' was used
     in a production by the Glasgow Citizens' Theatre in October 1979 (*Guardian*
     review, 15 October 1979). In TS the stage direction is not '*Sensation*', but the more
     restrictive: '*Freddy reels. Higgins falls back on the divan*'. In the rehearsal for the 1914
     production at His Majesty's, Shaw told Mrs Campbell that if the line is said 'self-
     possessedly' it will 'kill the act' (RN2). In LC both instances of 'bloody' (Liza's at
     line 421, and Clara's at line 463) are marked with a pencilled 'X', but they were not
     censored. See Introduction, p. xxii–xxiv, and Appendix II.

filthy and beastly; though I do think it horrible and unladylike. But this last is really too much. Dont you think so, Colonel Pickering? 435

PICKERING

Dont ask me. Ive been away in India for several years; and manners have changed so much that I sometimes dont know whether I'm at a respectable dinner-table or in a ship's 440 forecastle.

CLARA

It's all a matter of habit. Theres no right or wrong in it. Nobody means anything by it. And it's so quaint, and gives such a smart emphasis to things that are not in themselves very witty. I find 445 the new small talk delightful and quite innocent.

MRS EYNSFORD HILL [rising]

Well, after that, I think it's time for us to go.

PICKERING and HIGGINS rise.

CLARA [rising] 450

Oh yes: we have three at-homes to go to still. Goodbye, Mrs Higgins. Goodbye, Colonel Pickering. Goodbye, Professor Higgins.

HIGGINS [coming grimly at her from the divan, and accompanying her to the door] 455

Goodbye. Be sure you try on that small talk at the three at-homes. Dont be nervous about it. Pitch it in strong.

CLARA [all smiles]

I will. Goodbye. Such nonsense, all this early Victorian prudery!

HIGGINS [tempting her] 460

Such damned nonsense!

CLARA

Such bloody nonsense!

MRS EYNSFORD HILL [convulsively]

Clara! 465

CLARA

Ha! ha! [She goes out radiant, conscious of being thoroughly up to date, and is heard descending the stairs in a stream of silvery laughter]

FREDDY [to the heavens at large] 470

Well, I ask you. [He gives it up, and comes to MRS HIGGINS] Goodbye.

MRS HIGGINS [shaking hands]

Goodbye. Would you like to meet Miss Doolittle again?

FREDDY [*eagerly*]   475
    Yes, I should, most awfully.

MRS HIGGINS
    Well, you know my days.

FREDDY
    Yes. Thanks awfully. Goodbye. [*He goes out*]   480

MRS EYNSFORD HILL
    Goodbye, Mr Higgins.

HIGGINS
    Goodbye. Goodbye.

MRS EYNSFORD HILL [*to* PICKERING]   485
    It's no use. I shall never be able to bring myself to use that
    word.

PICKERING
    Dont. It's not compulsory, you know. Youll get on quite well
    without it.   490

MRS EYNSFORD HILL
    Only, Clara is so down on me if I am not positively reeking with
    the latest slang. Goodbye.

PICKERING
    Goodbye. [*They shake hands*]   495

MRS EYNSFORD HILL [*to* MRS HIGGINS]
    You mustnt mind Clara. [PICKERING, *catching from her lowered
    tone that this is not meant for him to hear, discreetly joins* HIGGINS *at
    the window*] We're so poor! and she gets so few parties, poor child!
    She doesnt quite know. [MRS HIGGINS, *seeing that her eyes are*   500
    moist, takes her hand sympathetically and goes with her to the door]
    But the boy is nice. Dont you think so?

MRS HIGGINS
    Oh, quite nice. I shall always be delighted to see him.

MRS EYNSFORD HILL   505
    Thank you, dear. Goodbye. [*She goes out*]

HIGGINS [*eagerly*]
    Well? Is Eliza presentable [*he swoops on his mother and drags her
    to the ottoman, where she sits down in* ELIZA'*s place with her son
    on her left*]?   510

      PICKERING *returns to his chair on her right.*

MRS HIGGINS
    You silly boy, of course she's not presentable. She's a triumph of
    your art and of her dressmaker's; but if you suppose for a

moment that she doesnt give herself away in every sentence she   515
utters, you must be perfectly cracked about her.

PICKERING

But dont you think something might be done? I mean something
to eliminate the sanguinary element from her conversation.

MRS HIGGINS   520

Not as long as she is in Henry's hands.

HIGGINS [*aggrieved*]

Do you mean that *my* language is improper?

MRS HIGGINS

No, dearest: it would be quite proper – say on a canal barge: but   525
it would not be proper for her at a garden party.

HIGGINS [*deeply injured*]

Well I must say–

PICKERING [*interrupting him*]

Come, Higgins: you must learn to know yourself. I havnt heard   530
such language as yours since we used to review the volunteers
in Hyde Park twenty year ago.

HIGGINS [*sulkily*]

Oh, well, if *you* say so, I suppose I dont always talk like a
bishop.   535

MRS HIGGINS [*quieting* HENRY *with a touch*]

Colonel Pickering: will you tell me what is the exact state of
things in Wimpole Street?

PICKERING [*cheerfully: as if this completely changed the subject*]

Well, I have come to live there with Henry. We work together at   540
my Indian Dialects; and we think it more convenient–

MRS HIGGINS

Quite so. I know all about that: it's an excellent arrangement.
But where does this girl live?

HIGGINS   545

With us, of course. Where *should* she live?

531–2   *review the volunteers in Hyde Park twenty years ago* A reference to Pickering's miltary
past in reviewing parades of army volunteers in London's Hyde Park.

546   *should she live?* Originally (EM/NASH, C1916) '*would* [with emphasis] she live?'
Changed to 'should' (no emphasis) in C1931 and to '*should*' (with emphasis) in
C1941.

MRS HIGGINS

But on what terms? Is she a servant? If not, what is she?

PICKERING [*slowly*]

I think I know what you mean, Mrs Higgins.   550

HIGGINS

Well, dash me if *I* do! Ive had to work at the girl every day for
months to get her to her present pitch. Besides, she's useful. She
knows where my things are, and remembers my appointments
and so forth.   555

MRS HIGGINS

How does your housekeeper get on with her?

HIGGINS

Mrs Pearce? Oh, she's jolly glad to get so much taken off her
hands; for before Eliza came, *she* used to have to find things and   560
remind me of my appointments. But she's got some silly bee in
her bonnet about Eliza. She keeps saying 'you dont *think* sir':
doesnt she, Pick?

PICKERING

Yes: thats the formula. 'You dont *think* sir.' Thats the end of   565
every conversation about Eliza.

HIGGINS

As if I ever stop thinking about the girl and her confounded
vowels and consonants. I'm worn out, thinking about her, and
watching her lips and her teeth and her tongue, not to mention   570
her soul, which is the quaintest of the lot.

MRS HIGGINS

You certainly are a pretty pair of babies, playing with your live
doll.

HIGGINS   575

Playing! The hardest job I ever tackled: make no mistake about
that, mother. But you have no idea how frightfully interesting it
is to take a human being and change her into a quite different
human being by creating a new speech for her. It's filling up the
deepest gulf that separates class from class and soul from soul.   580

550   *Mrs Higgins* In RC2 Mrs Campbell wrote 'dull' to describe the scene from here to
      line 633 ('get a word in edgeways').

553   *present pitch* Followed in EM/NASH only by a stage direction for Higgins: '*Shuffling
      untidily*'.

555   *and so forth* Shaw wanted Tree to 'emphasize this' [sentence] – i.e., to stress Eliza's
      usefulnes to Higgins, as opposed to any romantic interest.

PICKERING [*drawing his chair closer to* MRS HIGGINS *and bend-
ing over to her eagerly*]

Yes: it's enormously interesting. I assure you, Mrs Higgins, we
take Eliza very seriously. Every week – every day almost – there
is some new change. [*Closer again*] We keep records of every   585
stage – dozens of gramophone disks and photographs–

HIGGINS [*assailing her at the other ear*]

Yes, by George: it's the most absorbing experiment I ever
tackled. She regularly fills our lives up: doesnt she, Pick?

PICKERING   590
We're always talking Eliza.

HIGGINS
Teaching Eliza.

PICKERING
Dressing Eliza.   595

MRS HIGGINS
What!

HIGGINS
Inventing new Elizas.

HIGGINS		You know, she has the most	600
	speaking	extraordinary quickness of ear:	
PICKERING	*together*	I assure you, my dear Mrs Higgins,	
		that girl	

HIGGINS		just like a parrot. Ive tried her with	
		every	605
PICKERING		is a genius. She can play the piano	
		quite beautifully.	

HIGGINS		possible sort of sound that a human	
		being can make	
PICKERING		We have taken her to classical	610
		concerts and to music	

HIGGINS		Continental dialects. African	
		dialects, Hottentot	
PICKERING		halls; and it's all the same to her: she	
		plays everything	615

613, 616 *Hottentot . . . clicks* The doubly articulated consonants of the language spoken by
Africa's Khoikhoi peoples. 'Hottentot' – from the Dutch for 'stutterer', i.e., the
'clicks' of the Khoisan language – is now considerd an offensive term for the
Khoikhoi.

HIGGINS	⎫	⎧ clicks, things it took me years to get
	⎬	⎨ hold of; and
PICKERING	⎭	⎩ she hears right off when she comes
		home, whether it's

HIGGINS ⎫ ⎧ she picks them up like a shot, right   620
⎬ ⎨ away, as if she had
PICKERING ⎭ ⎩ Beethoven and Brahms or Lehar
and Lionel Monckton;

HIGGINS ⎫ ⎧ been at it all her life.
PICKERING ⎬ ⎨ though six months ago, she'd never   625
⎭ ⎩ as much as touched a piano—

MRS HIGGINS [*putting her fingers in her ears, as they are by this*
time shouting one another down with an intolerable noise]
Sh-sh-sh–sh! [*They stop*]

PICKERING   630

I beg your pardon. [*He draws his chair back apologetically*]

HIGGINS

Sorry. When Pickering starts shouting nobody can get a word
in edgeways.

MRS HIGGINS   635

Be quiet, Henry. Colonel Pickering: dont you realize that when
Eliza walked into Wimpole Street, something walked in with her?

PICKERING

Her father did. But Henry soon got rid of him.

MRS HIGGINS   640

It would have been more to the point if her mother had. But as
her mother didnt something else did.

PICKERING

But what?

---

623   *Lionel Monckton* An eccelctic array of composers: German classical composers Ludwig
van Beethoven (1770–1827) and Johannes Brahms (1833–97), Hungarian opereretta
composer Franz Lehar (1870–1948), and English light musical composer Lionel
Monckton (1861–1924). Monckton's musical comedy *The Arcadians* had run at
London's Shaftesbury Theatre in 1909–11 for over 800 performances, and other
Monckton plays opened in London in 1910, 1911, and 1912 (*The Quaker Girl, The
Mousmé, The Dancing Mistress*). Lehar's *The Count of Luxembourg* ran for over three
hundred perfomances in London in 1911–12, and his *Gipsy Love* opened at Daly's
Theatre on 1 June 1912, just as Shaw was finishing *Pygmalion*.

636   *Be quiet, Henry* Shaw advised Mrs Pearce to 'Put your hand on H's mouth' at this
point (Dukore 147).

MRS HIGGINS [*unconsciously dating herself by the word*] 645
    A problem.

PICKERING
    Oh I see. The problem of how to pass her off as a lady.

HIGGINS
    I'll solve that problem. Ive half solved it already. 650

MRS HIGGINS
    No, you two infinitely stupid male creatures: the problem of
    what is to be done with her afterwards.

HIGGINS
    I dont see anything in that. She can go her own way, with all the 655
    advantages I have given her.

MRS HIGGINS
    The advantages of that poor woman who was here just now!
    The manners and habits that disqualify a fine lady from earning
    her own living without giving her a fine lady's income! Is that 660
    what you mean?

PICKERING [*indulgently, being rather bored*]
    Oh, that will be all right, Mrs Higgins. [*He rises to go*]

HIGGINS [*rising also*]
    We'll find her some light employment. 665

PICKERING
    She's happy enough. Dont you worry about her. Goodbye. [*He
    shakes hands as if he were consoling a frightened child, and makes
    for the door*]

HIGGINS 670
    Anyhow, theres no good bothering now. The thing's done.
    Goodbye, mother. [*He kisses her, and follows* PICKERING]

PICKERING [*turning for a final consolation*]
    There are plenty of openings. We'll do whats right. Goodbye.

HIGGINS [*to* PICKERING *as they go out together*] 675
    Lets take her to the Shakespear exhibition at Earls Court.

676 *Shakespear exhibition at Earls Court* An exhibition on 'the architecture, life,
manners, sports, pastimes, music, and notably the drama of Shakespeare's age' (*The
Times*, 17 January 1912) was held in a specially constructed set of buildings at Earl's
Court from May to September 1912. It was sponsored by the Shakespeare
Memorial Committee, whose objective was to establish a National Theatre in
honour of Shakespeare, and of which Shaw was a member.

PICKERING

    Yes: lets. Her remarks will be delicious.

HIGGINS

    She'll mimic all the people for us when we get home.   680

PICKERING

    Ripping. [*Both are heard laughing as they go downstairs*]

MRS HIGGINS [*rises with an impatient bounce, and returns to her work at the writing-table. She sweeps a litter of disarranged papers out of the way; snatches a sheet of paper from her stationery case;* 685 *and tries resolutely to write. At the third line she gives it up; flings down her pen; grips the table angrily and exclaims*]

    Oh, men! men!! men!!!

*   *   *

Clearly Eliza will not pass as a duchess yet; and Higgins's bet remains unwon. But the six months are not yet exhausted; and 690 just in time Eliza does actually pass as a princess. For a glimpse of how she did it imagine an Embassy in London one summer evening after dark. The hall door has an awning and a carpet across the sidewalk to the kerb, because a grand reception is in progress. A small crowd is lined up to see the guests arrive. 695

A Rolls-Royce car drives up. Pickering in evening dress, with medals and orders, alights, and hands out Eliza, in opera cloak, evening dress, diamonds, fan, flowers and all accessories. Higgins follows. The car drives off; and the three go up the steps and into the house, the door opening for them as they approach. 700

Inside the house they find themselves in a spacious hall from which the grand staircase rises. On the left are the arrangements for the gentlemen's cloaks. The male guests are depositing their hats and wraps there.

On the right is a door leading to the ladies' cloakroom. Ladies 705 are going in cloaked and coming out in splendor. Pickering whispers to Eliza and points out the ladies' room. She goes into it. Higgins and Pickering take off their overcoats and take tickets for them from the attendant.

One of the guests, occupied in the same way, has his back 710 turned. Having taken his ticket, he turns round and reveals

---

688   *Oh, men! men!! men!!!* In all editions prior to C1941 Act III ends here.

himself as an important looking young man with an astonishingly hairy face. He has an enormous moustache, flowing out into luxuriant whiskers. Waves of hair cluster on his brow. His hair is cropped closely at the back, and glows with oil. Otherwise he is very smart. He wears several worthless orders. He is evidently a foreigner, guessable as a whiskered Pandour from Hungary; but in spite of the ferocity of his moustache he is amiable and genially voluble. 715

Recognizing Higgins, he flings his arms wide apart and approaches him enthusiastically. 720

WHISKERS

Maestro, maestro. [*He embraces* HIGGINS *and kisses him on both cheeks*] You remember me?

HIGGINS 725

No I dont. Who the devil are you?

WHISKERS

I am your pupil: your first pupil, your best and greatest pupil. I am little Nepommuck, the marvellous boy. I have made your name famous throughout Europe. You teach me phonetic. You cannot forget *me*. 730

HIGGINS

Why dont you shave?

NEPOMMUCK

I have not your imposing appearance, your chin, your brow. Nobody notices me when I shave. Now I am famous: they call me Hairy Faced Dick. 735

HIGGINS

And what are you doing here among all these swells?

NEPOMMUCK 740

I am interpreter. I speak 32 languages. I am indispensable at these international parties. You are great cockney specialist: you place a man anywhere in London the moment he open his mouth. I place any man in Europe.

A FOOTMAN *hurries down the grand staircase and comes to* 745
NEPOMMUCK.

FOOTMAN

You are wanted upstairs. Her Excellency cannot understand the Greek gentleman.

717 *Pandour from Hungary* Hungarian guard or policeman

NEPOMMUCK   750

Thank you, yes, immediately.

THE FOOTMAN *goes and is lost in the crowd.*

NEPOMMUCK [*to* HIGGINS]

This Greek diplomatist pretends he cannot speak nor understand English. He cannot deceive me. He is the son of a   755
Clerkenwell watchmaker. He speaks English so villainously that
he dare not utter a word of it without betraying his origin. I help
him to pretend; but I make him pay through the nose. I make
them all pay. Ha ha! [*He hurries upstairs*]

PICKERING   760

Is this fellow really an expert? Can he find out Eliza and
blackmail her?

HIGGINS

We shall see. If he finds her out I lose my bet.

ELIZA *comes from the cloakroom and joins them.*   765

PICKERING

Well, Eliza, now for it. Are you ready?

LIZA

Are you nervous, Colonel?

PICKERING   770

Frightfully. I feel exactly as I felt before my first battle. It's the
first time that frightens.

LIZA

It is not the first time for me, Colonel. I have done this fifty
times – hundreds of times – in my little piggery in Angel Court   775
in my day-dreams. I am in a dream now. Promise me not to let
Professor Higgins wake me; for if he does I shall forget
everything and talk as I used to in Drury Lane.

PICKERING

Not a word, Higgins. [*To* ELIZA] Now ready?   780

LIZA

Ready.

PICKERING

Go.

They mount the stairs, HIGGINS *last.* PICKERING *whispers to*   785
THE FOOTMAN *on the first landing.*

FIRST LANDING FOOTMAN

Miss Doolittle, Colonel Pickering, Professor Higgins.

SECOND LANDING FOOTMAN

Miss Doolittle, Colonel Pickering, Professor Higgins.   790

At the top of the staircase the Ambassador and his wife, with NEPOMMUCK *at her elbow, are receiving.*

HOSTESS [*taking* ELIZA's *hand*]
How d'ye do?

HOST [*same play*]   795
How d'ye do? How d'ye do, Pickering?

LIZA [*with a beautiful gravity that awes her* HOSTESS]
How do you do? [*She passes on to the drawing room*]

HOSTESS
Is that your adopted daughter, Colonel Pickering? She will make   800
a sensation.

PICKERING
Most kind of you to invite her for me. [*He passes on*]

HOSTESS [*to* NEPOMMUCK]
Find out all about her.   805

NEPOMMUCK [*bowing*]
Excellency– [*he goes into the crowd*]

HOST
How d'ye do, Higgins? You have a rival here tonight. He
introduced himself as your pupil. Is he any good?   810

HIGGINS
He can learn a language in a fortnight – knows dozens of them.
A sure mark of a fool. As a phonetician, no good whatever.

HOSTESS
How d'ye do, Professor?   815

HIGGINS
How do you do? Fearful bore for you this sort of thing. Forgive
my part in it. [*He passes on*]

In the drawing room and its suite of salons the reception is in
full swing. Eliza passes through. She is so intent on her ordeal   820
that she walks like a somnambulist in a desert instead of a débu-
tante in a fashionable crowd. They stop talking to look at her,
admiring her dress, her jewels, and her strangely attractive self.
Some of the younger ones at the back stand on their chairs to see.

The Host and Hostess come in from the staircase and   825
mingle with their guests. Higgins, gloomy and contemptuous
of the whole business, comes into the group where they are
chatting.

821 *somnambulist* sleepwalker

HOSTESS

Ah, here is Professor Higgins: he will tell us. Tell us all about   830
the wonderful young lady, Professor.

HIGGINS [*almost morosely*]

What wonderful young lady?

HOSTESS

You know very well. They tell me there has been nothing like   835
her in London since people stood on their chairs to look at
Mrs Langtry.

NEPOMMUCK *joins the group, full of news.*

HOSTESS

Ah, here you are at last, Nepommuck. Have you found out all   840
about the Doolittle lady?

NEPOMMUCK

I have found out all about her. She is a fraud.

HOSTESS

A fraud! Oh no.   845

NEPOMMUCK

Yes, yes. She cannot deceive me. Her name cannot be Doolittle.

HIGGINS

Why?

NEPOMMUCK   850

Because Doolittle is an English name. And she is not English.

HOSTESS

Oh, nonsense! She speaks English perfectly.

NEPOMMUCK

Too perfectly. Can you shew me any English woman who   855
speaks English as it should be spoken? Only foreigners who
have been taught to speak it speak it well.

HOSTESS

Certainly she terrified me by the way she said How d'ye do. I
had a schoolmistress who talked like that; and I was mortally   860
afraid of her. But if she is not English what is she?

NEPOMMUCK

Hungarian.

ALL THE REST

Hungarian!   865

---

837   *Mrs Langtry* English actress (1853–1929) – an American citizen from
1887 – and society celebrity who numbered among her many lovers the Prince of
Wales (the future Edward VI).

NEPOMMUCK

Hungarian. And of royal blood. I am Hungarian. My blood is
royal.

HIGGINS

Did you speak to her in Hungarian?   870

NEPOMMUCK

I did. She was very clever. She said 'Please speak to me in
English: I do not understand French.' French! She pretends not
to know the difference between Hungarian and French.
Impossible: she knows both.   875

HIGGINS

And the blood royal? How did you find that out?

NEPOMMUCK

Instinct, maestro, instinct. Only the Magyar races can produce
that air of the divine right, those resolute eyes. She is a princess. 880

HOST

What do you say, Professor?

HIGGINS

I say an ordinary London girl out of the gutter and taught to
speak by an expert. I place her in Drury Lane.   885

NEPOMMUCK

Ha ha ha! Oh, maestro, maestro, you are mad on the subject of
cockney dialects. The London gutter is the whole world for you.

HIGGINS [*to the* HOSTESS]

What does your Excellency say?   890

HOSTESS

Oh, of course I agree with Nepommuck. She must be a princess
at least.

HOST

Not necessarily legitimate, of course. Morganatic perhaps. But   895
that is undoubtedly her class.

HIGGINS

I stick to my opinion.

HOSTESS

Oh, you are incorrigible.   900

    The group breaks up, leaving HIGGINS *isolated.* PICKERING
joins him.

879 *Magyar races* i.e., Hungarian
895 *Morganatic* Not entitled to claim the possessions or title of a spouse of higher social
    rank.

PICKERING

>Where is Eliza? We must keep an eye on her.

>>ELIZA *joins them.* 905

LIZA

>I dont think I can bear much more. The people all stare so at me. An old lady has just told me that I speak exactly like Queen Victoria. I am sorry if I have lost your bet. I have done my best; but nothing can make me the same as these people. 910

PICKERING

>You have not lost it, my dear. You have won it ten times over.

HIGGINS

>Let us get out of this. I have had enough of chattering to these fools. 915

PICKERING

>Eliza is tired; and I am hungry. Let us clear out and have supper somewhere.

ACT IV

The Wimpole Street laboratory. Midnight. Nobody in the room. The clock on the mantelpiece strikes twelve. The fire is not alight: it is a summer night. Presently HIGGINS *and* PICKERING *are heard on the stairs.*

HIGGINS [*calling down to* PICKERING]

I say, Pick: lock up, will you? I shant be going out again.

PICKERING

Right. Can Mrs Pearce go to bed? We dont want anything more, do we?

HIGGINS

Lord, no!

    ELIZA *opens the door and is seen on the lighted landing in all the finery in which she has just won* HIGGINS*'s bet for him. She comes to the hearth, and switches on the electric lights there. She is tired: her pallor contrasts strongly with her dark eyes and hair; and her expression is almost tragic. She takes off her cloak; puts her fan and gloves on the piano; and sits down on the bench, brooding and silent.* HIGGINS, *in evening dress, with overcoat and hat, comes in, carrying a smoking jacket which he has picked up downstairs. He takes off the hat and overcoat; throws them carelessly on the newspaper stand; disposes of his coat in the same way; puts on the smoking jacket; and throws himself wearily into the easy-chair at the hearth.* PICKERING, *similarly attired, comes in. He also takes off his hat and overcoat, and is about to throw them on* HIGGINS*'s when he hesitates.*

PICKERING

I say: Mrs Pearce will row if we leave these things lying about in the drawing room.

---

18 *brooding and silent* EM/NASH, C1916, and C1931 all have a slightly different description of Eliza's entry: '*ELIZA opens the door and is seen on the lighted landing in opera cloak, brilliant evening dress, and diamonds, with fan, flowers, and all accessories. She comes to the hearth, and switches on the electric light there. She is tired; her pallor contrasts strongly with her dark eyes and hair; and her expression is almost tragic. She takes off her cloak, puts her fan and flowers on the piano, and sits down on the bench, brooding and silent*'.

HIGGINS

Oh, chuck them over the bannisters into the hall. She'll find   30
them there in the morning and put them away all right. She'll
think we were drunk.

PICKERING

We are, slightly. Are there any letters?

                                                                  35

HIGGINS

I didn't look. [PICKERING *takes the overcoats and hats and goes
downstairs.* HIGGINS *begins half singing half yawning an air from*
La Fanciulla del Golden West. *Suddenly he stops and exclaims*] I
wonder where the devil my slippers are!

   ELIZA *looks at him darkly; then rises suddenly and leaves the*   40
room.

   HIGGINS *yawns again, and resumes his song.* PICKERING
returns, with the contents of the letterbox in his hand.

PICKERING

Only circulars, and this coroneted billet-doux for you. [*He*   45
*throws the circulars into the fender, and posts himself on the
hearthrug, with his back to the grate*]

HIGGINS [*glancing at the billet-doux*]

Money-lender. [*He throws the letter after the circulars*]

   ELIZA *returns with a pair of large down-at-heel slippers. She*   50
places them on the carpet before HIGGINS, *and sits as before without a word.*

HIGGINS [*yawning again*]

Oh Lord! What an evening! What a crew! What a silly tom-
foolery! [*He raises his shoe to unlace it, and catches sight of the*   55
*slippers. He stops unlacing and looks at them as if they had
appeared there of their own accord*] Oh! theyre there, are they?

---

38   *La Fanciulla del Golden West* A three-act opera by Giacomo Puccini (1858–1924),
     the correct Italian title of which is *La fanciulla del West* (normally translated as *The
     Girl of the Golden West*, the title of the 1905 David Belasco play on which the opera
     is based). It premièred at the Metropolitan Opera House in New York on 10
     December 1910, and was first seen in England at Covent Garden on 29 May 1911. It
     was produced again at Covent Garden on 15 July 1912, shortly after Shaw had com-
     pleted *Pygmalion*, but there is no record of Shaw ever having seen it – though
     presumably Higgins had (see below, note on line 60).

45   *coroneted billet-doux* A love-letter with an embossed crest, as from nobility.
     Pickering is speaking ironically.

PICKERING [*stretching himself*]

Well, I feel a bit tired. It's been a long day. The garden party, a
dinner party, and the reception! Rather too much of a good   60
thing. But youve won your bet, Higgins. Eliza did the trick, and
something to spare, eh?

HIGGINS [*fervently*]

Thank God it's over!

    ELIZA *flinches violently; but they take no notice of her; and*   65
she recovers herself and sits stonily as before.

PICKERING

Were you nervous at the garden party? *I* was. Eliza didnt seem a
bit nervous.

HIGGINS   70

Oh, *she* wasnt nervous. I knew she'd be all right. No: it's the
strain of putting the job through all these months that has told
on me. It was interesting enough at first, while we were at the
phonetics; but after that I got deadly sick of it. If I hadnt backed
myself to do it I should have chucked the whole thing up two   75
months ago. It was a silly notion: the whole thing has been a
bore.

PICKERING

Oh come! the garden party was frightfully exciting. My heart
began beating like anything.   80

---

60 *and the reception!* Higgins's original boast was that 'in three months' he could 'pass
that girl [Eliza] off as a duchess at an ambassador's garden party'(Act I, lines
409–10). The actual wager that Pickering subsequently makes with Higgins gives
Higgins *six* months to get Eliza ready for the garden party (Act II, line 288). In the
original version of the play (EM/NASH, C1916, C1931), the garden party takes
place off-stage between Acts III and IV, and is followed (also off-stage) by a dinner
party and a visit to an opera (presumably *La fanciulla del West*). This is the 'long
day' referred to by Pickering in Act IV line 59. But when Shaw wrote the film scene
in which Eliza is put to the test, he made it an evening event at an ambassadorial
'grand reception' held in a 'drawing room and its suite of salons' and then included
the scene in his final version of the text of the play (C1941). There is no reference
in that scene, however, to a garden party – nor would it make sense since Eliza
would already have been subjected to her test by the time of the evening reception.
Nor is there any mention in the scene of a dinner party (or opera). Indeed, the
scene ends with Pickering saying that he is hungry, so 'Let us clear out and have
supper somewhere' (Act III, line 917).

HIGGINS

Yes, for the first three minutes. But when I saw we were going
to win hands down, I felt like a bear in a cage, hanging about
doing nothing. The dinner was worse: sitting gorging there
for over an hour, with nobody but a damned fool of a fash-   85
ionable woman to talk to! I tell you, Pickering, never again for
me. No more artificial duchesses. The whole thing has been
simple purgatory.

PICKERING

Youve never been broken in properly to the social routine.   90
[*Strolling over to the piano*] I rather enjoy dipping into it
occasionally myself: it makes me feel young again. Anyhow, it
was a great success: an immense success. I was quite frightened
once or twice because Eliza was doing it so well. You see, lots of
the real people cant do it at all: theyre such fools that they think   95
style comes by nature to people in their position; and so they
never learn. Theres always something professional about doing
a thing superlatively well.

HIGGINS

Yes: thats what drives me mad: the silly people dont know their   100
own silly business. [*Rising*] However, it's over and done with;
and now I can go to bed at last without dreading tomorrow.

  ELIZA'*s beauty becomes murderous.*

PICKERING

I think I shall turn in too. Still, it's been a great occasion: a   105
triumph for you. Goodnight. [*He goes*]

HIGGINS [*following him*]

Goodnight. [*Over his shoulder, at the door*] Put out the lights,
Eliza; and tell Mrs Pearce not to make coffee for me in the
morning: I'll take tea. [*He goes out*]   110

  ELIZA *tries to control herself and feel indifferent as she rises
and walks across to the hearth to switch off the lights. By the time
she gets there she is on the point of screaming. She sits down in*
HIGGINS'*s chair and holds on hard to the arms. Finally she gives
way and flings herself furiously on the floor, raging.*   115

HIGGINS [*in despairing wrath outside*]

What the devil have I done with my slippers? [*He appears at the
door*]

LIZA [*snatching up the slippers, and hurling them at him one after
the other with all her force*]   120
There are your slippers. And there. Take your slippers; and may
you never have a day's luck with them!

HIGGINS [*astounded*]
What on earth–! [*He comes to her*] Whats the matter? Get up.
[*He pulls her up*] Anything wrong?   125

LIZA [*breathless*]
Nothing wrong – with *you*. Ive won your bet for you, havnt I?
Thats enough for you. *I* dont matter, I suppose.

HIGGINS
You won my bet! You! Presumptuous insect! *I* won it. What did   130
you throw those slippers at me for?

LIZA
Because I wanted to smash your face. I'd like to kill you, you
selfish brute. Why didnt you leave me where you picked me out
of – in the gutter? You thank God it's all over, and that now you   135
can throw me back again there, do you? [*She crisps her fingers
frantically*]

HIGGINS [*looking at her in cool wonder*]
The creature is nervous, after all.

LIZA [*gives a suffocated scream of fury, and instinctively darts her   140
nails at his face*]!!

HIGGINS [*catching her wrists*]
Ah! would you? Claws in, you cat. How dare you shew your
temper to me? Sit down and be quiet. [*He throws her roughly
into the easy-chair*]   145

LIZA [*crushed by superior strength and weight*]
Whats to become of me? Whats to become of me?

HIGGINS
How the devil do I know whats to become of you? What does it
matter what becomes of you?   150

---

120   *with all her force* Shaw wanted Eliza to throw the slippers at Higgins with some
vigour. 'How carefully you avoided hurting him with the slippers; and how tenderly
he raised you and reciprocated your gentleness! I almost slept', Shaw complained to
Mrs Campbell (Dukore 150).

136–7   *crisps her fingers frantically* An unusual use of 'crisp' as a verb, meaning something
like 'curl' or 'crimp'.

LIZA

You dont care. I know you dont care. You wouldnt care if I was dead. I'm nothing to you – not so much as them slippers.

HIGGINS [*thundering*]

Those slippers.   155

LIZA [*with bitter submission*]

Those slippers. I didnt think it made any difference now.

A pause. ELIZA *hopeless and crushed.* HIGGINS *a little uneasy.*

HIGGINS [*in his loftiest manner*]

Why have you begun going on like this? May I ask whether you   160
complain of your treatment here?

LIZA

No.

HIGGINS

Has anybody behaved badly to you? Colonel Pickering? Mrs   165
Pearce? Any of the servants?

LIZA

No.

HIGGINS

I presume you dont pretend that *I* have treated you badly?   170

LIZA

No.

HIGGINS

I am glad to hear it. [*He moderates his tone*] Perhaps youre tired
after the strain of the day. Will you have a glass of champagne?   175
[*He moves towards the door*]

LIZA

No. [*Recollecting her manners*] Thank you.

HIGGINS [*good-humored again*]

This has been coming on you for some days. I suppose it was   180
natural for you to be anxious about the garden party. But thats
all over now. [*He pats her kindly on the shoulder. She writhes*]
Theres nothing more to worry about.

LIZA

No. Nothing more for *you* to worry about. [*She suddenly rises*   185
and gets away from him by going to the piano bench, where she
sits and hides her face] Oh God! I wish I was dead.

HIGGINS [*staring after her in sincere surprise*]

Why? In heaven's name, why? [*Reasonably, going to her*] Listen
to me, Eliza. All this irritation is purely subjective.   190

LIZA

I dont understand. I'm too ignorant.

HIGGINS

It's only imagination. Low spirits and nothing else. Nobody's
hurting you. Nothing's wrong. You go to bed like a good girl   195
and sleep it off. Have a little cry and say your prayers: that will
make you comfortable.

LIZA

I heard *your* prayers. 'Thank God it's all over!'

HIGGINS [*impatiently*]   200

Well, *dont* you thank God it's all over? Now you are free and
can do what you like.

LIZA [*pulling herself together in desperation*]

What am I fit for? What have you left me fit for? Where am I to
go? What am I to do? Whats to become of me?   205

HIGGINS [*enlightened, but not at all impressed*]

Oh, *thats* whats worrying you, is it? [*He thrusts his hands into
his pockets, and walks about in his usual manner, rattling the
contents of his pockets, as if condescending to a trivial subject out
of pure kindness*] I shouldnt bother about it if I were you. I   210
should imagine you wont have much difficulty in settling
yourself somewhere or other, though I hadnt quite realized that
you were going away. [*She looks quickly at him: he does not look
at her, but examines the dessert stand on the piano and decides
that he will eat an apple*] You might marry, you know. [*He bites   215
a large piece out of the apple and munches it noisily*] You see,
Eliza, all men are not confirmed old bachelors like me and the
Colonel. Most men are the marrying sort (poor devils!); and
youre not bad-looking: it's quite a pleasure to look at you
sometimes – not now, of course, because youre crying and   220
looking as ugly as the very devil; but when youre all right and
quite yourself, youre what I should call attractive. That is, to the
people in the marrying line, you understand. You go to bed and
have a good nice rest; and then get up and look at yourself in
the glass; and you wont feel so cheap.   225

---

219 *not bad-looking* On this line Shaw told Higgins 'dont attend to' Eliza; 'Poke the fire
     & dont make a sympathetic point on "attractive" ' (RN2).
224 *a good nice rest* One might expect 'a good *night's* rest', but it is 'nice' in all editions
     of the play.

ELIZA *again looks at him, speechless, and does not stir.*

The look is quite lost on him: he eats his apple with a dreamy expression of happiness, as it is quite a good one.

HIGGINS [*a genial afterthought occurring to him*]

I daresay my mother could find some chap or other who would   230
do very well.

LIZA

We were above that at the corner of Tottenham Court Road.

HIGGINS [*waking up*]

What do you mean?   235

LIZA

I sold flowers. I didnt sell myself. Now youve made a lady of me
I'm not fit to sell anything else. I wish youd left me where you
found me.

HIGGINS [*slinging the core of the apple decisively into the grate*]   240

Tosh, Eliza. Dont you insult human relations by dragging all
this cant about buying and selling into it. You neednt marry the
fellow if you dont like him.

LIZA

What else am I to do?   245

HIGGINS

Oh, lots of things. What about your old idea of a florist's shop?
Pickering could set you up in one: he has lots of money.
[*Chuckling*] He'll have to pay for all those togs you have been
wearing today; and that, with the hire of the jewellery, will make   250
a big hole in two hundred pounds. Why, six months ago you
would have thought it the millennium to have a flower shop of
your own. Come! youll be all right. I must clear off to bed: I'm
devilish sleepy. By the way, I came down for something: I forget
what it was.   255

LIZA

Your slippers.

HIGGINS

Oh yes, of course. You shied them at me. [*He picks them up, and
is going out when she rises and speaks to him*]   260

LIZA

Before you go, sir—

HIGGINS [*dropping the slippers in his surprise at her calling him Sir*]
Eh?

LIZA   265

Do my clothes belong to me or to Colonel Pickering?

HIGGINS [*coming back into the room as if her question were the very climax of unreason*]

What the devil use would they be to Pickering?

LIZA   270

He might want them for the next girl you pick up to experiment on.

HIGGINS [*shocked and hurt*]

Is *that* the way you feel towards us?

LIZA   275

I dont want to hear anything more about that. All I want to know is whether anything belongs to me. My own clothes were burnt.

HIGGINS

But what does it matter? Why need you start bothering about that in the middle of the night?   280

LIZA

I want to know what I may take away with me. I dont want to be accused of stealing.

HIGGINS [*now deeply wounded*]

Stealing! You shouldnt have said that, Eliza. That shews a want   285
of feeling.

LIZA

I'm sorry. I'm only a common ignorant girl; and in my station I have to be careful. There cant be any feelings between the like of you and the like of me. Please will you tell me what belongs   290
to me and what doesnt?

HIGGINS [*very sulky*]

You may take the whole damned houseful if you like. Except the jewels. Theyre hired. Will that satisfy you? [*He turns on his heel and is about to go in extreme dudgeon*]   295

LIZA [*drinking in his emotion like nectar, and nagging him to provoke a further supply*]

Stop, please. [*She takes off her jewels*] Will you take these to your room and keep them safe? I dont want to run the risk of their being missing.   300

HIGGINS [*furious*]

Hand them over. [*She puts them into his hands*] If these belonged to me instead of to the jeweller, I'd ram them down your ungrateful throat. [*He perfunctorily thrusts them into his pockets, unconsciously decorating himself with the protruding ends*   305
of the chains]

LIZA [*taking a ring off*]

This ring isnt the jeweller's: it's the one you bought me in Brighton. I dont want it now. [HIGGINS *dashes the ring violently into the fireplace, and turns on her so threateningly that she* 310 *crouches over the piano with her hands over her face, and exclaims*] Dont you hit me.

HIGGINS

Hit you! You infamous creature, how dare you accuse me of such a thing? It is you who have hit me. You have wounded me 315 to the heart.

LIZA [*thrilling with hidden joy*]

I'm glad. Ive got a little of my own back, anyhow.

HIGGINS [*with dignity, in his finest professional style*]

You have caused me to lose my temper: a thing that has hardly 320 ever happened to me before. I prefer to say nothing more tonight. I am going to bed.

LIZA [*pertly*]

Youd better leave a note for Mrs Pearce about the coffee; for she wont be told by me. 325

HIGGINS [*formally*]

Damn Mrs Pearce; and damn the coffee; and damn you; and [*wildly*] damn my own folly in having lavished my hard-earned knowledge and the treasure of my regard and intimacy on a heartless guttersnipe. [*He goes out with impressive decorum, and* 330 *spoils it by slamming the door savagely*]

ELIZA *goes down on her knees on the hearthrug to look for the ring. When she finds it she considers for a moment what to do with it. Finally she flings it down on the dessert stand and goes upstairs in a tearing rage.* 335

* * *

335 *tearing rage* In EM, C1916, and C1931 Act IV ends differently. Immediately after Higgins's angry exit, 'ELIZA *smiles for the first time; expresses her feelings by a wild pantomime in which an imitation of* HIGGINS'*s exit is confused with her own triumph; and finally goes down on her knees on the hearthrug to look for the ring*'.

The furniture of Eliza's room has been increased by a big wardrobe and a sumptuous dressing-table. She comes in and switches on the electric light. She goes to the wardrobe; opens it; and pulls out a walking dress, a hat, and a pair of shoes, which she throws on the bed. She takes off her evening dress and shoes: 340 then takes a padded hanger from the wardrobe; adjusts it carefully in the evening dress: and hangs it in the wardrobe, which she shuts with a slam. She puts on her walking shoes, her walking dress, and hat. She takes her wrist watch from the dressing-table and fastens it on. She pulls on her gloves; takes her vanity bag; 345 and looks into it to see that her purse is there before hanging it on her wrist. She makes for the door. Every movement expresses her furious resolution.

She takes a last look at herself in the glass.

She suddenly puts out her tongue at herself: then leaves the 350 room, switching off the electric light at the door.

Meanwhile, in the street outside, Freddy Eynsford Hill, lovelorn, is gazing up at the second floor, in which one of the windows is still lighted.

The light goes out. 355

FREDDY

Goodnight, darling, darling, darling.

ELIZA comes out, giving the door a considerable bang behind her.

LIZA 360

Whatever are you doing here?

FREDDY

Nothing. I spend most of my nights here: It's the only place where I'm happy. Dont laugh at me, Miss Doolittle.

LIZA 365

Dont you call me Miss Doolittle, do you hear? Liza's good enough for me. [She breaks down and grabs him by the shoulders] Freddy: you dont think I'm a heartless guttersnipe, do you?

FREDDY

Oh no, no, darling: how can you imagine such a thing? You are 370 the loveliest, dearest–

*He loses all self-control and smothers her with kisses. She, hungry
for comfort, responds. They stand there in one another's arms.*
An elderly police CONSTABLE *arrives.*

CONSTABLE [*scandalized*]   375

Now then! Now then!! Now then!!!

They release one another hastily.

FREDDY

Sorry, constable. Weve only just become engaged.

They run away.   380

The constable shakes his head, reflecting on his own courtship and on the vanity of human hopes. He moves off in the
opposite direction with slow professional steps.

The flight of the lovers takes them to Cavendish Square.
There they halt to consider their next move.   385

LIZA [*out of breath*]

He didnt half give me a fright, that copper. But you answered
him proper.

FREDDY

I hope I havnt taken you out of your way. Where were you   390
going?

LIZA

To the river.

FREDDY

What for?   395

LIZA

To make a hole in it.

FREDDY [*horrified*]

Eliza, darling. What do you mean? What's the matter?

LIZA   400

Never mind. It doesnt matter now. Theres nobody in the world
now but you and me, is there?

FREDDY

Not a soul.

They indulge in another embrace, and are again surprised by a   405
much younger CONSTABLE.

372–3 *hungry for comfort* Shaw's original direction for Eliza's response to Freddy's kiss was
'ELIZA *responds blissfully*' (HRC, SHAW 25.9, corrected proofs for C1941).

SECOND CONSTABLE

Now then, you two! What's this? Where do you think you are? Move along here, double quick.

FREDDY   410

As you say, sir, double quick.

They run away again, and are in Hanover Square before they stop for another conference.

FREDDY

I had no idea the police were so devilishly prudish.   415

LIZA

It's their business to hunt girls off the streets.

FREDDY

We must go somewhere. We cant wander about the streets all night.   420

LIZA

Cant we? I think it'd be lovely to wander about for ever.

FREDDY

Oh, darling.

They embrace again, oblivious of the arrival of a crawling taxi.   425
It stops.

TAXIMAN

Can I drive you and the lady anywhere, sir?

They start asunder.

LIZA   430

Oh, Freddy, a taxi. The very thing.

FREDDY

But, damn it, Ive no money.

LIZA

I have plenty. The Colonel thinks you should never go out   435
without ten pounds in your pocket. Listen. We'll drive about all night; and in the morning I'll call on old Mrs Higgins and ask her what I ought to do. I'll tell you all about it in the cab. And the police wont touch us there.

FREDDY   440

Righto! Ripping. [*To the* TAXIMAN] Wimbledon Common. [*They drive off*]

ACT V

MRS HIGGINS's *drawing room. She is at her writing-table as before.*
THE PARLORMAID *comes in.*

THE PARLORMAID [*at the door*]
Mr Henry, maam, is downstairs with Colonel Pickering.
MRS HIGGINS
Well, shew them up.
THE PARLORMAID
Theyre using the telephone, maam. Telephoning to the police,
I think.
MRS HIGGINS
What!
THE PARLORMAID [*coming further in and lowering her voice*]
Mr Henry is in a state, maam. I thought I'd better tell you.
MRS HIGGINS
If you had told me that Mr Henry was not in a state it would
have been more surprising. Tell them to come up when theyve
finished with the police. I suppose he's lost something.
THE PARLORMAID
Yes, maam. [*Going*]
MRS HIGGINS
Go upstairs and tell Miss Doolittle that Mr Henry and the
Colonel are here. Ask her not to come down til I send for her.
THE PARLORMAID
Yes, maam.
        HIGGINS *bursts in. He is, as* THE PARLORMAID *has said, in a*
state.
HIGGINS
Look here, mother: heres a confounded thing!
MRS HIGGINS
Yes, dear. Good morning. [*He checks his impatience and kisses*
her, whilst THE PARLORMAID *goes out*] What is it?
HIGGINS
Eliza's bolted.
MRS HIGGINS [*calmly continuing her writing*]
You must have frightened her.

HIGGINS

    Frightened her! nonsense! She was left last night, as usual, to
turn out the lights and all that; and instead of going to bed she
changed her clothes and went right off: her bed wasnt slept in.
She came in a cab for her things before seven this morning; and   40
that fool Mrs Pearce let her have them without telling me a
word about it. What am I to do?

MRS HIGGINS

    Do without, I'm afraid, Henry. The girl has a perfect right to
leave if she chooses.   45

HIGGINS [*wandering distractedly across the room*]

    But I cant find anything. I dont know what appointments Ive
got. I'm – [PICKERING *comes in.* MRS HIGGINS *puts down her
pen and turns away from the writing-table*]

PICKERING [*shaking hands*]   50

    Good morning, Mrs Higgins. Has Henry told you? [*He sits
down on the ottoman*]

HIGGINS

    What does that ass of an inspector say? Have you offered a
reward?   55

MRS HIGGINS [*rising in indignant amazement*]

    You dont mean to say you have set the police after Eliza?

HIGGINS

    Of course. What are the police for? What else could we do? [*He
sits in the Elizabethan chair*]   60

PICKERING

    The inspector made a lot of difficulties. I really think he
suspected us of some improper purpose.

MRS HIGGINS

    Well, of course he did. What right have you to go to the police   65
and give the girl's name as if she were a thief, or a lost umbrella,
or something? Really! [*She sits down again, deeply vexed*]

HIGGINS

    But we want to find her.

PICKERING   70

    We cant let her go like this, you know, Mrs Higgins. What were
we to do?

MRS HIGGINS

    You have no more sense, either of you, than two children. Why–
    THE PARLORMAID *comes in and breaks off the conversation.*   75

THE PARLORMAID
Mr Henry: a gentleman wants to see you very particular. He's
been sent on from Wimpole Street.

HIGGINS
Oh, bother! I cant see anyone now. Who is it?   80

THE PARLORMAID
A Mr Doolittle, sir.

PICKERING
Doolittle! Do you mean the dustman?

THE PARLORMAID   85
Dustman! Oh no, sir: a gentleman.

HIGGINS [springing up excitedly]
By George, Pick, it's some relative of hers that she's gone to.
Somebody we know nothing about. [To the parlormaid] Send
him up, quick.   90

THE PARLORMAID
Yes, sir. [She goes]

HIGGINS [eagerly, going to his mother]
Genteel relatives! now we shall hear something. [He sits down in
the Chippendale chair]   95

MRS HIGGINS
Do you know any of her people?

PICKERING
Only her father: the fellow we told you about.

THE PARLORMAID [announcing]   100
Mr Doolittle. [She withdraws]

   DOOLITTLE enters. He is resplendently dressed as for a fashionable wedding, and might, in fact, be the bridegroom. A flower
in his buttonhole, a dazzling silk hat, and patent leather shoes
complete the effect. He is too concerned with the business he has   105
come on to notice MRS HIGGINS. He walks straight to HIGGINS,
and accosts him with vehement reproach.

DOOLITTLE [indicating his own person]
See here! Do you see this? You done this.

HIGGINS   110
Done what, man?

---

105   complete the effect In EM/NASH, C1916, and C1931 Doolittle is dressed slightly dif-
      ferently: 'He is brilliantly dressed in a new fashionable frock-coat, with white
      waist-coat and gray trousers. A flower in his button-hole, a dazzling silk hat, and
      patent-leather shoes complete the effect'.

DOOLITTLE

This, I tell you. Look at it. Look at this hat. Look at this coat.

PICKERING

Has Eliza been buying you clothes? 115

DOOLITTLE

Eliza! not she. Why would she buy me clothes?

MRS HIGGINS

Good morning, Mr Doolittle. Wont you sit down?

DOOLITTLE [*taken aback as he becomes conscious that he has* 120
forgotten his hostess]

Asking your pardon, maam. [*He approaches her and shakes her
proffered hand*] Thank you. [*He sits down on the ottoman, on*
PICKERING's *right*] I am that full of what has happened to me
that I cant think of anything else. 125

HIGGINS

What the dickens *has* happened to you?

DOOLITTLE

I shouldnt mind if it had only *happened* to me: anything might
happen to anybody and nobody to blame but Providence, as 130
you might say. But this is something that *you* done to me: yes,
you, Enry Iggins.

HIGGINS

Have you found Eliza?

DOOLITTLE 135

Have you lost her?

HIGGINS

Yes.

DOOLITTLE

You have all the luck, you have. I aint found her; but she'll find 140
me quick enough now after what you done to me.

MRS HIGGINS

But what has my son done to you, Mr Doolittle?

DOOLITTLE

Done to me! Ruined me. Destroyed my happiness. Tied me up 145
and delivered me into the hands of middle class morality.

HIGGINS [*rising intolerantly and standing over* DOOLITTLE]

Youre raving. Youre drunk. Youre mad. I gave you five pounds.
After that I had two conversations with you, at half-a-crown an
hour. Ive never seen you since. 150

132 *Enry Iggins* Henry Higgins didn't become Enry Iggins until C1941.

DOOLITTLE

Oh! Drunk am I? Mad am I? Tell me this. Did you or did you not write a letter to an old blighter in America that was giving five millions to found Moral Reform Societies all over the world, and that wanted you to invent a universal language for him?   155

HIGGINS

What! Ezra D. Wannafeller! He's dead. [*He sits down again carelessly*]   160

DOOLITTLE

Yes: he's dead; and I'm done for. Now did you or did you not write a letter to him to say that the most original moralist at present in England, to the best of your knowledge, was Alfred Doolittle, a common dustman?   165

HIGGINS

Oh, after your first visit I remember making some silly joke of the kind.

DOOLITTLE

Ah! You may well call it a silly joke. It put the lid on me right enough. Just give him the chance he wanted to shew that   170 Americans is not like us: that they reckonize and respect merit in every class of life, however humble. Them words is in his blooming will, in which, Henry Higgins, thanks to your silly joking, he leaves me a share in his Pre-digested Cheese Trust worth three thousand a year on condition that I lecture for his   175 Wannafeller Moral Reform World League as often as they ask me up to six times a year.

HIGGINS

The devil he does! Whew! [*Brightening suddenly*] What a lark!

---

154 *Moral Reform Societies* Doolittle isn't making it up. Such societies were a staple of Victorian and Edwardian British and American society, tackling with evangelical fervour issues such as prostitution, alcohol, and Godlessness.

158 *Ezra D. Wannafeller* Fictitious, but likely a satiric combination of the names of two successful American businessmen – John Wanamaker (1838–1922) and J.D. Rockefeller (1839–1937).

173 *Henry Higgins* Doolittle occasionally remembers to aspirate.

175 *three thousand a year* In the Sequel, Shaw says Doolittle has four thousand a year (below, p. 133).

PICKERING   180

A safe thing for you, Doolittle. They wont ask you twice.

DOOLITTLE

It aint the lecturing I mind. I'll lecture them blue in the face, I
will, and not turn a hair. It's making a gentleman of me that I
object to. Who asked him to make a gentleman of me? I was   185
happy. I was free. I touched pretty nigh everybody for money
when I wanted it, same as I touched you, Enry Iggins. Now I am
worrited: tied neck and heels; and everybody touches me for
money. It's a fine thing for you, says my solicitor. Is it? says I.
You mean it's a good thing for you, I says. When I was a poor   190
man and had a solicitor once when they found a pram in the
dust cart, he got me off, and got shut of me and got me shut of
him as quick as he could. Same with the doctors: used to shove
me out of the hospital before I could hardly stand on my legs,
and nothing to pay. Now they finds out that I'm not a healthy   195
man and cant live unless they looks after me twice a day. In the
house I'm not let do a hand's turn for myself: somebody else
must do it and touch me for it. A year ago I hadnt a relative in
the world except two or three that wouldnt speak to me. Now
Ive fifty, and not a decent week's wages among the lot of them. I 200
have to live for others and not for myself: thats middle class
morality. *You* talk of losing Eliza. Dont you be anxious: I bet
she's on my doorstep by this: she that could support herself
easy by selling flowers if I wasnt respectable. And the next one
to touch me will be you, Enry Iggins. I'll have to learn to speak 205
middle class language from you, instead of speaking proper
English. Thats where *youll* come in; and I daresay thats what
you done it for.

MRS HIGGINS

But, my dear Mr Doolittle, you need not suffer all this if   210
you are really in earnest. Nobody can force you to accept
this bequest. You can repudiate it. Isnt that so, Colonel
Pickering?

PICKERING

I believe so.   215

DOOLITTLE [*softening his manner in deference to her sex*]

Thats the tragedy of it, maam. It's easy to say chuck it; but I
havnt the nerve. Which of us has? We're all intimidated.
Intimidated, maam: thats what we are. What is there for me if I

107

chuck it but the workhouse in my old age? I have to dye my hair   220
already to keep my job as a dustman. If I was one of the
deserving poor, and had put by a bit, I could chuck it; but then
why should I, acause the deserving poor might as well be
millionaires for all the happiness they ever has. They dont know
what happiness is. But I, as one of the undeserving poor, have   225
nothing between me and the pauper's uniform but this here
blasted three thousand a year that shoves me into the middle
class. (Excuse the expression, maam; youd use it yourself if you
had my provocation.) Theyve got you every way you turn: it's a
choice between the Skilly of the workhouse and the Char Bydis   230
of the middle class; and I havnt the nerve for the workhouse.
Intimidated: thats what I am. Broke. Bought up. Happier men
than me will call for my dust, and touch me for their tip; and I'll
look on helpless, and envy them. And thats what your son has
brought me to. [*He is overcome by emotion*]   235

MRS HIGGINS
Well, I'm very glad youre not going to do anything foolish,
Mr Doolittle. For this solves the problem of Eliza's future. You
can provide for her now.

DOOLITTLE [*with melancholy resignation*]   240
Yes, maam: I'm expected to provide for everyone now, out of
three thousand a year.

HIGGINS [*jumping up*]
Nonsense! he cant provide for her. He shant provide for her.
She doesnt belong to him. I paid him five pounds for her.   245
Doolittle: either youre an honest man or a rogue.

DOOLITTLE [*tolerantly*]
A little of both, Henry, like the rest of us: a little of both.

---

220 *dye my hair* Doolittle dyes his hair to disguise his age. In Act II of Shaw's *Major
Barbara* Shirley complains that he is 'to be thrown into the gutter and my job given
to a young man that can do it no better than me because Ive black hair that goes
white at the first change' – a problem, he says, that 'three pennorth o hair dye'
might solve.

230 *Skilly . . . Char Bydis* Doolittle's version of Scylla and Charybdis in the Greek myth
of the perils posed by the sea-monster Scylla and the whirlpool Charybdis as sailors
navigated between them (usually assumed to be in the Straits of Messina between
Italy and Sicily). Doolittle also neatly puns on the skilly (an unappetising gruel)
traditionally served in Victorian and Edwardian prisons and workhouses.

HIGGINS

Well, you took that money for the girl; and you have no right to   250
take her as well.

MRS HIGGINS

Henry: dont be absurd. If you want to know where Eliza is, she
is upstairs.

HIGGINS [*amazed*]   255

Upstairs!!! Then I shall jolly soon fetch her downstairs. [*He
makes resolutely for the door*]

MRS HIGGINS [*rising and following him*]

Be quiet, Henry. Sit down.

HIGGINS   260

I–

MRS HIGGINS

Sit down, dear; and listen to me.

HIGGINS

Oh very well, very well, very well. [*He throws himself ungraciously*   265
on the ottoman, with his face towards the windows] But I think
you might have told us this half an hour ago.

MRS HIGGINS

Eliza came to me this morning. She told me of the brutal way
you two treated her.   270

HIGGINS [*bouncing up again*]

What!

PICKERING [*rising also*]

My dear Mrs Higgins, she's been telling you stories. We didnt
treat her brutally. We hardly said a word to her; and we parted   275
on particularly good terms. [*Turning on* HIGGINS] Higgins: did
you bully her after I went to bed?

---

269   *Eliza came to me this morning* In all editions prior to C1941 Mrs Higgins has
another sentence between this one and the next: 'She passed the night partly walking about in a rage, partly trying to throw herself into the river and being afraid to,
and partly in the Carlton Hotel'. There is a slightly different version in TS, where
Shaw has Eliza 'sleeping under the [blank] in the Carlton Hotel'; rather than filling
in the blank, Shaw chose to put her in the more dignified position of simply being
in the hotel. However, in view of the changed ending of Act IV, which has Eliza
spending the night with Freddy in a taxi, Shaw needed to delete Mrs Higgins's
account of Eliza's nocturnal activities. The Carlton Hotel is where Pickering stayed
when he arrived in London from India (Act I, line 437) – hence Eliza's thought of
seeking temporary refuge there.

HIGGINS

Just the other way about. She threw my slippers in my face. She
behaved in the most outrageous way. I never gave her the   280
slightest provocation. The slippers came bang into my face the
moment I entered the room – before I had uttered a word. And
used perfectly awful language.

PICKERING [*astonished*]

But why? What did we do to her?   285

MRS HIGGINS

I think I know pretty well what you did. The girl is naturally
rather affectionate, I think. Isnt she, Mr Doolittle?

DOOLITTLE

Very tender-hearted, maam. Takes after me.   290

MRS HIGGINS

Just so. She had become attached to you both. She worked very
hard for you, Henry. I dont think you quite realize what anything in the nature of brain work means to a girl of her class.
Well, it seems that when the great day of trial came, and she did   295
this wonderful thing for you without making a single mistake,
you two sat there and never said a word to her, but talked
together of how glad you were that it was all over and how you
had been bored with the whole thing. And then you were
surprised because she threw your slippers at you! *I* should have   300
thrown the fire-irons at you.

HIGGINS

We said nothing except that we were tired and wanted to go to
bed. Did we, Pick?

PICKERING [*shrugging his shoulders*]   305

That was all.

MRS HIGGINS [*ironically*]

Quite sure?

PICKERING

Absolutely. Really, that was all.   310

MRS HIGGINS

You didnt thank her, or pet her, or admire her, or tell her how
splendid she'd been.

282–3 *And used perfectly awful language* EM has 'she' before 'used', but the pronoun is
dropped from all subsequent editions.

HIGGINS [*impatiently*]

But she knew all about that. We didnt make speeches to her, if   315
thats what you mean.

PICKERING [*conscience stricken*]

Perhaps we were a little inconsiderate. Is she very angry?

MRS HIGGINS [*returning to her place at the writing-table*]

Well, I'm afraid she wont go back to Wimpole Street, especially   320
now that Mr Doolittle is able to keep up the position you have
thrust on her; but she says she is quite willing to meet you on
friendly terms and to let bygones be bygones.

HIGGINS [*furious*]

Is she, by George? Ho!   325

MRS HIGGINS

If you promise to behave yourself, Henry, I'll ask her to come
down. If not, go home: for you have taken up quite enough of
my time.

HIGGINS   330

Oh, all right. Very well. Pick: you behave yourself. Let us put
on our best Sunday manners for this creature that we picked
out of the mud. [*He flings himself sulkily into the Elizabethan
chair*]

DOOLITTLE [*remonstrating*]   335

Now, now, Enry Iggins! Have some consideration for my
feelings as a middle class man.

MRS HIGGINS

Remember your promise, Henry. [*She presses the bell-button on
the writing-table*] Mr Doolittle: will you be so good as to step   340
out on the balcony for a moment. I dont want Eliza to have the
shock of your news until she has made it up with these two
gentlemen. Would you mind?

DOOLITTLE

As you wish, lady. Anything to help Henry to keep her off my   345
hands. [*He disappears through the window*]

   THE PARLORMAID *answers the bell.* PICKERING *sits down in*
DOOLITTLE's *place.*

MRS HIGGINS

Ask Miss Doolittle to come down, please.   350

THE PARLORMAID

Yes, maam. [*She goes out*]

MRS HIGGINS

Now, Henry: be good.

HIGGINS   355

I am behaving myself perfectly.

PICKERING

He is doing his best, Mrs Higgins.

> *A pause.* HIGGINS *throws back his head; stretches out his legs;*
> *and begins to whistle.*   360

MRS HIGGINS

Henry, dearest, you dont look at all nice in that attitude.

HIGGINS [*pulling himself together*]

I was not trying to look nice, mother.

MRS HIGGINS   365

It doesnt matter, dear. I only wanted to make you speak.

HIGGINS

Why?

MRS HIGGINS

Because you cant speak and whistle at the same time.   370

> HIGGINS *groans. Another very trying pause.*

HIGGINS [*springing up, out of patience*]

Where the devil is that girl? Are we to wait here all day?

> ELIZA *enters, sunny, self-possessed, and giving a staggeringly*
> *convincing exhibition of ease of manner. She carries a little work-*   375
> *basket, and is very much at home.* PICKERING *is too much taken*
> *aback to rise.*

LIZA

How do you do, Professor Higgins? Are you quite well?

HIGGINS [*choking*]   380

Am I– [*He can say no more*]

LIZA

But of course you are: you are never ill. So glad to see you again,
Colonel Pickering. [*He rises hastily; and they shake hands*] Quite
chilly this morning, isnt it? [*She sits down on his left. He sits*   385
beside her]

HIGGINS

Dont you dare try this game on me. I taught it to you; and it
doesnt take me in. Get up and come home; and dont be a fool.

> ELIZA *takes a piece of needlework from her basket, and begins*   390
> *to stitch at it, without taking the least notice of this outburst.*

MRS HIGGINS

Very nicely put, indeed, Henry. No woman could resist such an
invitation.

HIGGINS 395

You let her alone, mother. Let her speak for herself. You will jolly
soon see whether she has an idea that I havnt put into her head or
a word that I havnt put into her mouth. I tell you I have created
this thing out of the squashed cabbage leaves of Covent Garden;
and now she pretends to play the fine lady with me. 400

MRS HIGGINS [placidly]

Yes, dear; but youll sit down, wont you?

HIGGINS sits down again, savagely.

LIZA [to PICKERING, taking no apparent notice of HIGGINS, and
working away deftly] 405

Will you drop me altogether now that the experiment is over,
Colonel Pickering?

PICKERING

Oh dont. You mustnt think of it as an experiment. It shocks
me, somehow. 410

LIZA

Oh, I'm only a squashed cabbage leaf–

PICKERING [impulsively]

No.

LIZA [continuing quietly] 415

– but I owe so much to you that I should be very unhappy if
you forgot me.

PICKERING

It's very kind of you to say so, Miss Doolittle.

LIZA 420

It's not because you paid for my dresses. I know you are generous
to everybody with money. But it was from you that I learnt really
nice manners; and that is what makes one a lady, isnt it? You see
it was so very difficult for me with the example of Professor
Higgins always before me. I was brought up to be just like him, 425
unable to control myself, and using bad language on the slightest
provocation. And I should never have known that ladies and
gentlemen didnt behave like that if you hadnt been there.

HIGGINS

Well!! 430

PICKERING

Oh, thats only his way, you know. He doesnt mean it.

LIZA

Oh, I didnt mean it either, when I was a flower girl. It was only

my way. But you see I did it; and thats what makes the   435
difference after all.

PICKERING

No doubt. Still, he taught you to speak; and I couldnt have
done that, you know.

LIZA [*trivially*]   440

Of course: that is his profession.

HIGGINS

Damnation!

LIZA [*continuing*]

It was just like learning to dance in the fashionable way: there   445
was nothing more than that in it. But do you know what began
my real education?

PICKERING

What?

LIZA [*stopping her work for a moment*]   450

Your calling me Miss Doolittle that day when I first came to
Wimpole Street. That was the beginning of self-respect for me.
[*She resumes her stitching*] And there were a hundred little things
you never noticed, because they came naturally to you. Things
about standing up and taking off your hat and opening doors–   455

PICKERING

Oh, that was nothing.

LIZA

Yes: things that shewed you thought and felt about me as if
I were something better than a scullery-maid; though of course   460
I know you would have been just the same to a scullery-maid if
she had been let into the drawing room. *You* never took off
your boots in the dining room when I was there.

PICKERING

You mustnt mind that. Higgins takes off his boots all over the   465
place.

LIZA

I know. I am not blaming him. It is his way, isnt it? But it made
such a difference to me that you didnt do it. You see, really and
truly, apart from the things anyone can pick up (the dressing   470

---

460   *scullery-maid* The scullery is a small room adjacent to the kitchen used mainly for
washing dishes. Shaw's Mrs Warren (in *Mrs Warren's Profession*) worked as a
scullery-maid before becoming a prostitute.

and the proper way of speaking, and so on), the difference
between a lady and a flower girl is not how she behaves, but how
she's treated. I shall always be a flower girl to Professor Higgins,
because he always treats me as a flower girl, and always will; but
I know I can be a lady to you, because you always treat me as a   475
lady, and always will.

MRS HIGGINS
Please dont grind your teeth, Henry.

PICKERING
Well, this is really very nice of you, Miss Doolittle.   480

LIZA
I should like you to call me Eliza, now, if you would.

PICKERING
Thank you. Eliza, of course.

LIZA   485
And I should like Professor Higgins to call me Miss Doolittle.

HIGGINS
I'll see you damned first.

MRS HIGGINS
Henry! Henry!   490

PICKERING [*laughing*]
Why dont you slang back at him? Dont stand it. It would do
him a lot of good.

LIZA
I cant. I could have done it once but now I cant go back to it.   495
You told me, you know, that when a child is brought to a foreign
country, it picks up the language in a few weeks, and forgets its
own. Well, I am a child in your country. I have forgotten my
own language, and can speak nothing but yours. Thats the real
break-off with the corner of Tottenham Court Road. Leaving   500
Wimpole Street finishes it.

PICKERING [*much alarmed*]
Oh! but youre coming back to Wimpole Street, arnt you? Youll
forgive Higgins?

---

495   *cant go back to it* For C1941 Shaw deleted a sentence after this one: 'Last night,
      when I was wandering about, a girl spoke to me; and I tried to get back into the old
      way with her; but it was no use'.

HIGGINS [*rising*]   505

Forgive! Will she, by George! Let her go. Let her find out how she can get on without us. She will relapse into the gutter in three weeks without me at her elbow.

DOOLITTLE *appears at the centre window. With a look of dignified reproach at* HIGGINS, *he comes slowly and silently to his*   510 *daughter, who, with her back to the window, is unconscious of his approach.*

PICKERING

He's incorrigible, Eliza. You wont relapse, will you?

LIZA   515

No: not now. Never again. I have learnt my lesson. I dont believe I could utter one of the old sounds if I tried. [DOOLITTLE *touches her on her left shoulder. She drops her work, losing her self-possession utterly at the spectacle of her father's splendor*] A-a-a-a-a-ah-ow-ooh!   520

HIGGINS [*with a crow of triumph*]

Aha! Just so. A-a-a-a-ahowooh! A-a-a-a-ahowooh! A-a-a-a-ahowooh! Victory! Victory! [*He throws himself on the divan, folding his arms, and spraddling arrogantly*]

DOOLITTLE   525

Can you blame the girl? Dont look at me like that, Eliza. It aint my fault. Ive come into some money.

---

506   *Will she, by George!* RC has additional dialogue here:

    LIZA

      No thank you. If it were only you, I shouldnt mind perhaps; but a duchess cant live in a house where shes treated as a scullery-maid.

    MRS HIGGINS

      And by a mere professional man, too.

    HIGGINS [*sardonically*]

      Ha!

    PICKERING

      But think, Eliza. What are you to do?

    LIZA

      Oh, Professor Higgins has been most kind and considerate about that. He thought of a number of things I can do. He thinks I am quite good-looking enough to induce somebody to marry me: I have only to ask. And there is my old ambition: a florist's shop.

    PICKERING [*scandalized*]

      Oh no, no. Thatll never do.

    HIGGINS [*rising and prowling savagely between his chair and the door*]

      Let her go . . .

524   *spraddling* spreading his legs wide apart

LIZA

You must have touched a millionaire this time, dad.

DOOLITTLE   530

I have. But I'm dressed something special today. I'm going to
St George's, Hanover Square. Your stepmother is going to marry
me.

LIZA [*angrily*]

Youre going to let yourself down to marry that low common   535
woman!

PICKERING [*quietly*]

He ought to, Eliza. [*To* DOOLITTLE] Why has she changed her
mind?

DOOLITTLE [*sadly*]   540

Intimidated, Governor. Intimidated. Middle class morality
claims its victim. Wont you put on your hat, Liza, and come
and see me turned off?

LIZA

If the Colonel says I must, I–I'll [*almost sobbing*] I'll demean   545
myself. And get insulted for my pains, like enough.

DOOLITTLE

Dont be afraid: she never comes to words with anyone now,
poor woman! respectability has broke all the spirit out of her.

PICKERING [*squeezing* ELIZA*'s elbow gently*]   550

Be kind to them, Eliza. Make the best of it.

LIZA [*forcing a little smile for him through her vexation*]

Oh well, just to shew theres no ill feeling. I'll be back in a
moment. [*She goes out*]

DOOLITTLE [*sitting down beside* PICKERING]   555

I feel uncommon nervous about the ceremony, Colonel. I wish
youd come and see me through it.

PICKERING

But youve been through it before, man. You were married to
Eliza's mother.   560

DOOLITTLE

Who told you that, Colonel?

---

532 *St George's, Hanover Square* An early eighteenth-century Anglican church, a
favoured location for society weddings.

PICKERING
Well, nobody told me. But I concluded – naturally–

DOOLITTLE   565
No: that aint the natural way, Colonel: it's only the middle class way. My way was always the undeserving way. But dont say nothing to Eliza. She dont know: I always had a delicacy about telling her.

PICKERING   570
Quite right. We'll leave it so, if you dont mind.

DOOLITTLE
And youll come to the church, Colonel, and put me through straight?

PICKERING   575
With pleasure. As far as a bachelor can.

MRS HIGGINS
May I come, Mr Doolittle? I should be very sorry to miss your wedding.

DOOLITTLE   580
I should indeed be honored by your condescension, maam; and my poor old woman would take it as a tremenjous compliment. She's been very low, thinking of the happy days that are no more.

MRS HIGGINS [*rising*]
I'll order the carriage and get ready. [*The men rise, except*   585
HIGGINS] I shant be more than fifteen minutes. [*As she goes to the door* ELIZA *comes in, hatted and buttoning her gloves*] I'm going to the church to see your father married, Eliza. You had better come in the brougham with me. Colonel Pickering can go on with the bridegroom.   590

    MRS HIGGINS *goes out.* ELIZA *comes to the middle of the room between the centre window and the ottoman.* PICKERING *joins her.*

DOOLITTLE
Bridegroom! What a word! It makes a man realize his position,   595
somehow. [*He takes up his hat and goes towards the door*]

PICKERING
Before I go, Eliza, do forgive Higgins and come back to us.

LIZA
I dont think dad would allow me. Would you, dad?   600

---

600   *dad* 'papa' in EM/NASH, C1916, and C1931.

118

DOOLITTLE [*sad but magnanimous*]

They played you off very cunning, Eliza, them two sportsmen. If it had been only one of them, you could have nailed him. But you see, there was two; and one of them chaperoned the other, as you might say. [*To* PICKERING] It was artful of you, Colonel: but I bear no malice: I should have done the same myself. I been the victim of one woman after another all my life, and I dont grudge you two getting the better of Liza. I shant interfere. It's time for us to go, Colonel. So long, Henry. See you in St George's, Eliza. [*He goes out*]

PICKERING [*coaxing*]

Do stay with us, Eliza. [*He follows* DOOLITTLE]

ELIZA *goes out on the balcony to avoid being alone with* HIGGINS. *He rises and joins her there. She immediately comes back into the room and makes for the door; but he goes along the balcony quickly and gets his back to the door before she reaches it.*

HIGGINS

Well, Eliza, youve had a bit of your own back, as you call it. Have you had enough? and are you going to be reasonable? Or do you want any more?

LIZA

You want me back only to pick up your slippers and put up with your tempers and fetch and carry for you.

HIGGINS

I havnt said I wanted you back at all.

LIZA

Oh, indeed. Then what are we talking about?

HIGGINS

About you, not about me. If you come back I shall treat you just as I have always treated you. I cant change my nature; and I dont intend to change my manners. My manners are exactly the same as Colonel Pickering's.

LIZA

Thats not true. He treats a flower girl as if she was a duchess.

HIGGINS

And I treat a duchess as if she was a flower girl.

LIZA

I see. [*She turns away composedly, and sits on the ottoman, facing the window*] The same to everybody.

HIGGINS

Just so.

LIZA

Like father.

HIGGINS [*grinning, a little taken down*]

Without accepting the comparison at all points, Eliza, it's quite   645
true that your father is not a snob, and that he will be quite at
home in any station of life to which his eccentric destiny may
call him. [*Seriously*] The great secret, Eliza, is not having bad
manners or good manners or any other particular sort of
manners, but having the same manner for all human souls: in   650
short, behaving as if you were in Heaven, where there are no
third-class carriages, and one soul is as good as another.

LIZA

Amen. You are a born preacher.

HIGGINS [*irritated*]   655

The question is not whether I treat you rudely, but whether you
ever heard me treat anyone else better.

LIZA [*with sudden sincerity*]

I dont care how you treat me. I dont mind your swearing at me.
I shouldnt mind a black eye: Ive had one before this. But   660
[*standing up and facing him*] I wont be passed over.

HIGGINS

Then get out of my way; for I wont stop for you. You talk about
me as if I were a motor bus.

LIZA   665

So you are a motor bus: all bounce and go, and no consideration for anyone. But I can do without you: dont think I
cant.

HIGGINS

I know you can. I told you you could.   670

LIZA [*wounded, getting away from him to the other side of the
ottoman with her face to the hearth*]

I know you did, you brute. You wanted to get rid of me.

HIGGINS

Liar.   675

LIZA.

Thank you. [*She sits down with dignity*]

HIGGINS

You never asked yourself, I suppose, whether *I* could do
without *you*.   680

LIZA [*earnestly*]

Dont you try to get round me. Youll *have* to do without me.

HIGGINS [*arrogant*]

I can do without anybody. I have my own soul: my own spark
of divine fire. But [*with sudden humility*] I shall miss you, Eliza.   685
[*He sits down near her on the ottoman*] I have learnt something
from your idiotic notions: I confess that humbly and gratefully.
And I have grown accustomed to your voice and appearance. I
like them, rather.

LIZA   690

Well, you have both of them on your gramophone and in your
book of photographs. When you feel lonely without me, you
can turn the machine on. It's got no feelings to hurt.

HIGGINS

I cant turn your soul on. Leave me those feelings; and you can   695
take away the voice and the face. They are not you.

LIZA

Oh, you *are* a devil. You can twist the heart in a girl as easy as
some could twist her arms to hurt her. Mrs Pearce warned me.
Time and again she has wanted to leave you; and you always got   700
round her at the last minute. And you dont care a bit for her.
And you dont care a bit for me.

HIGGINS

I care for life, for humanity; and you are a part of it that has
come my way and been built into my house. What more can   705
you or anyone ask?

LIZA

I wont care for anybody that doesnt care for me.

HIGGINS

Commercial principles, Eliza. Like [*reproducing her Covent*   710
Garden pronunciation with professional exactness] s'yollin voylets
[selling violets], isnt it?

LIZA

Dont sneer at me. It's mean to sneer at me.

HIGGINS   715

I have never sneered in my life. Sneering doesnt become either the
human face or the human soul. I am expressing my righteous
contempt for Commercialism. I dont and wont trade in affection.
You call me a brute because you couldnt buy a claim on me by
fetching my slippers and finding my spectacles. You were a fool: I   720
think a woman fetching a man's slippers is a disgusting sight: did I

712   [*selling violets*] Shaw's bracketed insertion.

ever fetch *your* slippers? I think a good deal more of you for throwing them in my face. No use slaving for me and then saying you want to be cared for: who cares for a slave? If you come back, come back for the sake of good fellowship; for youll get nothing 725 else. Youve had a thousand times as much out of me as I have out of you; and if you dare to set up your little dog's tricks of fetching and carrying slippers against my creation of a Duchess, Eliza, I'll slam the door in your silly face.

LIZA 730

What did you do it for if you didnt care for me?

HIGGINS [*heartily*]

Why, because it was my job.

LIZA

You never thought of the trouble it would make for me. 735

HIGGINS

Would the world ever have been made if its maker had been afraid of making trouble? Making life means making trouble. Theres only one way of escaping trouble; and thats killing things. Cowards, you notice, are always shrieking to have troublesome 740 people killed.

LIZA

I'm no preacher: I dont notice things like that. I notice that you dont notice me.

HIGGINS [*jumping up and walking about intolerantly*] 745

Eliza: youre an idiot. I waste the treasures of my Miltonic mind by spreading them before you. Once for all, understand that I go my way and do my work without caring twopence what happens to either of us. I am not intimidated, like your father and your stepmother. So you can come back or go to the devil: 750 which you please.

LIZA

What am I to come back for?

HIGGINS [*bouncing up on his knees on the ottoman and leaning over it to her*] 755

For the fun of it. Thats why I took you on.

LIZA [*with averted face*]

And you may throw me out tomorrow if I dont do everything you want me to?

HIGGINS 760

Yes: and you may walk out tomorrow if I dont do everything *you* want me to.

LIZA

And live with my stepmother?

HIGGINS 765

Yes, or sell flowers.

LIZA

Oh! If I only *could* go back to my flower basket! I should be independent of both you and father and all the world! Why did you take my independence from me? Why did I give it up? I'm 770 a slave now, for all my fine clothes.

HIGGINS

Not a bit. I'll adopt you as my daughter and settle money on you if you like. Or would you rather marry Pickering?

LIZA [*looking fiercely round at him*] 775

I wouldnt marry *you* if you asked me; and youre nearer my age than what he is.

HIGGINS [*gently*]

Than he is: not 'than what he is'.

LIZA [*losing her temper and rising*] 780

I'll talk as I like. Youre not my teacher now.

HIGGINS [*reflectively*]

I dont suppose Pickering would, though. He's as confirmed an old bachelor as I am.

LIZA 785

Thats not what I want; and dont you think it. Ive always had chaps enough wanting me that way. Freddy Hill writes to me twice and three times a day, sheets and sheets.

HIGGINS [*disagreeably surprised*]

Damn his impudence! [*He recoils and finds himself sitting on his* 790 *heels*]

LIZA

He has a right to if he likes, poor lad. And he does love me.

HIGGINS [*getting off the ottoman*]

You have no right to encourage him. 795

LIZA

Every girl has a right to be loved.

HIGGINS

What! By fools like that?

LIZA 800

Freddy's not a fool. And if he's weak and poor and wants me, may be he'd make me happier than my betters that bully me and dont want me.

HIGGINS

Can he *make* anything of you? Thats the point. 805

LIZA

Perhaps I could make something of him. But I never thought of us making anything of one another; and you never think of anything else. I only want to be natural.

HIGGINS 810

In short, you want me to be as infatuated about you as Freddy? Is that it?

LIZA

No I dont. Thats not the sort of feeling I want from you. And dont you be too sure of yourself or of me. I could have been a 815 bad girl if I'd liked. Ive seen more of some things than you, for all your learning. Girls like me can drag gentlemen down to make love to them easy enough. And they wish each other dead the next minute.

HIGGINS 820

Of course they do. Then what in thunder are we quarrelling about?

LIZA [*much troubled*]

I want a little kindness. I know I'm a common ignorant girl, and you a book-learned gentleman; but I'm not dirt under 825 your feet. What I done [*correcting herself*] what I did was not for the dresses and the taxis: I did it because we were pleasant together and I come – came – to care for you; not to want you to make love to me, and not forgetting the difference between us, but more friendly like. 830

HIGGINS

Well, of course. Thats just how I feel. And how Pickering feels. Eliza: youre a fool.

LIZA

Thats not a proper answer to give me. [*She sinks on the chair at* 835 *the writing-table in tears*]

HIGGINS

It's all youll get until you stop being a common idiot. If youre going to be a lady, youll have to give up feeling neglected if the men you know dont spend half their time snivelling over you and 840 the other half giving you black eyes. If you cant stand the coldness of my sort of life, and the strain of it, go back to the gutter. Work til youre more a brute than a human being; and then cuddle and squabble and drink til you fall asleep. Oh, it's a fine life, the life of

the gutter. It's real: it's warm: it's violent: you can feel it through   845
the thickest skin: you can taste it and smell it without any training
or any work. Not like Science and Literature and Classical Music
and Philosophy and Art. You find me cold, unfeeling, selfish, dont
you? Very well: be off with you to the sort of people you like.
Marry some sentimental hog or other with lots of money, and a   850
thick pair of lips to kiss you with and a thick pair of boots to kick
you with. If you cant appreciate what youve got, youd better get
what you can appreciate.

LIZA [*desperate*]

Oh, you *are* a cruel tyrant. I cant talk to you: you turn everything   855
against me: I'm always in the wrong. But you know very well all
the time that youre nothing but a bully. You know I cant go back
to the gutter, as you call it, and that I have no real friends in the
world but you and the Colonel. You know well I couldnt bear to
live with a low common man after you two; and it's wicked and   860
cruel of you to insult me by pretending I could. You think I must
go back to Wimpole Street because I have nowhere else to go but
father's. But dont you be too sure that you have me under your
feet to be trampled on and talked down. I'll marry Freddy, I will,
as soon as I'm able to support him.   865

865   *as soon as I'm able to support him* 'as soon as hes able to support me' in EM/NASH,
C1916, and C1931. The dialogue then continued:
HIGGINS [*sitting down beside her*]
Rubbish! You shall marry an ambassador. You shall marry the Governor-General of India
or the Lord Lieutenant of Ireland, or somebody who wants a deputy-queen. I'm not going
to have my masterpiece thrown away on Freddy.
LIZA
You think I like you to say that. But I havnt forgot what you said a moment ago; and I
wont be coaxed around as if I was a baby or a puppy. If I cant have kindness, I'll have
independence.
HIGGINS
Independence? Thats middle class blasphemy. We are all dependent on one another, every
soul of us on earth.
LIZA [*rising determinedly*]
I'll let you see whether I'm dependent on you. If you can preach, I can teach. I'll go and be
a teacher . . .
The dialogue as we now have it first appeared in C1941.

HIGGINS [*thunderstruck*]

Freddy!!! that young fool! That poor devil who couldnt get a job as an errand boy even if he had the guts to try for it! Woman: do you not understand that I have made you a consort for a king?

LIZA   870

Freddy loves me: that makes him king enough for me. I dont want him to work: he wasnt brought up to it as I was. I'll go and be a teacher.

HIGGINS

Whatll you teach, in heaven's name?   875

LIZA

What you taught me. I'll teach phonetics.

HIGGINS

Ha! ha! ha!

LIZA.   880

I'll offer myself as an assistant to that hairyfaced Hungarian.

HIGGINS [*rising in a fury*]

What! That impostor! that humbug! that toadying ignoramus! Teach him my methods! my discoveries! You take one step in his direction and I'll wring your neck. [*He lays hands on her*] Do   885
you hear?

LIZA [*defiantly non-resistant*]

Wring away. What do I care? I knew youd strike me some day. [*He lets her go, stamping with rage at having forgotten himself, and recoils so hastily that he stumbles back into his seat on the ottoman*] 890
Aha! Now I know how to deal with you. What a fool I was not to think of it before! You cant take away the knowledge you gave me. You said I had a finer ear than you. And I can be civil and kind to people, which is more than you can. Aha! [*Purposely dropping her aitches to annoy him*] Thats done you, Enry Iggins,   895
it az. Now I dont care that [*snapping her fingers*] for your bullying and your big talk. I'll advertize it in the papers that your duchess is only a flower girl that you taught, and that she'll teach anybody to be a duchess just the same in six months for a thousand guineas. Oh, when I think of myself crawling under   900

---

881   *hairyfaced Hungarian* In EM/NASH, C1916, and C1931 Eliza says she will offer herself as an assistant to a 'Professor Nepean', but in view of the additional scene in Act III of C1941 that introduces Professor Nepommuck ('the hairyfaced Hungarian') Shaw dispensed with Professor Nepean.

896   *it az* In EM/NASH, C1916, and C1931 the sentence merely reads 'Aha! Thats done you, Henry Higgins, it has'.

your feet and being trampled on and called names, when all the
time I had only to lift up my finger to be as good as you, I could
just kick myself.

HIGGINS [*wondering at her*]

You damned impudent slut, you! But it's better than snivelling; 905
better than fetching slippers and finding spectacles, isnt it?
[*Rising*] By George, Eliza, I said I'd make a woman of you; and I
have. I like you like this.

LIZA

Yes: you can turn round and make up to me now that I'm not 910
afraid of you, and can do without you.

HIGGINS

Of course I do, you little fool. Five minutes ago you were like a
millstone round my neck. Now youre a tower of strength: a
consort battleship. You and I and Pickering will be three old 915
bachelors instead of only two men and a silly girl.

    MRS HIGGINS *returns, dressed for the wedding.* ELIZA
instantly becomes cool and elegant.

MRS HIGGINS

The carriage is waiting, Eliza. Are you ready? 920

LIZA

Quite. Is the Professor coming?

MRS HIGGINS

Certainly not. He cant behave himself in church. He makes
remarks out loud all the time on the clergyman's pronunciation. 925

LIZA

Then I shall not see you again, Professor. Goodbye. [*She goes to
the door*]

MRS HIGGINS [*coming to* HIGGINS]

Goodbye, dear. 930

HIGGINS

Goodbye, mother. [*He is about to kiss her, when he recollects
something*] Oh, by the way, Eliza, order a ham and a Stilton
cheese, will you? And buy me a pair of reindeer gloves, number

---

915 *consort battleship* For the 1920 revival of the play at the Aldwych Theatre (directed
by Shaw), Higgins (C. Aubrey Smith) took Eliza's (Mrs Campbell) arm on this line.
Eliza, said Shaw, must then 'instantly throw him off with implacable pride; and this
is the note until the final "Buy them yourself" ' (*Theatrics* 155). (See Appendix III.2
for this ending of the play.)

933 *by the way, Eliza* 'be scornful' at this point, Shaw instructed Mrs Campbell
(Shaw/Campbell, p. 180).

eights, and a tie to match that new suit of mine. You can choose   935
the color. [*His cheerful, careless, vigorous voice shews that he is
incorrigible*]

LIZA [*disdainfully*]

Number eights are too small for you if you want them lined with
lamb's wool. You have three new ties that you have forgotten in   940
the drawer of your washstand. Colonel Pickering prefers double
Gloucester to Stilton; and you dont notice the difference. I
telephoned Mrs Pearce this morning not to forget the ham. What
you are to do without me I cannot imagine. [*She sweeps out*]

MRS HIGGINS   945

I'm afraid youve spoilt that girl, Henry. I should be uneasy
about you and her if she were less fond of Colonel Pickering.

HIGGINS

Pickering! Nonsense: she's going to marry Freddy. Ha ha!
Freddy! Freddy!! Ha ha ha ha ha!!!!!   950

[*He roars with laughter as the play ends*]

---

935   *new suit of mine* in EM/NASH, C1916, and C1931 Eliza is instructed to buy the suit
      at 'Eale and Binman's', presumably a fashionable gentleman's store, but not traced.

939–44   *Number eights ... I cannot imagine* This speech by Eliza does not appear until
      C1941. For earlier endings see Appendix III.

[SEQUEL]¹

The rest of the story need not be shewn in action,² and indeed, would hardly need telling if our imaginations were not so enfeebled by their lazy dependence on the ready-mades and reach-me-downs of the ragshop in which Romance keeps its stock of 'happy endings' to misfit all stories. Now, the history of Eliza Doolittle, though called a romance because the transfiguration it records seems exceedingly improbable, is common enough. Such transfigurations have been achieved by hundreds of resolutely ambitious young women since Nell Gwynne³ set them the example by playing queens and fascinating kings in the theatre in which she began by selling oranges. Nevertheless, people in all directions have assumed, for no other reason than that she became the heroine of a romance, that she must have married the hero of it. This is unbearable, not only because her little drama, if acted on such a thoughtless assumption, must be spoiled, but because the true sequel is patent to anyone with a sense of human nature in general, and of feminine instinct in particular.

Eliza, in telling Higgins she would not marry him if he asked, was not coquetting: she was announcing a well-considered decision. When a bachelor interests, and dominates, and teaches, and becomes important to a spinster, as Higgins with Eliza, she always, if she has character enough to be capable of it, considers very seriously indeed whether she will play for becoming that bachelor's wife, especially if he is so little interested in marriage that a determined and devoted woman might capture him if she set herself resolutely to do it. Her decision will depend a good deal on whether she is really free to choose; and that, again, will depend on her age and income. If she is at the end of her youth, and has no security for her livelihood, she will marry him because she must marry anybody who will provide for her. But at Eliza's age a good-looking girl does not feel that pressure: she feels free to pick and choose. She is therefore guided by her instinct in the matter. Eliza's instinct tells her not to marry Higgins. It does not tell her to give him up. It is not in the slightest doubt as to his

---

1 Shaw added the 'Sequel', without giving it a title, in C1916. He made no revisions for subsequent editions of the play.
2 Shaw did, however, show it in action in a never-used 1934 film scenario for Pygmalion (see Appendix III.5).
3 Nell Gwynne (or Gwyn or Gwynn, 1650–87) rose from orange girl at Drury Lane Theatre to famous actress and eventually to mistress of Charles II.

remaining one of the strongest personal interests in her life. It would be very sorely strained if there was another woman likely to supplant her with him. But as she feels sure of him on that last point, she has no doubt at all as to her course, and would not have any, even if the difference of twenty years in age, which seems so great to youth, did not exist between them.

As our own instincts are not appealed to by her conclusion, let us see whether we cannot discover some reason in it. When Higgins excused his indifference to young women on the ground that they had an irresistible rival in his mother, he gave the clue to his inveterate old-bachelordom. The case is uncommon only to the extent that remarkable mothers are uncommon. If an imaginative boy has a sufficiently rich mother who has intelligence, personal grace, dignity of character without harshness, and a cultivated sense of the best art of her time to enable her to make her house beautiful, she sets a standard for him against which very few women can struggle, besides effecting for him a disengagement of his affections, his sense of beauty, and his idealism from his specifically sexual impulses. This makes him a standing puzzle to the huge number of uncultivated people who have been brought up in tasteless homes by commonplace or disagreeable parents, and to whom, consequently, literature, painting, sculpture, music, and affectionate personal relations come as modes of sex if they come at all. The word passion means nothing else to them; and that Higgins could have a passion for phonetics and idealize his mother instead of Eliza, would seem to them absurd and unnatural. Nevertheless, when we look round and see that hardly anyone is too ugly or disagreeable to find a wife or a husband if he or she wants one, whilst many old maids and bachelors are above the average in quality and culture, we cannot help suspecting that the disentanglement of sex from the associations with which it is commonly confused, a disentanglement which persons of genius achieve by sheer intellectual analysis, is sometimes produced or aided by parental fascination.

Now, though Eliza was incapable of thus explaining to herself Higgins's formidable powers of resistance to the charm that prostrated Freddy at the first glance, she was instinctively aware that she could never obtain a complete grip of him, or come between him and his mother (the first necessity of the married woman). To put it shortly, she knew that for some mysterious reason he had not the makings of a married man in him, according to her conception of a husband as one to whom she would be his nearest and fondest and warmest interest. Even had there been no mother-rival, she would still have refused to accept an interest in herself that was secondary to philosophic interests. Had Mrs Higgins died, there would still have been Milton and the Universal Alphabet. Landor's remark[4] that to those who have the greatest power of loving, love is a secondary affair, would not have recommended Landor to Eliza. Put that along with her resentment of Higgins's domineering superiority, and her mistrust of his coaxing cleverness in getting round her and evading her wrath when he had gone too far with his impetuous bullying, and you will see that Eliza's instinct had good grounds for warning her not to marry her Pygmalion.

And now, whom did Eliza marry? For if Higgins was a predestinate old bachelor, she was most certainly not a predestinate old maid. Well, that can be told very shortly to those who have not guessed it from the indications she has herself given them.

Almost immediately after Eliza is stung into proclaiming her considered determination not to marry Higgins, she mentions the fact that young Mr Frederick Eynsford Hill is pouring out his love for her daily through the post. Now Freddy is young, practically twenty years younger than Higgins: he is a gentleman (or, as Eliza would qualify him, a toff), and speaks like one. He is nicely dressed, is treated by the Colonel as an equal, loves her unaffectedly, and is not her master, nor ever likely to dominate her in spite of his advantage of social standing. Eliza has no use for the foolish romantic tradition that all women love to be mastered, if not actually bullied and beaten. 'When you go to women' says Nietzsche 'take your whip with you'.[5] Sensible despots have never confined that precaution to women: they have taken their whips with them when they have dealt with men, and been slavishly idealized by the men over whom they have flourished the whip much more than by women. No doubt there are slavish women as well as slavish men; and women, like men, admire those that are stronger than themselves. But to admire a strong person and to live under that strong person's thumb are two different things. The weak may not be admired and hero-worshipped; but they are by no means disliked or shunned; and they never seem to have the least difficulty in marrying people who are too good for them. They may fail in emergencies; but life is not one long emergency: it is mostly a string of situations for which no exceptional strength is needed, and with which even rather weak people can cope if they have a stronger partner to help them out. Accordingly, it is a truth everywhere in evidence that strong

---

4 Walter Savage Landor (1775–1865), English poet and writer, but the 'remark' to which Shaw refers has not been traced.
5 From chapter 18 of Friedrich Nietzsche's (1844–1900) *Also sprach Zarathustra* [*Thus Spoke Zarathustra*], 1883–5.

people, masculine or feminine, not only do not marry stronger people, but do not shew any preference for them in selecting their friends. When a lion meets another with a louder roar 'the first lion thinks the last a bore'.[6] The man or woman who feels strong enough for two, seeks for every other quality in a partner than strength.

The converse is also true. Weak people want to marry strong people who do not frighten them too much; and this often leads them to make the mistake we describe metaphorically as 'biting off more than they can chew'. They want too much for too little; and when the bargain is unreasonable beyond all bearing, the union becomes impossible: it ends in the weaker party being either discarded or borne as a cross, which is worse. People who are not only weak, but silly or obtuse as well, are often in these difficulties.

This being the state of human affairs, what is Eliza fairly sure to do when she is placed between Freddy and Higgins? Will she look forward to a lifetime of fetching Higgins's slippers or to a lifetime of Freddy fetching hers? There can be no doubt about the answer. Unless Freddy is biologically repulsive to her, and Higgins biologically attractive to a degree that overwhelms all her other instincts, she will, if she marries either of them, marry Freddy.

And that is just what Eliza did.

Complications ensued; but they were economic, not romantic. Freddy had no money and no occupation. His mother's jointure, a last relic of the opulence of Largelady Park, had enabled her to struggle along in Earlscourt with an air of gentility, but not to procure any serious secondary education for her children, much less give the boy a profession. A clerkship at thirty shillings a week was beneath Freddy's dignity, and extremely distasteful to him besides. His prospects consisted of a hope that if he kept up appearances somebody would do something for him. The something appeared vaguely to his imagination as a private secretaryship or a sinecure of some sort. To his mother it perhaps appeared as a marriage to some lady of means who could not resist her boy's niceness. Fancy her feelings when he married a flower girl who had become disclassed under extraordinary circumstances which were now notorious!

It is true that Eliza's situation did not seem wholly ineligible. Her father, though formerly a dustman, and now fantastically disclassed, had become extremely popular in the smartest society by a social talent which

6 From William Barnes Rhodes's (1772–1826) popular burlesque, *Bombastes Furioso* (1822): 'So have I heard on Afric's burning shore/Another lion give a grievous roar,/And the first lion thought the last a bore'.

triumphed over every prejudice and every disadvantage. Rejected by the middle class, which he loathed, he had shot up at once into the highest circles by his wit, his dustmanship (which he carried like a banner), and his Nietzschean transcendence of good and evil. At intimate ducal dinners he sat on the right-hand of the Duchess; and in country houses he smoked in the pantry and was made much of by the butler when he was not feeding in the dining room and being consulted by cabinet ministers. But he found it almost as hard to do all this on four thousand a year as Mrs Eynsford Hill to live in Earlscourt on an income so pitiably smaller that I have not the heart to disclose its exact figure. He absolutely refused to add the last straw to his burden by contributing to Eliza's support.

Thus Freddy and Eliza, now Mr and Mrs Eynsford Hill, would have spent a penniless honeymoon but for a wedding present of £500 from the Colonel to Eliza. It lasted a long time because Freddy did not know how to spend money, never having had any to spend, and Eliza, socially trained by a pair of old bachelors, wore her clothes as long as they held together and looked pretty, without the least regard to their being many months out of fashion. Still, £500 will not last two young people for ever; and they both knew, and Eliza felt as well, that they must shift for themselves in the end. She could quarter herself on Wimpole Street because it had come to be her home; but she was quite aware that she ought not to quarter Freddy there, and that it would not be good for his character if she did.

Not that the Wimpole Street bachelors objected. When she consulted them, Higgins declined to be bothered about her housing problem when that solution was so simple. Eliza's desire to have Freddy in the house with her seemed of no more importance than if she had wanted an extra piece of bedroom furniture. Pleas as to Freddy's character, and the moral obligation on him to earn his own living, were lost on Higgins. He denied that Freddy had any character, and declared that if he tried to do any useful work some competent person would have the trouble of undoing it: a procedure involving a net loss to the community, and great unhappiness to Freddy himself, who was obviously intended by Nature for such light work as amusing Eliza, which, Higgins declared, was a much more useful and honorable occupation than working in the city. When Eliza referred again to her project of teaching phonetics, Higgins abated not a jot of his violent opposition to it. He said she was not within ten years of being qualified to meddle with his pet subject; and as it was evident that the Colonel agreed with him, she felt she could not go against them in this grave matter, and that she had no right, without Higgins's consent, to exploit the knowledge he had given her; for his knowledge seemed to her as much his private property as his watch: Eliza was no communist. Besides, she was superstitiously devoted to them both, more entirely and frankly after her marriage than before it.

It was the Colonel who finally solved the problem, which had cost him much perplexed cogitation. He one day asked Eliza, rather shyly, whether she had quite given up her notion of keeping a flower shop. She replied that she had thought of it, but had put it out of her head, because the Colonel had said, that day at Mrs Higgins's, that it would never do. The Colonel confessed that when he said that, he had not quite recovered from the dazzling impression of the day before. They broke the matter to Higgins that evening. The sole comment vouchsafed by him very nearly led to a serious quarrel with Eliza. It was to the effect that she would have in Freddy an ideal errand boy.

Freddy himself was next sounded on the subject. He said he had been thinking of a shop himself; though it had presented itself to his pennilessness as a small place in which Eliza should sell tobacco at one counter whilst he sold newspapers at the opposite one. But he agreed that it would be extraordinarily jolly to go early every morning with Eliza to Covent Garden and buy flowers on the scene of their first meeting: a sentiment which earned him many kisses from his wife. He added that he had always been afraid to propose anything of the sort, because Clara would make an awful row about a step that must damage her matrimonial chances, and his mother could not be expected to like it after clinging for so many years to that step of the social ladder on which retail trade is impossible.

This difficulty was removed by an event highly unexpected by Freddy's mother. Clara, in the course of her incursions into those artistic circles which were the highest within her reach, discovered that her conversational qualifications were expected to include a grounding in the novels of Mr H. G. Wells.[7] She borrowed them in various directions so energetically that she swallowed them all within two months. The result was a conversion of a kind quite common today. A modern Acts of the Apostles would fill fifty whole Bibles if anyone were capable of writing it.

Poor Clara, who appeared to Higgins and his mother as a disagreeable and ridiculous person, and to her own mother as in some inexplicable way a social failure, had never seen herself in either light; for, though to some extent ridiculed and mimicked in West Kensington like everybody

7 Wells (1866–1946) was a prolific novelist, historian, and journalist, whose friendship with Shaw – though often tested – lasted over forty years. See J. Percy Smith, ed., *Bernard Shaw and H.G. Wells* (Toronto, 1995).

else there, she was accepted as a rational and normal – or shall we say inevitable? – sort of human being. At worst they called her The Pusher; but to them no more than to herself had it ever occurred that she was pushing the air, and pushing it in a wrong direction. Still, she was not happy. She was growing desperate. Her one asset, the fact that her mother was what the Epsom greengrocer called a carriage lady, had no exchange value, apparently. It had prevented her from getting educated, because the only education she could have afforded was education with the Earlscourt greengrocer's daughter. It had led her to seek the society of her mother's class; and that class simply would not have her, because she was much poorer than the greengrocer, and, far from being able to afford a maid, could not afford even a housemaid, and had to scrape along at home with an illiberally treated general servant. Under such circumstances nothing could give her an air of being a genuine product of Largelady Park. And yet its tradition made her regard a marriage with anyone within her reach as an unbearable humiliation. Commercial people and professional people in a small way were odious to her. She ran after painters and novelists; but she did not charm them; and her bold attempts to pick up and practise artistic and literary talk irritated them. She was, in short, an utter failure, an ignorant, incompetent, pretentious, unwelcome, penniless, useless little snob; and though she did not admit these disqualifications (for nobody ever faces unpleasant truths of this kind until the possibility of a way out dawns on them) she felt their effects too keenly to be satisfied with her position.

Clara had a startling eyeopener when, on being suddenly wakened to enthusiasm by a girl of her own age who dazzled her and produced in her a gushing desire to take her for a model, and gain her friendship, she discovered that this exquisite apparition had graduated from the gutter in a few months time. It shook her so violently, that when Mr H. G. Wells lifted her on the point of his puissant pen, and placed her at the angle of view from which the life she was leading and the society to which she clung appeared in its true relation to real human needs and worthy social structure, he effected a conversion and a conviction of sin comparable to the most sensational feats of General Booth or Gypsy Smith.[8] Clara's snobbery went bang. Life suddenly began to move with her. Without knowing how or why, she began to make friends and enemies. Some of the acquaintances to whom she had been a tedious or indifferent or

---

8 William Booth (1829–1912), founder of the Salvation Army, and Rodney 'Gypsy' Smith (1860–1947), born of gypsy parents and a prominent member of the Salvation Army until dismissed for accepting personal gifts.

ridiculous affliction, dropped her; others became cordial. To her amazement she found that some 'quite nice' people were saturated with Wells, and that this accessibility to ideas was the secret of their niceness. People she had thought deeply religious and had tried to conciliate on that tack with disastrous results, suddenly took an interest in her, and revealed a hostility to conventional religion which she had never conceived possible except among the most desperate characters. They made her read Galsworthy;[9] and Galsworthy exposed the vanity of Largelady Park and finished her. It exasperated her to think that the dungeon in which she had languished for so many unhappy years had been unlocked all the time, and that the impulses she had so carefully struggled with and stifled for the sake of keeping well with society, were precisely those by which alone she could have come into any sort of sincere human contact. In the radiance of these discoveries, and the tumult of their reaction, she made a fool of herself as freely and conspicuously as when she so rashly adopted Eliza's expletive in Mrs Higgins's drawing room; for the newborn Wellsian had to find her bearings almost as ridiculously as a baby; but nobody hates a baby for its ineptitudes, or thinks the worse of it for trying to eat the matches; and Clara lost no friends by her follies. They laughed at her to her face this time; and she had to defend herself and fight it out as best she could.

When Freddy paid a visit to Earlscourt (which he never did when he could possibly help it) to make the desolating announcement that he and his Eliza were thinking of blackening the Largelady scutcheon by opening a shop, he found the little household already convulsed by a prior announcement from Clara that she also was going to work in an old furniture shop in Dover Street, which had been started by a fellow Wellsian. This appointment Clara owed, after all, to her old social accomplishment of Push. She had made up her mind that, cost what it might, she would see Mr Wells in the flesh; and she had achieved her end at a garden party. She had better luck than so rash an enterprise deserved. Mr Wells came up to her expectations. Age had not withered him, nor could custom stale his infinite variety[10] in half an hour. His pleasant neatness and compactness, his small hands and feet, his teeming ready brain, his unaffected accessibility, and a certain fine apprehensiveness which stamped him as susceptible from his topmost hair to his tipmost toe, proved irresistible.

9 John Galsworthy (1867–1933), playwright and novelist, whose widely read novels about the Forsyte family began in 1906 with *A Man of Property*.

10 An allusion to Enobarbus's praise of Cleopatra in Shakespeare's *Antony and Cleopatra* (Act II, Scene ii): 'Age cannot wither her, nor custom stale / Her infinite variety'.

Clara talked of nothing else for weeks and weeks afterwards. And as she happened to talk to the lady of the furniture shop, and that lady also desired above all things to know Mr Wells and sell pretty things to him, she offered Clara a job on the chance of achieving that end through her.

And so it came about that Eliza's luck held, and the expected opposition to the flower shop melted away. The shop is in the arcade of a railway station not very far from the Victoria and Albert Museum;[11] and if you live in that neighborhood you may go there any day and buy a buttonhole from Eliza.

Now here is a last opportunity for romance. Would you not like to be assured that the shop was an immense success, thanks to Eliza's charms and her early business experience in Covent Garden? Alas! the truth is the truth: the shop did not pay for a long time, simply because Eliza and her Freddy did not know how to keep it. True, Eliza had not to begin at the very beginning; she knew the names and prices of the cheaper flowers; and her elation was unbounded when she found that Freddy, like all youths educated at cheap, pretentious, and thoroughly inefficient schools, knew a little Latin. It was very little, but enough to make him appear to her a Porson or Bentley,[12] and to put him at his ease with botanical nomenclature. Unfortunately he knew nothing else; and Eliza, though she could count money up to eighteen shillings or so, and had acquired a certain familiarity with the language of Milton from her struggles to qualify herself for winning Higgins's bet, could not write out a bill without utterly disgracing the establishment. Freddy's power of stating in Latin that Balbus[13] built a wall and that Gaul was divided into three parts did not carry with it the slightest knowledge of accounts or business: Colonel Pickering had to explain to him what a cheque book and a bank account meant. And the pair were by no means easily teachable. Freddy backed up Eliza in her obstinate refusal to believe that they could save money by engaging a bookkeeper with some knowledge of the business. How, they argued, could you possibly save money by going to extra expense when you already could not make both ends meet? But the Colonel, after making the ends meet over and over again, at last gently insisted; and Eliza, humbled to the dust by having to beg from him so

11 The Victoria and Albert Museum was established in 1852 as the South Kensington Museum, and renamed in 1899 in honour of Queen Victoria and Prince Albert. Eliza's shop would have been at the South Kensington station (opened in 1868).

12 Richard Porson (1759–1808) and Richard Bentley (1662–1742) were both distinguished classical scholars.

13 Lucius Cornelius Balbus was Julius Caesar's private secretary and chief engineer.

often, and stung by the uproarious derision of Higgins, to whom the notion of Freddy succeeding at anything was a joke that never palled, grasped the fact that business, like phonetics, has to be learned.

On the piteous spectacle of the pair spending their evenings in shorthand schools and polytechnic classes, learning bookkeeping and typewriting with incipient junior clerks, male and female, from the elementary schools, let me not dwell. There were even classes at the London School of Economics,[14] and a humble personal appeal to the director of that institution to recommend a course bearing on the flower business. He, being a humorist, explained to them the method of the celebrated Dickensian essay on Chinese Metaphysics by the gentleman who read an article on China and an article on Metaphysics and combined the information.[15] He suggested that they should combine the London School with Kew Gardens.[16] Eliza, to whom the procedure of the Dickensian gentleman seemed perfectly correct (as in fact it was) and not in the least funny (which was only her ignorance), took the advice with entire gravity. But the effort that cost her the deepest humiliation was a request to Higgins, whose pet artistic fancy, next to Milton's verse, was calligraphy, and who himself wrote a most beautiful Italian hand, that he would teach her to write. He declared that she was congenitally incapable of forming a single letter worthy of the least of Milton's words; but she persisted; and again he suddenly threw himself into the task of teaching her with a combination of stormy intensity, concentrated patience, and occasional bursts of interesting disquisition on the beauty and nobility, the august mission and destiny, of human handwriting. Eliza ended by acquiring an extremely uncommercial script which was a positive extension of her personal beauty, and spending three times as much on stationery as anyone else because certain qualities and shapes of paper became indispensable to her. She could not even address an envelope in the usual way because it made the margins all wrong.

Their commercial schooldays were a period of disgrace and despair for the young couple. They seemed to be learning nothing about flower shops. At last they gave it up as hopeless, and shook the dust of the shorthand schools, and the polytechnics, and the London School of Economics from their feet for ever. Besides, the business was in some mysterious way beginning to take care of itself. They had somehow forgotten their

14 The London School of Economics was founded by Fabian Society members, including Shaw, in 1895, with a focus on teaching and research in politics and economics.

15 As explained by Mr Pott in chapter 51 of *The Pickwick Papers*.

16 The Royal Botanic Gardens at Kew, west of London.

objections to employing other people. They came to the conclusion that their own way was the best, and that they had really a remarkable talent for business. The Colonel, who had been compelled for some years to keep a sufficient sum on current account at his bankers to make up their deficits, found that the provision was unnecessary: the young people were prospering. It is true that there was not quite fair play between them and their competitors in trade. Their week-ends in the country cost them nothing, and saved them the price of their Sunday dinners; for the motor car was the Colonel's; and he and Higgins paid the hotel bills. Mr F. Hill, florist and greengrocer (they soon discovered that there was money in asparagus; and asparagus led to other vegetables), had an air which stamped the business as classy; and in private life he was still Frederick Eynsford Hill, Esquire. Not that there was any swank about him: nobody but Eliza knew that he had been christened Frederick Challoner. Eliza herself swanked like anything.

That is all. That is how it has turned out. It is astonishing how much Eliza still manages to meddle in the housekeeping at Wimpole Street in spite of the shop and her own family. And it is notable that though she never nags her husband, and frankly loves the Colonel as if she were his favorite daughter, she has never got out of the habit of nagging Higgins that was established on the fatal night when she won his bet for him. She snaps his head off on the faintest provocation, or on none. He no longer dares to tease her by assuming an abysmal inferiority of Freddy's mind to his own. He storms and bullies and derides; but she stands up to him so ruthlessly that the Colonel has to ask her from time to time to be kinder to Higgins; and it is the only request of his that brings a mulish expression into her face. Nothing but some emergency or calamity great enough to break down all likes and dislikes, and throw them both back on their common humanity – and may they be spared any such trial! – will ever alter this. She knows that Higgins does not need her, just as her father did not need her. The very scrupulousness with which he told her that day that he had become used to having her there, and dependent on her for all sorts of little services, and that he should miss her if she went away (it would never have occurred to Freddy or the Colonel to say anything of the sort) deepens her inner certainty that she is 'no more to him than them slippers'; yet she has a sense, too, that his indifference is deeper than the infatuation of commoner souls. She is immensely interested in him. She has even secret mischievous moments in which she wishes she could get him alone, on a desert island, away from all ties and with nobody else in the world to consider, and just drag him off his pedestal and see him making love like any common man. We all have private imaginations of that sort. But when it comes to business, to the life that she really leads as distinguished from the life of dreams and fancies, she likes Freddy and she likes the Colonel; and she does not like Higgins and Mr Doolittle. Galatea never does quite like Pygmalion: his relation to her is too godlike to be altogether agreeable.

APPENDIX I

Discarded Scenes

Shaw's original version of *Pygmalion*, as represented in the shorthand
script (HRC SHAW 24.7) and the typescript transcription of the shorthand (HRC SHAW 24.5), contains two discarded sections of dialogue,
never included in any published or acted version of the play. The first is
in Act III, beginning after Mrs Higgins's regret that 'my celebrated son
has no manners', and her advice to the Eynsford Hills (including Freddy,
who enters earlier than in Shaw's revised version) that they 'musnt mind
him' (Act III, line 167 in this edition). (The formatting of the dialogue
has been modified from the typescript original to conform with Shaw's
practices as reflected in this edition.)

HIGGINS
  Oh, theres nothing wrong with my manners. [*Resuming his
  catechism*] *You* dont mind, do you?
MRS EYNSFORD HILL
  Oh, not at all.   5
HIGGINS [*to* MISS EYNSFORD HILL]
  Do you?
MISS EYNSFORD HILL [*rising to the occasion*]
  Of course I do. Youre the rudest man I ever met.
MRS HIGGINS [*laughs*] !!!   10
HIGGINS [*laughing also*]
  Well, isnt it just as good fun as the other thing, anyhow?
MRS HIGGINS
  You have forgotten to apologize to Mr Eynsford Hill.
FREDDY [*blushing*]   15
  Oh, not at all. When a chap has a sister he gets accustomed to
  home truths. [MISS EYNSFORD HILL *looks daggers*]
HIGGINS [*breaking a momentary silence*]
  I daresay youre right. *We* were a lot of brothers with just one
  little sister at the tail end of the family. We spoilt her like   20
  anything. But it must be a devil of a thing to have an older sister,
  especially if she has a bit of a tongue.

FREDDY

It is; and no mistake.

MRS HIGGINS [*to* MISS EYNSFORD HILL, *who is furious*]   25

I was an elder sister, Miss Eynsford Hill. Imagine my feelings! I
have been elder sistering and mothering all my life; and this is
my reward.

MISS EYNSFORD HILL [*disarmed*]

We are fellow-sufferers. I am older than Freddy, I am sorry   30
to say.

MRS HIGGINS

Are you, by George!

MISS EYNSFORD HILL

I am delighted to find that I look younger.   35

HIGGINS

You dont. I should say there is a good six years between ...
[PARLOUR MAID *returns*]

The second section of dialogue also occurs in Act III, after Eliza and he
Eynsford Hills have left Mrs Higgins's home and Mrs Higgins is trying to
determine what's to become of Eliza when Higgins has completed his
experiment with her. The section begins in this edition at line 636.

MRS HIGGINS

Be quiet, Henry. Colonel Pickering: have you known Henry
long enough to find him out?

HIGGINS

What the–   5

MRS HIGGINS

Be quiet, Henry. I am speaking to Colonel Pickering, not to you.

PICKERING

I dont quite understand. Found out what?

MRS HIGGINS   10

Found out that he is the most selfish of created beings.

HIGGINS

The old story–

MRS HIGGINS

Do hold your tongue, Henry, to oblige me.   15

HIGGINS

O, very well, very well. Have it your own way. I have devoted
my life to the regeneration of the Human race through the

most difficult science in the world; and then I am told I am
selfish. Go on. Go on. 20

PICKERING

I find him a very good fellow, Mrs Higgins. I get on very well
with him.

MRS HIGGINS

No doubt. He *is* a very good fellow. 25

HIGGINS

Thank you.

MRS HIGGINS [*continuing*]

If he were not, he would be in prison or in the Cape Police, or
some other refuge for gentlemen criminals. He has always been 30
a headstrong, ungovernable, perfectly unscrupulous boy; and if
it were not that by the mercy of heaven his impulses are mostly
good ones I dont know what would have become of him.

PICKERING

We are all creatures of impulse, Mrs Higgins. 35

MRS HIGGINS

Dont talk nonsense, Colonel Pickering.

HIGGINS [*uproariously*]

Ha ha! Ha ha! Your turn now, Pick.

MRS HIGGINS 40

Less noise, Henry, please. [*To* PICKERING] Soldiering may be a
matter of impulse: at least it doesnt seem to require much
forethought in our army; but housekeeping and mothering and
women's work in general teach them some conscience and
consideration, dont they? 45

PICKERING

Yes; but what is all this leading to, my dear lady?

MRS HIGGINS

Patience, Colonel: I am not as amusing as Eliza; but what I say
is for your good. 50

PICKERING

I am sure of that, Mrs Higgins.

HIGGINS

Ha ha! O Lord! If you could only see your face, Pick!

MRS HIGGINS 55

When Eliza walked into Wimpole Street, something walked in
with her.

PICKERING

Her father did . . .

APPENDIX II

The Censor's Report on *Pygmalion*

In order to obtain a licence (prescribed by the 1843 Theatres Act) for a public performance of *Pygmalion*, the manager of the theatre intending to produce the play was required to submit the script, normally at least two weeks before the planned opening, to the Office of the Lord Chamberlain (with a fee of two guineas), where an official known as the Examiner of Plays read the play to determine its suitability (or not) for performance. In most cases approval was routine, but in the case of Shaw – given his previous disputes with the Lord Chamberlain's Office (see Introduction, p. xvii-iii) – the Examiner, G.S. Street, wrote a report for his superiors, here published for the first time. The script submitted for licensing was a printed copy in which the author is identified only as 'a Fellow of the Royal Society of Literature', though it is clear that Street quickly cottoned on to who the author was. The script is in the British Library, Add Ms 66056F, no. 2442. The licence is dated 26 February 1914. There are two copies of Street's report (dated 23 February 1914), a holograph and a typed copy. It is interesting to speculate on what passage Street had in mind as one of 'genuine and tender feeling', and Street was clearly one of the very earliest of readers to misinterpret the ending of the play.

It is understood that this is by Bernard Shaw and on internal evidence no one else could have written it. It is in his happiest light manner, and contains, what is unusual with him, a passage of genuine and tender feeling.

The Pygmalion of the play is one Higgins, a professor of Phonetics who boasts that in a short time he can turn anyone into anything so far as speech goes. He wagers with his friend, a Colonel, that he can make Liza, a flower girl, pass for a duchess at an ambassador's garden party. The first three acts are taken up with preliminaries and education. An amusing character, the girl's father, boasts himself one of the 'undeserving poor' and preaches a diverting morality. In the fourth act, Liza is transformd into a lady in speech and manners and has won Higgins his triumph. But he and the Colonel have reckoned without her feelings. They have all lived together – all this is quite innocent, of course – and she is outraged by their discussing the success of the experiment as though she was an automaton and not a human being. She runs away and in the fifth act they find they cannot do without her: in the end she consents to come back and it is clear [she] will be treated humanly as a daughter or sister. She, of course, is Galatea.

The Play is entirely without offence, except perhaps to the opinions of old-fashioned people who must be accustomed to having their opinions offended in modern dialogue. I notice, however, one detail. On page 46 [p. 74 of this edition], the word 'bloody' slips out of the as yet only partially educated Liza and on the next page a silly young woman uses it under the impression that it is part of the new 'small talk'. The word is not used in anger, of course, and the incident is merely funny. I think it would be a mistake to be particular about it, but since the word has been forbidden in other plays – in a different sort of connection, however – I mention it.

Recommended for License.

APPENDIX III

The Endings of Pygmalion[1]

1. The original ending (EM/NASH, C1916, C1931) [Transcription from C1931]

LIZA

Then I shall not see you again, Professor. Goodbye. [*She goes to the door*]

MRS HIGGINS [*coming to* HIGGINS]

Goodbye, dear. 5

HIGGINS

Goodbye, mother. [*He is about to kiss her, when he recollects something*] Oh, by the way, Eliza, order a ham and a Stilton cheese, will you? And buy me a pair of reindeer gloves, number eights, and a tie to match that new suit of mine, at Eale & 10 Binman's. You can choose the color. [*His cheerful, careless, vigorous voice shews that he is incorrigible*][2]

LIZA [*disdainfully*]

Buy them yourself. [*She sweeps out*]

MRS HIGGINS 15

I'm afraid youve spoiled that girl, Henry. But never mind, dear: I'll buy you the tie and gloves.

HIGGINS [*sunnily*][3]

Oh, dont bother. She'll buy em all right enough. Goodbye.

They kiss. MRS HIGGINS *runs out.* HIGGINS, *left alone, rattles* 20
his cash in his pocket; chuckles; and disports himself in a highly self-satisfied manner.[4]

---

1   See Introduction, pp. xxv–xxix, for discussion of the variant endings of *Pygmalion*.
2   The stage direction is not present in RC1 or LC.
3   The stage direction is '*cheerfully*' in RC1 and LC.
4   The stage direction in RC1 and LC ends after '*chuckles*', as it does in the 1913 original publication of the play in German. The translation given of the German text in an unauthorized summary of the play in the *New York Times* on 30 November 1913 is 'He kisses her. Mrs Higgins hurries out. Higgins, left alone, chinks the coins in his pocket and snickers', which is accurate except for 'He kisses her', the German text reading 'Sie küssen sich' – 'they kiss each other'. (*Pygmalion. Komödie in fünf Akten* [Berlin, 1913], p. 109.)

2. The Aldwych Theatre ending (1920)

For the revival of *Pygmalion* at the Aldwych Theatre that ran from 10 February 1920 to 17 April 1920 (78 performances) Shaw devised a new (unpublished) ending. It is described in a letter to Mrs Campbell (Eliza), undated but c. 5 February 1920: 'When Eliza emancipates herself – when Galatea comes to life – she must not relapse. She must retain her pride and triumph to the end. When Higgins takes your arm on "consort battleship" you must instantly throw him off with implacable pride; and this is the note until the final "Buy them yourself" [see Appendix III.1]. He will go out on the balcony to watch your departure; come back triumphantly into the room; exclaim "Galatea!" (meaning that the statue has come to life at last); and – curtain. Thus he gets the last word; and you get it too . . .' (*Theatrics* 155).

3. The changed ending (C1939)

LIZA

Then I shall not see you again, Professor. Goodbye. [*She goes to the door*]

MRS HIGGINS [*coming to* HIGGINS]

Goodbye, dear.   5

HIGGINS

Goodbye, mother. [*He is about to kiss her, when he recollects something*] Oh, by the way, Eliza, order a ham and a Stilton cheese, will you? And buy me a pair of reindeer gloves, number eights, and a tie to match that new suit of mine, at Eale &   10
Binman's. You can choose the color. [*His cheerful, careless, vigorous voice shews that he is incorrigible*]

LIZA [*disdainfully*]

Buy them yourself. [*She sweeps out*]

MRS HIGGINS   15

I'm afraid youve spoilt that girl, Henry. I should be uneasy about you and her if she were less fond of Colonel Pickering.

HIGGINS

Pickering! Nonsense: she's going to marry Freddy. Ha ha! Freddy! Freddy!! Ha ha ha ha ha!!!!!   20

[*He roars with laughter as the play ends*]

4. The final version (C1941)

LIZA

Then I shall not see you again, Professor. Goodbye. [*She goes to the door*]

MRS HIGGINS [*coming to* HIGGINS]

Goodbye, dear. 5

HIGGINS

Goodbye, mother. [*He is about to kiss her, when he recollects something*] Oh, by the way, Eliza, order a ham and a Stilton cheese, will you? And buy me a pair of reindeer gloves, number eights, and a tie to match that new suit of mine. You can choose 10 the color. [*His cheerful, careless, vigorous voice shews that he is incorrigible*]

LIZA [*disdainfully*]

Number eights are too small for you if you want them lined with lamb's wool. You have three new ties that you have forgotten in the 15 drawer of your washstand. Colonel Pickering prefers double Gloucester to Stilton; and you dont notice the difference. I telephoned Mrs Pearce this morning not to forget the ham. What you are to do without me I cannot imagine.

[*She sweeps out*] 20

MRS HIGGINS

I'm afraid youve spoilt that girl, Henry. I should be uneasy about you and her if she were less fond of Colonel Pickering.

HIGGINS

Pickering! Nonsense: she's going to marry Freddy. Ha ha! 25 Freddy! Freddy!! Ha ha ha ha ha!!!!! [*He roars with laughter as the play ends*]

5. Shaw's film ending (1934: BL Add Ms 50628 f. 35, dated by Shaw 1 October 1934; italics added)

[Scene] 49

Chelsea Embankment. MRS HIGGINS's *limousine standing opposite her door.* DOOLITTLE *holds the car door open in a courtly manner for* MRS HIGGINS, *who gets in. He gets in himself, leaving* ELIZA *on the pavement.*

FREDDY *appears.*   5

ELIZA

    Here he is, Mrs Higgins. May he come?

MRS HIGGINS

    Certainly, dear. Room for four.

ELIZA *kisses* FREDDY.   10

[Scene] 50

[HIGGINS *on balcony*] HIGGINS's *smile changes to an expression of fury. He shakes his fist at the kissing couple below.*

[Scene] 51

The Embankment.

ELIZA *cocks a snoot prettily at* HIGGINS, *and gets into the car.*

FREDDY *takes off his hat to* HIGGINS *in the Chaplin manner and*   15
follows ELIZA *into the car.*

The car drives off. Wedding March.

The End.

6. Shaw's alternative film ending (1938: HRC SHAW 25.7; italics added)[5]

SCENE 48

MRS HIGGINS's *limousine standing opposite her garden gate in Cheyne Walk. Inside the car are* ELIZA *and* FREDDY *looking out for* MRS HIGGINS.

HIGGINS *and his mother come out. He is over-coated and hatted exactly as in the first scene in Covent Garden.*   5

ELIZA *disappears into the back of the limousine to allow* FREDDY *to alight and open the door for* MRS HIGGINS.

HIGGINS [*staring at* FREDDY]

    Hallo! What the devil are *you* doing here?

5 Complete film script (carbon). First page has NOTE:
    'This scenario is not technically complete; but it indicates exactly what the producer has to work on in the studio, with all the omissions from and additions to the text of the original play. These are so extensive that the printed play should be carefully kept out of the studio, as it can only confuse and mislead the producer and the performers'. This copy is inscribed by Shaw: 'To Floryan Sobieniowski for translation into Polish'. Dated by Shaw 1 March 1938.

FREDDY
  Miss Doolittle invited me.

MRS HIGGINS
  How do you do, Mr Hill? I think you may call her Eliza now.

She gets into the car.

15

FREDDY [*still holding the car door open*]
  Coming, Professor?

ELIZA
  No, he is not coming. Get in quick. We are late.

FREDDY
  By the way, Professor, thanks awfully for promising to set us up   20
  in a flower shop. Her old dream, you know. A lady in a flower
  shop. We are most grateful.

ELIZA
  Sh-sh-sh, Freddy: I havent asked him yet.

She pulls him into the car.   25

ELIZA *slams the door of the limousine, which drives off, leaving*
HIGGINS *on the pavement, stranded and amazed.*

HIGGINS
  A squashed cabbage leaf! A lady in a flower shop!

SCENE 49[6]

A vision of the past.

Covent Garden as in Scene 13.[7] ELIZA *crouching over her basket,
and looking her dirtiest and most wretched.* HIGGINS *alone, looking
at her.*

5

ELIZA
  Poor girl! Hard enough for her to live without being worried
  and chivied. Ought to be ashamed of himself, unmanly coward.
  Let him mind his own business and leave a poor girl alone.

6 Written against this scene and the next, not in Shaw's hand, is 'Omit 49 & 50'.
7 The end of the rain storm outside St Paul's Church at the beginning of the film.

The old music from the church. HIGGINS *takes his hat off. The scene*
fades out and is replaced by   10

SCENE 50

A vision of the future.

A florist's shop in South Kensington, full of fashionable customers.
ELIZA *behind the counter, serving in great splendor. The name of the*
shopkeeper, F. HILL, is visible. Half the shop is stocked with vegetables.
FREDDY, *in apron and mild muttonchop whiskers is serving. Dream-*   5
like silence. Fade out into

SCENE 51

Back to Scene 48.

HIGGINS *standing rapt. A* POLICEWOMAN *comes along. She stops*
and looks curiously at HIGGINS, *who is quite unconscious of her,*
and visibly rapt.

POLICEWOMAN   5
    Anything wrong, sir?
HIGGINS [*waking up*]
    What?
POLICEWOMAN
    Anything wrong, sir?   10
HIGGINS [*impressively*]
    No: nothing wrong. A happy ending. A happy beginning. Good
    morning, madam.
POLICEWOMAN [*impressed*]
    Good morning, sir.   15

HIGGINS *raises his hat and stalks away majestically. The* POLICE-
WOMAN *stands at attention and salutes.*

THE END

7. Pascal's film ending (1938: HRC SHAW 25.8)[8]

[From where Eliza leaves Higgins with 'Goodbye Professor Higgins'.]

CLOSE SHOT. Higgins.

CLOSE SHOT. Eliza.

CLOSE SHOT. Higgins.

Hoot of Car off.

CAMERA PANS with him as he runs to window.   5

EXTERIOR MRS HIGGINS' HOUSE–DAY.
MED. SHOT. Shooting from window down into Street.
Freddy's car is drawn up at the kerb, with him seated in it. He
looks up [and] waves and smiles.
MED. SHOT. Freddy's car at kerb. Eliza hurries out of the   10
house, and gets into car.

MRS. HIGGINS' DRAWING ROOM–DAY.
MED. SHOT. Higgins leaves window, and runs out of shot.
EXTERIOR MRS HIGGINS' HOUSE–DAY.
MED. SHOT. Freddy's car driving off. Higgins comes running   15
out of house. Car drives round corner. Higgins runs u.s. to
corner.

EXTERIOR–EMBANKMENT–DAY.
LONG SHOT. Freddy's car travelling along the road. Traffic
also on road.   20

EXTERIOR–STREET CORNER–DAY.
CLOSE SHOT. Higgins at corner, looking out of shot after car.

MIX TO

EXTERIOR–EMBANKMENT–DAY.

8 Film script, signed by Pascal.

MED. SHOT. Higgins walks into shot from camera left, he   25
crosses road and CAMERA PANS along with him, as he walks
along pavement.

MIX TO

MED. CLOSE SHOT. Higgins striding along Embankment,
CAMERA TRACKING BACK before him (left to right).   30

MIX TO

CLOSE SHOT. Higgins striding along Embankment. CAMERA
TRACKING BACK before him (left to right).

EXTERIOR–BRIDGE–DAY.
MED. SHOT. Higgins striding across Bridge over Thames.   35
CAMERA TRACKING before him (left to right).

MIX TO

EXTERIOR–STREET–DAY.
MED. CLOSE SHOT. Higgins walking along Street, CAMERA
TRACKING before him (right to left).   40

MIX TO

CLOSE SHOT. Higgins walking very quickly along Street.
CAMERA TRACKING before him. He comes to his own house,
and hurries inside (right to left).

MIX TO   45

HIGGINS' LABORATORY–DAY.
MED. SHOT. on closed doors. Higgins throws them open and
CAMERA PANS with him across room to his desk. He picks up
record and smashes it over the motor of Playback. Picks up box of
chocolates and sits into chair. Cuff catches in switch of Playback.   50
CLOSE SHOT. Higgins in profile at desk.

PLAYBACK (ELIZA): Oo . . . I ain't dirty . . . I washed me face
and hands before I come I did.

PLAYBACK (HIGGINS): I shall make a Duchess of this draggle-tailed guttersnipe.　　55

PLAYBACK (ELIZA): A . . . ah . . . ahaou!

PLAYBACK (HIGGINS): In six months . . . in three . . .

He leans over and switches Playback off, then sits back in chair and puts head in hand, still in profile.

ELIZA'S VOICE (In perfect English): I washed my face and　60 hands before I came . . .

Higgins swings round in his chair and looks out of shot right of Camera . . .

ELIZA'S VOICE: . . . I did.

He swings back in chair with back to Camera.　　65

HIGGINS' VOICE: Where the devil are my slippers, Eliza?

FADE OUT
MUSIC
THE END